WITHDRAWN
HARVARD LIBRARY
WITHDRAWN

# *Ethics* AFTER *Auschwitz?*

# AMERICAN UNIVERSITY STUDIES

SERIES VII
THEOLOGY AND RELIGION

VOL. 305

PETER LANG
New York • Washington, D.C./Baltimore • Bern
Frankfurt • Berlin • Brussels • Vienna • Oxford

Carole J. Lambert

# *Ethics* AFTER *Auschwitz?*

## PRIMO LEVI'S & ELIE WIESEL'S RESPONSE

PETER LANG
New York • Washington, D.C./Baltimore • Bern
Frankfurt • Berlin • Brussels • Vienna • Oxford

Library of Congress Cataloging-in-Publication Data
Lambert, Carole J.
Ethics after Auschwitz?: Primo Levi's and
Elie Wiesel's response / Carole J. Lambert.
p. cm. — (American university studies. VII, Theology and religion; v. 305)
Includes bibliographical references and index.
1. Humanistic ethics. 2. Jewish ethics. 3. Holocaust, Jewish (1939–1945)—Influence.
4. Holocaust, Jewish (1939–1945)—Moral and ethical aspects. 5. Auschwitz
(Concentration camp). 6. Levi, Primo. 7. Wiesel, Elie, 1928–. I. Title.
BJ1360.L28   296.3'6—dc22   2010035825
ISBN 978-1-4331-0964-5
ISSN 0740-0446

Bibliographic information published by **Die Deutsche Nationalbibliothek**.
**Die Deutsche Nationalbibliothek** lists this publication in the "Deutsche
Nationalbibliografie"; detailed bibliographic data is available
on the Internet at http://dnb.d-nb.de/.

BJ
1360
.L28
2011

Cover illustration: Marc Chagall, "The Ladder"
© 2010 Artists Rights Society (ARS), New York / ADAGP, Paris

The paper in this book meets the guidelines for permanence and durability
of the Committee on Production Guidelines for Book Longevity
of the Council of Library Resources.

© 2011 Peter Lang Publishing, Inc., New York
29 Broadway, 18th floor, New York, NY 10006
www.peterlang.com

All rights reserved.
Reprint or reproduction, even partially, in all forms such as microfilm,
xerography, microfiche, microcard, and offset strictly prohibited.

Printed in Germany

*In memory of my most beloved and courageous brother:*
*Paul Braden Wilson, Jr.*
*(November 15, 1942–June 13, 1967)*
*Son of*
*Paul Braden Wilson, M.D. and Esther Elizabeth ("Betty") Roberts Wilson*

# Table of Contents

Acknowledgments ................................................................................. ix

Introduction ........................................................................................... 1

## PRACTICAL ETHICS

Chapter 1: "Thou shalt not kill" ............................................................ 23
Chapter 2: "Thou shalt not commit adultery" ..................................... 37
Chapter 3: "Thou shalt not steal" ......................................................... 49
Chapter 4: "Thou shalt not bear false witness against
            thy neighbour" ................................................................... 63
Chapter 5: "Thou shalt not covet thy neighbour's house" ................. 77

## ESSENTIAL SPIRITUALITY

Chapter 6: "I am the LORD thy God. . . . Thou shalt have
            no other gods before me" .................................................. 93
Chapter 7: "Thou shalt not make unto thee any graven image" ....... 107
Chapter 8: "Thou shalt not take the name of the LORD
            thy God in vain" ................................................................ 119
Chapter 9: "Remember the Sabbath day, to keep it holy" ................. 131
Chapter 10: "Honour thy father and thy mother" .............................. 143

Conclusion ............................................................................................. 155

Index ...................................................................................................... 173

# Acknowledgments

I thank Azusa Pacific University's President Jon R. Wallace, former Provost Michael M. Whyte, and Vice Provost for Graduate Programs and Research Paul W. Gray for granting me a three-month research and writing leave from May 15 to August 15, 2010, which enabled me to complete this book. Their ongoing support of my Holocaust studies and texts has greatly encouraged me. I am also grateful to Abbylin H. Sellers, my exceedingly competent research assistant, who miraculously and promptly found for me books and articles from all corners of the world. I am equally appreciative of Susan J. Ferrante, my superb administrative assistant, who formatted this text beautifully, graciously handled Office of Research matters in my absence, and patiently taught me important computer skills which forwarded this project immensely. Claudio Graziani, my Roman tutor, kindly taught me Italian weekly for three or more years, carefully checking and correcting my translations of Primo Levi's and others' Italian texts; I remain greatly indebted to him.

Theodore Zev Weiss, Director of the Holocaust Education Foundation in Skokie, Illinois, is instrumental in my growth as a scholar of Holocaust literature and ethics. His Holocaust Educational Foundation Fellowship to the Twelfth Summer Institute on the Holocaust and Jewish Civilization, June 17–29, 2007, enabled me to study with outstanding scholars from around the country all aspects of the Shoah. This theoretical and factual grounding was then supplemented by his Holocaust Educational Foundation Eastern European Seminar for Faculty, June 8–21, 2009, a study tour which permitted fourteen other scholars and me to visit Holocaust sites in Poland, the Czech Republic, and Germany. At the close of this tour I was able to reconnect in Brussels, Belgium, with Professor Albert Mingelgrün of the Université Libre de Bruxelles, who had been my professor of literature and literary critical theory during my Fulbright Fellowship there in the 1984–1985 school year and who now is also a scholar of Holocaust literature. I am grateful to him for his help with my doctoral dissertation years ago and for his brilliant assistance with the third chapter of this book.

Professor Alberto Cavaglion and Cristina Sara of the Museo Diffuso della Resistenza della Deportazione, della Guerra dei Diritti e della Libertà in Turin, Italy, welcomed me graciously and provided me with rich conversation and stimulating books and archives just as I was beginning this project in September 2007 and again on my return to Turin in 2008.

I also am very grateful to Jackie Pavlovic, Production Supervisor at Peter Lang (New York), who finalized the book and guaranteed the satisfactory reproduction of Marc Chagall's "The Ladder" on our cover for which I am especially indebted to Bella Meyer, head of the New York-based Chagall Estate, Stephanie Weber of the Marc Chagall Estate in New York, and Courtney Richter, the Rights Administrator of the Artists Rights Society in New York. Both Primo Levi and Elie Wiesel admired the works of Chagall; it brings me joy to unite these three great artists.

I cannot write a book without feeling loved and encouraged by my beloved husband of forty-four years, David Eugene Lambert. I pray he knows the depth of my love for him.

# Introduction

Both Primo Levi and Elie Wiesel avoided being chased naked by Nazi guards and *Sonderkommando* prisoners into the terrifying black boxes that were sealed and flooded with Zyklon-B gas at Auschwitz II-Birkenau. Some of Levi's friends and part of Wiesel's family died minutes after the lights were extinguished and the asphyxiation process began. Both authors, housed in the same barracks in the depths of hell, a dark reality even surpassing Dante Alighieri's vivid images portrayed in *The Inferno*, could have deservedly expressed rage and bitterness for the rest of their lives. Both, however, chose to speak, write, and work for a better world, never allowing the memory of those who did not survive to fade.

Why and how did they make this choice? What influenced their values before Auschwitz and their moral decision making after it? What can others who have suffered less devastating traumas learn from them? "The quest is in the question," Wiesel often tells his students at Boston University. This book is a quest for hope and goodness emerging from the Shoah's deepest "night."

Theologian Richard L. Rubenstein in a 2004 speech at Claremont McKenna College called Primo Levi "a kind of anti-Wiesel" writer whose rational, humanistic, and even atheistic response to his Auschwitz experience counters Elie Wiesel's orthodox Jewish mystical writings. Similarly Massimo Giuliani had stated in 2003, "In Levi, the approach [studying the Shoah as a historical event which can be analyzed to prevent further similar genocides rather than assigning it a '"sacred status"' as he feels Wiesel does] is rational, de-mythologizing, and anti-ideological, even toward itself. It is not his purpose to make the Holocaust sacred or the mere object of a museum. This difference in approach makes Levi a kind of 'anti-Wiesel'" (4). Opposing the views of Levi and Wiesel toward the Holocaust is appropriate in many ways, and yet there are more similarities between the two authors than first meet the eye. Most striking of all is their ethical goodness whose principles can be drawn from their lives and works. For example, both emphasize respect for human dignity, reject indifference to the sufferings of others, and refuse hate. Their ethical goodness is enacted in their shared goals of combating evil—forgetfulness of or indifference to the Holocaust being a prime evil—and promoting post-Holocaust peace.

Other points of comparison follow: Levi and Wiesel worked professionally, the first as a chemist and then a paint factory manager, the second as a journalist and then a university professor. They found time to write before their post-World War II marriages and then while raising their children. They expressed appreciation to those who helped them during and after the Shoah, and they became friends in 1983 (Belpoliti 273–75; Roth 211), realizing that they had been at Auschwitz at the same time, had even lived in the same barracks, but without contact between each other. Wiesel describes this eventful moment:

> we were friends. For a time, we were together in the same camp, in the same barracks. Without a doubt, we passed each other every day, unacquainted and unaware. He was a chemist and therefore useful; I was only a number. We encountered each other again *after* the war, thanks to a chance meeting at a cultural conference in Rome [Levi says Milan, as noted below, and so does Wiesel in *And the Sea Is Never Full: Memoirs, 1969—* 345]. Once bona fides were made, the bond was immediate. Our exchanges continued over the years. Equipped with survivors' code, we could read each other's minds. Just before his tragic suicide in 1987, he called me. His desperation haunts me still. I well remember the thought that occurred to me at the time: Here is proof that one can die at Auschwitz after Auschwitz. ("Why Memory?")

Rubenstein and Giuliani are correct that the contrasts between them are striking: Levi eschewed religion, more comfortable with rationalistic agnosticism while Wiesel remained an Orthodox Jew, a Hasid. Wiesel explains:

> I am still a Hasid. That means I still believe in what I believed as a child. I still love to sing and to tell stories. I still love whatever characterized the Hasidic movement in its early stages—a longing fervor, passion, and compassion, doing things together with other people. The Hasidic movement was a movement of friendship. This is why it has always had such a strong appeal to me. (Abrahamson, *Against III* 224)

Levi has criticized Israel's treatment of Palestinians while Wiesel has championed Israel (although he has worked behind the scenes to liberate some Palestinian prisoners) (Wiesel, *Conversations* 189). Levi introduces prehistoric characters and science fiction settings into some of his stories while Wiesel often includes mysticism and kabbalic references in his. Levi was rumored to be under consideration for a Nobel Prize for Literature in 1987 (Angier 717; Anissimov 403; Thomson 467), the year he died, while Wiesel was awarded a Nobel Prize for Peace in 1986.

Thus a Sephardic Italian Jew and an Ashkenazic Hungarian Jew with distinct biographical similarities and pronounced biographical differences arrive at an ethics of goodness which motivates their lives and leaves a lasting legacy for their readers. However, literary critic Sara R. Horowitz writes, "Like a black hole, the Holocaust swallowed up the structures—philosophical, theological, and humanistic—by which we order our lives" (41). If this statement is true, then how did Levi and Wiesel "order [their] lives" ethically? What do their memoirs, essays, speeches, novels, and poems offer as post-Holocaust "structures" worthy of study and perhaps emulation? How does each define "goodness" after experiencing the "black hole" of evil that was Auschwitz?

In *Primo Levi's Ordinary Virtues: From Testimony to Ethics* Robert S. C. Gordon affirms that Levi's ethics are the result of "a centrifugal impulse toward the 'ordinary', driving outwards from the 'black hole of Auschwitz'" (37). His book astutely focuses on Levi's sight, memory or response to trauma, his silence, usefulness, and practical intelligence as expressed in measuredness, practice, perspective, and inventiveness; Gordon then analyzes Levi's sense of community as nurtured by common sense, friendship, and storytelling, concluding with studies of his wit, irony, and playfulness. Gordon emphasizes an aspect of Levi's ethics that I shall enhance—the dignified freedom of a former slave: "Levi's ethics, as this book has argued throughout, are an ethics of the former slave, ever mindful of his experience of slavery and of its continued dangers, but fully enfranchised, attuned as a liberal citizen of the world. In other words, freedom is the ordinariness to which his ordinary virtues aspire" (290).

Like the Hebrew slaves liberated from Egypt long ago, Levi chose to follow the Decalogue given by God (Exodus 20), even though he could no longer believe in the God who seemed to have remained silent and passive at Auschwitz. Levi's ethical actions that often harmonize with those of Wiesel, who kept his orthodox faith while perpetually arguing with God about exactly that same silence and passivity, reflect a conception of humanity, a true "Mensch," which gives a human being, agnostic like Levi or Hasidic like Wiesel, dignity as well as the possibility of respecting others in ways that honor their dignity, too. The age difference between the two men while incarcerated at Auschwitz—Wiesel was only fifteen when he arrived while Levi was twenty-four, already a university graduate—may account for their religious choices. Wiesel, raised in the *shtetl* of Sighet, Hungary, knew only orthodox, Hasidic Judaism while Levi, an assimilated Italian Jew from Turin, was experienced in analyzing philosophies, theories, and chemical elements.

Ethics may be defined as "a system of moral principles." Philosopher and ethicist John K. Roth affirms, "Ethical imperatives direct attention and guide action" (66). Philosophers of ethics often begin with classical Greek and Roman thinkers such as Socrates, Plato, Aristotle, Cicero, Seneca, and others and then trace the evolution of this field of study, noting the influence of predecessors on ethical innovators. Not being a professional philosophical ethicist, I shall, on the contrary, inductively draw ethical principles from the words, actions, and texts of Levi and Wiesel. I call my method "narrative ethics": ethics drawn from lived and written narratives. This approach best fits my education in comparative literature; it is also compatible with Levi's and Wiesel's love of literature more than strictly philosophical works, although Levi lists Lucretius's *On Nature* (*Ricerca* 141) and Bertrand Russell's *The Conquest of Happiness* (*Ricerca* 169) among his favorite books while Wiesel readily admits to being heavily influenced by Albert Camus (Abrahamson, *Against III* 225; Kalfa 197). My "narrative ethics" methodology also echoes Levi's scientific inductive approach described by Mirna Cicioni: "Just as in *Se questo è un uomo,* [so in *La tregua*] he uses the natural scientist's inductive method to draw philosophical and ethical reflections from concrete, even trivial experiences and encounters" (45).

Both Levi and Wiesel have absorbed since birth one foundational ethical text: the Torah. I am utilizing the Ten Commandments as chapter headings of this book because, whether unconsciously as for Levi who clearly distinguished right from wrong without often citing them or consciously as for Wiesel who studies Torah daily, they served as influential, molding moral standards. Peter J. Haas has noted that "the central core of Judaism [which Reform Judaism claimed] was its moral laws as summarized and taught in the Ten Commandments. These moral standards could in most cases be clearly distinguished from the 'ceremonial laws,' which were the historically contingent way in which Jewish values expressed themselves" (53). Although neither Levi nor Wiesel would call themselves "Reform Jews," they nevertheless shared this emphasis on that "central core of Judaism." Alberto Cavaglion notes, "la Bibbia sta qui come imagine della tradizione ebraica che questi giovani ebrei laici [Levi and his intellectual friends] rispettano" ["the Bible is here like a symbol of Jewish tradition which these young secular Jews respect"] (9). "Biblical echoes" can be found in Levi's texts (Angier 217), while Wiesel has written prolifically about biblical stories and characters such as Cain and Abel (*A Jew Today* 160–61; *Et Où vas-tu?* 159). Both Levi and Wiesel, quite appropriately, have produced commentaries on Job (*La Ricerca delle radici* and *Job ou Dieu dans la tempête*). Myriam Anissimov affirms, "Levi had a phenomenal memory: he would quote whole sentences from books he had read in English. . . . and knew passages of the Authorized Version of the Bible by heart" (277). Further, "Levi also pored over the texts that make up the biblical and post-biblical literary corpus: the Pentateuch, the *Midrash*, the *Aggada*, and even the *Schulchan Aruch*" (Anissimov 340).

Theologian Rosemary Radford Ruether notes that "Judaism believes it has the commandments, can obey the commandments well enough to be in friendship with God, and yet the final resolution of the tension of letter and spirit is not yet" (244). The commandments "concretize God's presence in everyday life" (241), whether or not that presence is recognized by an agnostic like Levi as it is daily by a Hasid like Wiesel. Many biblical scholars agree that the first five commandments treat one's relationship to God and that the last five refer to one's relationship with others. Since Levi gave up on God shortly after his *bar mitzvah* at age thirteen, but, as a result, did not turn into an ethical nihilist, I am entitling my first five chapters after the last five commandments. These chapters discuss both authors' humanism, in particular their valuing of friendships (Practical Ethics). In the last five chapters (Essential Spirituality), titled after the first five commandments, I argue that Levi, as he aged, matured spiritually, not becoming a devout Jew but moving beyond atheistic humanism. I show that this eccentric spirituality to some extent fulfilled the first five commandments and manifested itself in ethical actions similar to those of Wiesel, a believer in God. The commandment, however, which differentiates their actions most of all is "Remember the Sabbath day, to keep it holy." Wiesel begins his Sabbath preparations on Friday and strictly follows Sabbath traditions until its conclusion at nightfall on Saturday. Levi did not follow Sabbath rituals and may have even committed suicide on a Sabbath morning.

I have chosen to use the King James Version biblical translation of the ten commandments from the twentieth chapter of Exodus for my chapter headings because these words were traditionally memorized by children in awe of their "thee's" and "thou's," at least English speaking children of my and previous generations, and this was probably "the Authorized Version" which Anissimov says that Levi memorized. I wanted to retain that awesome resonance when discussing these commandments' influence on Levi and Wiesel. I generally draw from Levi's original texts in Italian and Wiesel's in French, providing my own translations of these in brackets following the Italian or French citation, unless otherwise indicated. Occasionally, I also include German citations, again followed by my own translations of these in brackets.

I try to let the ethical insights of Levi and Wiesel "dialogue" with each other as I show how their agreements are nuanced by their original presuppositions, secular rationalism predominating in Levi's voice and religious mysticism permeating Wiesel's perspectives. Here are some ethical principles both writers share that I have derived from their words, actions, and written texts and that will recur in my chapters: *The voice of the other must be heard and respected, regardless of his or her religion, race, or nationality; hatred is unacceptable.* Wiesel starkly asserts, "La haine, c'est le mal; c'est la face visible du mal" ["Hatred, it is evil; it is the visible face of evil"] (*Et où vas-tu?* 164). Both Levi and Wiesel have refused hatred, particularly hatred of Germans. Levi explained in a letter to his German translator of *If This Is a Man* (*Se questo è un uomo?*), "'I never harbored hatred for the German people. And if I had felt that way, I would be cured of it after having known you [Heinz Riedt]. I do not understand, I cannot tolerate the fact that a man should be judged not for what he is but because of the group to which he happens to belong'" (*The Drowned and the Saved* 174). In his moving admonition to tourists at Auschwitz, Levi wrote: "Visitor, observe the remains of this camp and consider: Whatever country you come from, you are not a stranger. Act so that your journey is not useless, and our deaths not useless. For you and your sons, the ashes of Auschwitz hold a message. Act so that the fruit of hatred, whose traces you have seen here, bears no more seed, either tomorrow or forever after" (quoted in Guinness 66).

Wiesel recognized that he was incapable of hate on his first visit back to Germany shortly after World War II (Wiesel, *Silences* 119). He also explained to an interviewer in 1974, "You must transpose the hate into something creative. As a writer you transpose hate into something you write, a novel. You express what you feel, and the hate becomes something else. But do not hate" (Abrahamson, *Against III* 227). Further, he believes that "the purpose of literature is to correct injustice" (Edelman 10); hatred risks perpetrating further injustices, not correcting them.

Wiesel even makes respect for others a key point of his teaching at Boston University: "My first goal is to inspire students to respect one another, which means they should be there to help each other, not to judge one another. . . . This is the first and most important value I want to pass on to my students: respect, that students would respect every fellow student and every fellow human being. How can I ask them to respect the dead if I don't ask them to respect the living? And the other way around" (Rittner, "An Interview" 34).

*Friends are essential to physical, psychological, and emotional survival.* Wiesel explains, "Those [in Auschwitz] who retreated to a universe limited to their own bodies had less chance of getting out alive, while to live for a brother, a friend, an ideal helped you hold out longer" (*Memoirs* 80–81). Levi describes how his unconditional commitment to Alberto helped them both to survive as they daily shared all food, goods, and information that they obtained at Auschwitz. Levi narrates in *Il systema periodico* ("Cerio") how he and Alberto even established a little underground business selling lighters which they fabricated from materials stolen from I. G. Farben. Levi named both of his children after Lorenzo, his second close friend at Auschwitz, an Italian laborer, not a prisoner, who daily hid extra soup rations for him, thus increasing Levi's and Alberto's caloric intake beyond the starvation level set by the Nazis. Once Levi remarked, "'I am faithful in friendship" (quoted in Angier 83), and he was indeed.

Wiesel has repeatedly affirmed that his father was his best friend at Auschwitz, although he wished that his childhood friends from Sighet had also been with him:

> In the camp I thought of my childhood friends, and of all those who had formed part of my inner landscape. Sadly we did not stay together. They left with the first transports and I a week later, with the last. In the camp there were no friends to remind me of my childhood. In the camp I had no more childhood. I had only my father, my best friend, my only friend. (*Memoirs* 49)

[H]ow could I recall my friends of those days without mentioning the best, the most devoted, the most generous of them all—my father? I lived only for him. And by him. He needed me—and I him—to live one more day, one more hour. I knew it and he knew it. I see him again and, at the core of my being, I feel a nameless sorrow: nothing has replaced that friendship. (*From the Kingdom* 83)

Wiesel and his father shared what they could in order to ensure their survival, and they tried to shield each other from fully understanding the physical, emotional, and spiritual pain each was personally feeling. This altruism served to keep them both alive to such an extent that Wiesel claims that he died within himself after his father was murdered in January 1945 (*Memoirs* 94) and that he was merely a walking corpse when the American soldiers liberated Buchenwald in April 1945 (*Memoirs* 95–97).

*Commitment to parents, siblings, spouses, and children is right and essential; it provides stability in life and encouragement to risk writing.* Both Levi and Wiesel remained faithful to their wives and committed to their children. However, Levi's intense love for his mother caused him despair when the dementia resulting from her multiple strokes left her confused and bed ridden in their home in Turin. He compared her to a "*Muselmann*" at Auschwitz (Angier 718), "the worn out man, whose intellect is dying or dead" (Levi, *Drowned* 142), and his despair over her mental and physical deterioration probably contributed to the deep depression which preceded his death. Carole Angier notes, "from 1978 onwards his depressions were triggered very largely by his mother's decline, and by its consequences" (602); "everyone knew that his mother's illness was consuming him, that it was a main factor in his depression, even the most important of all" (729).

After Wiesel's father's death in Buchenwald in January 1945, he admits that he had no more desire to live: "For all practical purposes, I had become one of the 'Mussulmen' [sic] drifting beyond life, into death as into water, no longer hungry, thirsty, or sleepy, fearing neither death nor beatings. . . . I did not line up for bread and soup. I waited for nothing and no one. I drifted through time and sank into a dreamless sleep. When I woke up, I didn't know where I was" (*Memoirs* 95).

Wiesel's mother turning from him on the train platform at Auschwitz II-Birkenau without saying "good-bye"—his last time to see her—also caused him grief. He would have loved to have received her embrace, blessing, and adieu, but their fatigue, the commotion of disembarking from their cattle car and undergoing "Dr." Josef Mengele's *Selektion* by the tracks, and the separation of all men from women made a mother's loving good-bye to her fifteen-year-old son impossible. He writes, "We were taken away before I could tell my mother goodbye, before I could kiss her hand and beg her forgiveness for the wrongs I must have done her, before I could squeeze Tsipouka, my little sister, to my heart. What remains of that night like no other is an irremediable sense of loss, of parting. My mother and my little sister left, and I never said goodbye" (*Memoirs* 77).

*Writing is cathartic, for it helps to verbalize the unspeakable while memorializing the dead; it also serves as a healthy outlet for intense anger while easing a tendency toward bitterness.* Horowitz wisely notes, "Holocaust fiction puts into words what customarily remains outside the flow of historical narrative: the sufferings, resistances, aspirations of the individuals ravaged by genocide" (39). Although not fiction but tragically a part of his second memoir, Levi's Hurbinek, the very young child at Auschwitz who never learned words, exemplifies her affirmation. Hurbinek would have died without having ever been known to those outside of this "night" if Levi had not described him in detail, as well as the prisoners' compassionate attempts to bring him into the humanity that speaking a language ensures (Cicioni 43; Levi, *La tregua* 228). In 1955 Levi wrote, "It is not permissible to forget, nor is it permissible to keep silent. If we fall silent, who then will speak? Certainly not the perpetrators and their accomplices. If we fail to bear witness, in a not too distant future we could well see the deeds of Nazi bestiality relegated by their very enormity to the status of legend. It is vital, therefore, to speak out" (*Black* 3).

Wiesel is also known for speaking for those murdered during the Shoah, but he nuances Levi's affirmation above by noting that such memorializing of the dead is a huge burden for the survivor to bear: "For the camp survivor life is a battle not only for the dead but also against them. Locked in the grip of the dead, he fears that by freeing himself, he is abandoning them. Hence the near-impossibility of loving, or believing in humanity" (*Memoirs* 298–99). His life testifies to his overcoming this "near-impossibility."

*Indifference is unacceptable, for evil must be verbally and artistically fought; witnesses need to speak up and serve as legitimate bridges between those who were "there," living and dead, and those who were not "there."* One of Levi's biographers, Carole Angier, notes, "The main longing of his life was to cross frontiers, to bridge gaps, to heal divisions. If he couldn't always do it in life, he could and did do it in writing" (82). Indeed, Levi affirms:

> From my very first book, *If This Is a Man*, I have wanted my writings, even if the name on the front cover is mine, to be read as collective works, as a voice that represented other voices. And even more than that, I wanted them to be an opening, a bridge between us and our readers, especially if they were young. It is very agreeable for us ex-deportees to sit round a table and tell each other of our far-off adventures, but it serves little purpose. As long as we are alive, it is up to us to speak, but to other people, to those who were not yet born, so that they know 'how far it can go.' (*Black* 96)

Wiesel also feels committed to link the dead with the living: "We must serve as living, integral links between the dead and the future generations so as to save the dead from death and the others from forgetfulness" (Abrahamson, *Against II* 385). He candidly explained to a student at the University of Oregon in 1975, "I write to explore my own self as much as I write in order to help you explore yourself. I believe that basically, and ontologically, there is only one person in the world. That is the beauty, really, of our teaching: there is only one person. That means the 'I' in me and the 'I' in you is the same 'I.' Between our deepest zones there is a bridge" (Abrahamson, *Against III* 230–31).

In his short acceptance speech in Genoa after having received the "Primo Levi" prize in 1992 (five years after Levi's death), Wiesel spoke about the ethics both he and Levi shared and their mutual mission resulting from enacting those ethics: "Condividemmo un'ossessione: portare testimonianza" ["We shared one obsession: bearing witness"] ("Io e Primo Levi" 204). He continues, "Se solo la gente potesse ricordare ciò che noi ricordiamo, loro [Shoah victims] pensavano, la società sarebbe guarita dai mali del pregiudizio, del bigottismo, del fanatismo, dall'odio, dalla violenza e dagli spargimenti di sangue. Nel nostro gergo etica e memoria erano deventati sinonimi" ["If only people were able to remember what we remember, they thought, society would be cured of the evils of prejudice, bigotism, fanaticism, hatred, violence, and the shedding of blood. In our lingo, ethics and memory had become synonomous"] (207). He concedes at the close of his acceptance address that "il concetto di umanità nell'uomo è stato concepito, se non condannato, a rimanere fragile" ["the concept of humanity in man has been conceived, if not condemned, to remain fragile"] (207–08). Wiesel and Levi have spent their post-Holocaust lives shoring up this fragile concept.

*Working for justice on earth takes precedent over waiting for supernatural miraculous interventions from heaven or splendid rewards in heaven.* Angier continues, "The rejection of injustice is one of Primo Levi's greatest themes, in both life and work. He had a passion for equality" (154). Shortly before his death, Levi acknowledged that he was not a "believer" but that he wished he could be (Camon 67). Hence his acts of goodness stemmed from a strong sense of justice that should occur in this world without any hope of retribution or reward in the next world.

Wiesel, as a student of kabbala, admits to doing good as a part of the process of *tikkun*—preparing the world for the eventual coming of the Messiah. Gershom Scholem explains, "Extinction of the stain, restoration of harmony—that is the meaning of the Hebrew word *Tikkun*, which is the term employed by the Kabbalists after the period of the Zohar, for man's task in this world" (233). Zachary Braiterman elaborates:

> The world's creation entails a powerful surge of destructive force shattering the mystical structure that forms the Godhead. With the breaking of the vessels, God and the world are torn into pieces. In response, human acts of *tikkun* (mending, repair) help restore this broken Godhead to a state of primordial wholeness. The kabbalist conducts this *tikkun* by performing mitzvot with mystical intentions. (144–45)

David R. Blumenthal more simply defines *tikkun* as the "process of meditatively bringing wholeness to persons, actions, the cosmos, and God" (156). Wiesel's working for justice on earth cannot be divorced from his Hasidic, kabbalistic spirituality whose moral mysticism is frequently evident in his texts. However, he cautions, "Mystics are part of my life, that is why I tell stories of miracles. But I believe in knowledge more than in miracle-making" (*Conversations* 187). His activism has extended beyond defending Jewish concerns to speaking out "wherever men and women are suffering injustice"—apartheid in South Africa, Indians in South America, nuclear threats, and even Armenians: "we are obsessed with the idea that being human means sharing our humanity" (*Conversations* 158).

Despite Levi's self-proclaimed inability to believe in God, some spirituality can also be demonstrated in his texts and life. Both Levi and Wiesel comment on prayer. Levi refused it, as described in *Survival in*

*Auschwitz*, when Kuhn thanks God for not being selected for the gas chamber and Levi despises him for his insensitivity before those who were chosen (129–30). Hence Levi's reason for rejecting Kuhn's prayer is his elevation of love for others, thus manifesting a foundational Jewish ethical principle. Wiesel continued to pray at Auschwitz and Buchenwald until after his liberation by the Americans. He and his father, although famished and exhausted, rose early, borrowed a prayer shawl, and prayed at great cost to themselves:

> In the morning my father and I would rise before the general wake up call and go to a nearby block where someone had traded a dozen rations of bread for a pair of phylacteries (tefillin). We would strap them onto our left arm and forehead, quickly recite the ritual blessings, then pass them on to the next person. A few dozen prisoners thereby sacrificed their sleep, and sometimes their rations of bread or coffee, to perform the mitzvah, the commandment to wear the tefillin. (*Memoirs* 82)

Despite his ongoing disputes with God, Wiesel still prays while no one knows if Levi prayed before his death on April 11, 1987. Rabbi Elio Toaff, the chief rabbi of Rome, who attended an exhibition there when Levi spoke in 1975 (Thomson 345), states that Levi telephoned him that fateful Saturday morning (Thomson 499, Angier 718), claiming that Levi said, "'I don't know how I can go on. My mother's ill with cancer—every time I look at her I remember the faces of those men stretched out on their plank-beds at Auschwitz'" (Thomson 499). Levi was not close to the Rabbi, and so this admission seems extraordinary for him to make as well as inaccurate perhaps in the Rabbi's memory since his mother was not suffering from cancer but rather strokes and progressive dementia and physical debilities. As will be shown below, other friends had heard Levi speak of his deep grief resulting from his mother's suffering and his depression because of it as well as his seeing her to be all too similar to dying Auschwitz prisoners. If Rabbi Toaff's assertion is true—that Levi did indeed call him just minutes before his death—then it is a testimony to his latent spirituality and desire for spiritual help.

Missing from these ethical principles is a strong affirmation of forgiveness by victims of perpetrators, a particularly Christian value that should not be imposed on these Jewish authors. Levi states clearly, "No, I have not forgiven any of the culprits, nor am I willing to forgive a single one of them, unless he has shown (with deeds, not words, and not too long afterwards) that he has become conscious of the crimes and errors . . . and is determined to condemn them, uproot them, from his conscience and from that of others" (quoted in Roth 124). Elie Wiesel says that he has not forgiven any perpetrators because none have asked him for forgiveness. He explains, "No, 'You shall love your enemy' is not written. . . . One does not forgive one's enemy, unless he asks one's forgiveness. We do not have to love our enemy. Why should we? He seeks only to kill us. To love him would be unnatural" (*Evil and Exile* 46). Shocking some around him, Wiesel even prayed at Auschwitz-Birkenau in January 1995 that God would not forgive those who had killed the children there. When questioned about this prayer he later explained:

> I am asking God not to forgive the murderers. I pray God not to forgive them. And I hope He hasn't done so. Remember one thing: I believe the question is really the wrong question, because forgiveness, even if it is permitted in certain cases, presupposes an admission of guilt, contrition, and remorse. I have not seen the killers express remorse or contrition, much less guilt, so why is this question even being raised? (Rittner, *"Good News"* 125)

My anecdotal experience of researching the life and works of Primo Levi in Italy and Elie Wiesel in France suggests that many Italians affirm Levi to be *their* premier Holocaust survivor/writer (Cicioni 127) while many French claim Wiesel (despite his American citizenship) as *their* foremost Shoah survivor/writer. The two are rarely linked together, perhaps for nationalistic reasons, but maybe also for linguistic reasons—Levi, fluent in French, has had his works translated poorly into French (Cavaglion 33; Angier 511) while Wiesel's literary language is French and he does not speak Italian. Fortunately, French and friendship firmly united the two authors.

Ian Thomson, however, has suggested that a friendship between Levi and Wiesel may not have really existed. He writes:

> On 27 August [1983], in an effort to dissipate his frustrations, Levi travelled to Milan to meet the survivor-spokesman Elie Wiesel, who was due to promote an Italian translation of his Jewish folk-story collection [*Célébration hassidique*]. Levi was not very fond of Wiesel, or rather of what he stood for. Wiesel had cornered a sentimental middle-brow Jewish market and made a celebrity cult of his survivor status. Perhaps Levi was a little envious. . . . Wiesel claimed to have had a great friendship with him in Auschwitz, though Levi had persistently denied it. ('We never met at Auschwitz, or if we did, I've forgotten.'). If Levi envied Wiesel's success, a part of Wiesel surely envied Levi his higher literary standing and intellectual ballast. Before taking part in a public interview, the survivors were taken to lunch

by [Armando] Verdiglione at the Hotel Duomo opposite the Cathedral. Wiesel ate very little. And as the meal progressed, Verdiglione detected a certain *froideur* between the men. (416)

This account is not in accord with Daniela Amsallem's personal letter from Levi of April 11, 1984, in which he states: '"La rencontre avec Wiesel a été brève mais très cordiale. Je l'ai trouvé fascinant, plein de chaleur humaine; nous sommes devenus amis en quelques minutes, et malgré les énormes différences d'origine et d'éducation, nous nous sommes trouvés en accord sur presque tous les sujets. Mais je le trouve bien meilleur que ses livres; ceux-ce me semblent littéraires, 'voulus', exhibés'" ["The meeting with Wiesel was brief but very cordial. I found him to be fascinating, full of human warmth; we became friends in a few minutes, and in spite of the enormous differences in origin and education, we found ourselves in agreement on almost every subject. But I find him much better than his books; these seem to me literary, 'forcibly written,' flaunted"] (Amsallem 243).

Perhaps the two accounts can be refined and somewhat synthesized based on Wiesel's and Levi's other texts. Wiesel has never claimed to have known Levi at Auschwitz, as noted above ("He was a chemist and therefore useful; I was only a number" ["Why Memory?"]), and neither author writes from a motive of envy. The task of being witnesses to the Shoah supersedes that of a search for personal grandeur. Also, it is clear that their writing styles often differ—Wiesel's esoteric, often complicated mystical novels could have been annoying to Levi whose frequently concise, scientifically neutral tone stands in stark contrast to Wiesel's meditations. (As Gordon notes, "Not for Levi a childhood of faith, Kabbala, Yiddish, and the 'shtetl' (Wiesel)" [16].) However, even Levi admits to allowing himself to take on a religious persona under the guise of "poetry": "à travers la poésie moi aussi, homme laïque, je peux atteindre l'état d'esprit du croyant" ["by means of poetry, I also, a secular man, can attain the spiritual state of a believer"] (Amsallem 265). What is most significant for our book here is Levi's affirmation that, despite their diverse origins, Levi and Wiesel agreed "sur presque tous les sujets," doubtlessly including ethics.

The chapters which follow intend to demonstrate this ethical concord through a selective analysis of both authors' lives and works. In Chapter 1, "Thou shalt not kill," I provide insights into how the Nazi system appropriated Western culture's understandings of the "good," "true," and "beautiful," as well as "freedom." I note how compassion is sometimes incompatible with what is reasonable, and I show how this is demonstrated in three of Wiesel's fictional works: *Dawn*, *The Fifth Son*, and *A Beggar in Jerusalem*. I conclude the chapter with evidence that suggests that Levi's tragic death was not a suicide but an accident.

Chapter 2, "Thou shalt not commit adultery," discusses Wiesel's and Levi's committed love for and admiration of their wives Marion and Lucia, respectively. It answers the question of whether or not two authors faithful to their wives can write powerful scenes of wayward sexuality in their novels by commenting on passages from Wiesel's *The Accident* and Levi's *If Not Now, When?*

Chapter 3, "Thou shalt not steal," emphasizes the alteration of values that the Auschwitz victim had to undergo in order to survive. Primo Levi learned how to "organize" or steal adroitly while Elie Wiesel almost starved to death because of his fear of being punished for stealing. Levi's and Wiesel's critiques of the "thieves of time," those who steal themes and experiences from the Shoah and distort them for popular literary and visual art or even deny them entirely, is amplified by my brief summaries of Belgian scholar Albert Mingelgrün's analyses of four of such works: Philip K. Dick's *Le maître du Haut Château* [*The Man in the High Castle*], Norman Spinrad's *Rêve de fer* [*The Iron Dream*], Antoine Volodine's *Alto Solo*, and Maurice G. Dantec's *Les racines du mal* [*Roots of Evil*]. The chapter concludes with my own analysis of Amélie Nothomb's *Acide sulfurique: Roman* [*Sulfuric Acid: A Novel*] which dares to place "Pietro Livi" in a concentration camp created for the ongoing televised reality show, "Concentration."

Chapter 4, "Thou shalt not bear false witness against thy neighbour," includes a detailed comparison of Wiesel's and Levi's "witness," that is, their perceptions of particular events experienced during their sojourns in Auschwitz in 1944 until Wiesel's forced departure with his father for Gleiwitz and Buchenwald in January 1945 as recorded in their superb memoirs, *Night* and *Survival in Auschwitz*: the dehumanization that occurred immediately upon their arrivals; their ongoing, gnawing hunger; their harsh experiences during roll-calls on the *Appellplatz*; their viewings of cruel hangings there; their suffering through Dr. Mengele's October 1944 *Selektion*, and their experiences in the *Krankenbau* [hospital]. This chapter concludes with a brief comparison and contrast of their writing styles as memoirists.

Chapter 5, "Thou shalt not covet thy neighbour's house," verifies how Levi and Wiesel have never coveted others' homes but rather have found "home" in their own ways, Levi clinging to his birthplace on Corso Re Umberto in Turin and Wiesel finding "home" in his heart as he often lived out of a suitcase in Paris until arriving in New York as a young journalist. Levi's journey home after the Shoah as described in his *The Reawakening* is analyzed along with his hero Mendel's search for a home in *If Not Now, When?* Wiesel's transatlantic boat ride with European/Israeli refugees bound for Brazil, at first a journey that finds him completely consumed by his writing of his original version of *Night* in Yiddish (*Un di velt hot geshvign*), is described followed by an acknowledgement of the lack of "homes" in his first four fictional texts: *Dawn, The Accident, The Town Beyond the Wall,* and *The Gates of the Forest*. The ethical material in these five chapters grouped under the rubric of "Practical Ethics" is followed by five more chapters elucidating the "Essential Spirituality" motivating both men.

Predominantly based on their memoirs and conversations, Chapter 6, "I am the LORD thy God. . . . Thou shalt have no other gods before me," juxtaposes Levi's and Wiesel's beliefs, Levi's agnosticism and Wiesel's Hasidism, as well as their shared understanding of what it means to be truly "human"—manifesting an irrational, compassionate care for others, especially the weakest— which counters the social Darwinian "survival of the fittest" ethics enacted by many Nazis.

Chapter 7, "Thou shalt not make unto thee any graven image," explores the possibility that Levi may have made an idol out of humankind while Wiesel retained his troubled faith in God. Their spiritualities begin to merge, however, when Wiesel declares that "spiritual and humanistic are the same" (Personal interview); loving humans may equate with loving God, whether Levi recognizes this or not. An analysis of Franz Kafka's *The Trial*, interesting to both authors, shows how Josef K., definitely not a "Mensch," succumbs to a phantom bureaucracy, an idol perhaps even more dangerous than a visible god or dictator.

In Chapter 8, "Thou shalt not take the name of the LORD thy God in vain," I explore Levi's rejection of faith in God, from childhood on, and Wiesel's struggle to continue to believe in God after Auschwitz, especially as demonstrated in his dark play, *The Trial of God*. Does having God be defended by Sam, the devil, violate this commandment? A study of the meaning of both the commandment and the drama tries to answer this question.

Chapter 9, "Remember the Sabbath day, to keep it holy," examines the history and meaning of the Sabbath according to Scripture, hence its need for all observant Jews to honor it weekly. It also shows how medieval Christians, including Augustine, criticized and eventually persecuted Jews for exactly that observance, leading to the Nazi Aryan doctrine that God's chosen people were no longer the Jews but instead the Aryan race, personified in Germans with blond hair and blue eyes. This chapter concludes with analyses of Wiesel's and Levi's versions of the medieval legend of the Golem, Rabbi Judah Loew ben Bezalel, the Maharal of Prague's creation to help his persecuted people: Wiesel's *The Golem* and Levi's "Il servo."

Chapter 10, "Honour thy father and thy mother," chronicles how Levi and Wiesel honored their parents, Levi's father dying at home from cancer in 1942 while Wiesel witnessed his father's brutal murder at Buchenwald in January 1945. Wiesel's mother was probably killed by the Nazis the night of his family's arrival in Auschwitz in May 1944 while Levi cared for his frail, demented mother in his home until his death in April 1987; she survived him by four more years. Levi's frequent depressions, including the last, are related to his pain at seeing his mother turn into what he remembered as the "*Muselmänner*" of Auschwitz, the emaciated men, reduced to skin and bones, the living dead, who probably were unaware of their surroundings in their moribund condition. Wiesel has sensitively written a novel, *The Forgotten*, which chronicles a Shoah survivor's loss of memory due to Alzheimer's disease and his son's efforts to cope with this situation. An analysis of it concludes this chapter.

These last five chapters demonstrate Levi's and Wiesel's struggles to cope with God Who seems to have abandoned them and their people during the Shoah. The Conclusion returns to the questions raised in this Introduction and those elucidated throughout the text, especially if there can be "ethics after Auschwitz" in a postmodern, post-Holocaust world.

# Works Cited

Abrahamson, Irving, ed. *Against Silence: The Voice and Vision of Elie Wiesel.Vol. II.* New York: Holocaust Library, 1985. Print.

Abrahamson, Irving, ed. *Against Silence: The Voice and Vision of Elie Wiesel.Vol. III.* New York: Holocaust Library, 1985. Print.

Alighieri, Dante. *The Divine Comedy of Dante Alighieri: Inferno.* Trans. Allen Mandelbaum. New York: Bantam Books, 1982. Print.

Amsallem, Daniela. *Primo Levi au miroir de son oeuvre: Le témoin, L'écrivain, Le chimiste.* Lyon: Editions du Cosmogone, 2001. Print.

Angier, Carole. *The Double Bond: Primo Levi a Biography.* New York: Farrar, Straus and Giroux, 2002. Print.

Anissimov, Myriam. *Primo Levi: Tragedy of an Optimist.* Trans. Steve Cox. London: Aurum Press, 1998. Print.

Belpoliti, Marco, and Robert Gordon, eds. *The Voice of Memory: Interviews [with Primo Levi] 1961–1987.* Trans. Robert Gordon. New York: The New Press, 2001. Print.

*The Bible, The Authorized or King James Version.* Nashville, Tennessee: The Southwestern Company, 1902. Print.

Blumenthal, David R. *Facing the Abusing God: A Theology of Protest.* Louisville, KY: Westminster John Knox Press, 1993. Print.

Braiterman, Zachary. *(God) after Auschwitz: Tradition and Change in Post-Holocaust Jewish Thought.* Princeton: Princeton UP, 1998. Print.

Camon, Ferdinando. *Conversations with Primo Levi.* Trans. John Shepley. Marlboro, VT: Marlboro Press, 1989. Print.

Cavaglion, Alberto, and Elisabetta Ruffini. *Primo Levi: I giorni e le opere.* Torino: Museo Diffuso della Resistenza della Deportazione, della Guerra dei Diritti e della Libertà, 2007. Print.

Cicioni, Mirna. *Primo Levi: Bridges of Knowledge.* Oxford: Berg, 1995. Print.

Dantec, Maurice G. *Les racines du mal.* Paris: Gallimard, 1995. Print.

Dick, Philip K. *Le maître du Haut Château.* Trans. Jacques Parsons. Paris: Club du Livre d'Anticipation, coll. J'ai lu, no. 567, 1970. Print.

Edelman, Lily. "A Conversation with Elie Wiesel." *Responses to Elie Wiesel.* Ed. Harry James Cargas. New York: Persea Books, 1978. 9–22. Print.

"Ethics." *The Random House College Dictionary. Revised Edition.* 1983. Print.

Giuliani, Massimo. *A Centaur in Auschwitz: Reflections on Primo Levi's Thinking.* Lanham, Maryland: Lexington Books, 2003. Print.

Gordon, Robert S. C. *Primo Levi's Ordinary Virtues: From Testimony to Ethics.* Oxford: Oxford UP, 2001. Print.

Guinness, Os. *Long Journey Home.* New York: Doubleday, 2001. Print.

Haas, Peter J. *Morality after Auschwitz: The Radical Challenge of the Nazi Ethic.* Philadelphia: Fortress Press, 1992. Print.

Horowitz, Sara R. *Voicing the Void: Muteness and Memory in Holocaust Fiction.* Albany: State University of New York Press, 1977. Print.

Kafka, Franz. *The Trial.* Trans. Willa and Edwin Muir. New York: Schocken Books, 1974. Print.

Kalfa, Ariane, and Michaël de Saint Cheron. *Elie Wiesel en Hommage*. Paris: Les Editions du Cerf, 1998. Print.
Levi, Primo. *The Black Hole of Auschwitz*. Ed. Marco Belpoliti. Trans. Sharon Wood. Malden, MA: Polity Press, 2005. Print.
Levi, Primo. *The Drowned and the Saved*. Trans. Raymond Rosenthal. New York: Vintage International, 1989. Print.
Levi, Primo. *If Not Now, When?* Trans. William Weaver. New York: Penguin Books, 1995. Print.
Levi, Primo. *If This Is a Man*. Trans. Stuart Woolf. New York: First Collier Books Trade Edition, 1993. Print.
Levi, Primo. *The Reawakening*. Trans. Stuart Woolf. New York: A Touchstone Book, 1995. Print.
Levi, Primo. *La Ricerca delle radici*. Turin: Einaudi, 1981. Print.
Levi, Primo. *Se questo è un uomo*. Opere I. Torino: Einaudi, 1987. 1–212. Print.
Levi, Primo. "Il servo." Opere III. Torino: Einaudi, 1990. 338–46. Print.
Levi, Primo. *Il sistema periodico*. Opere I. Torino: Einaudi, 1987. 428–649. Print.
Levi, Primo. *Survival in Auschwitz: The Nazi Assault on Humanity*. Trans. Stuart Woolf. New York: A Touchstone Book Simon & Schuster, 1996. Print.
Levi, Primo. *La tregua*. Opere I. Torino: Einaudi, 1987. 213–425. Print.
Nothomb, Amélie. *Acide sulfurique: Roman*. Paris: Albin Michel, 2005. Print.
Rittner, Carol. "An Interview with Elie Wiesel." *Elie Wiesel: Between Memory and Hope*. Ed. Carol Rittner. New York: New York UP, 1990. 30–41. Print.
Rittner, Carol, and John K. Roth, ed. *"Good News" after Auschwitz? Christian Faith within a Post-Holocaust World*. Macon, GA: Mercer UP, 2001. Print.
Roth, John K. *Ethics During and After the Holocaust: In the Shadow of Birkenau*. New York: Palgrave Macmillan, 2007. Print.
Rubenstein, Richard L. "Gray into Black: The Case of Mordecai Chaim Rumkowski." Gray Zones: Ambiguity and Compromise in the Holocaust and Its Aftermath. Claremont McKenna College. Claremont, CA. 7 Feb. 2004. Address.
Ruether, Rosemary Radford. *Faith and Fratricide: The Theological Roots of Anti-Semitism*. New York: The Seabury Press, 1974. Print.
Scholem, Gershom. *Major Trends in Jewish Mysticism*. New York: Schocken Books, 1954. Print.
Spinrad, Norman. *Rêve de fer*. Trans. Jean-Michel Boissier. Paris: Pocket, coll. *Folio SF*, no. 239, 1992. Print.
Thomson, Ian. *Primo Levi: A Life*. New York: Metropolitan Books Henry Holt and Company, 2002. Print.
Volodine, Antoine. *Alto Solo*. Paris: Minuit, 1991. Print.
Wiesel, Elie. *The Accident*. Trans. Anne Borchardt. New York: Bantam Books, 1982. Print.
Wiesel, Elie. *A Beggar in Jerusalem*. Trans. Lily Edelman and the Author. New York: Schocken Books, 1970. Print.
Wiesel, Elie. *Célébration hassidique*. Paris: Le Seuil, 1976. Print.
Wiesel, Elie. *Conversations*. Ed. Robert Franciosi. Jackson: U of Mississippi P, 2002. Print.
Wiesel, Elie. *Dawn*. Trans. Frances Frenaye. New York: Bantam Books, 1982. Print.
Wiesel, Elie. *Et où vas-tu?* Paris: Éditions du Seuil, 2004. Print.

Wiesel, Elie. *The Fifth Son*. Trans. Marion Wiesel. New York: Warner Books, 1985. Print.
Wiesel, Elie. *The Forgotten*. Trans. Stephen Becker. New York: Schocken Books, 1992. Print.
Wiesel, Elie. *From the Kingdom of Memory: Reminiscences*. New York: Summit Books, 1990. Print.
Wiesel, Elie. *The Gates of the Forest*. Trans. Frances Frenaye. New York: Schocken Books, 1982. Print.
Wiesel, Elie. *The Golem: The Story of a Legend as told by Elie Wiesel and illustrated by Mark Podwal*. Trans. Anne Borchardt. New York: Summit Books, 1983. Print.
Wiesel, Elie. "Io e Primo Levi." *Nuova Antologia* 127 (1992): 204–08. Print.
Wiesel, Elie. *A Jew Today*. Trans. Marion Wiesel. New York: Random House, 1978. Print.
Wiesel, Elie. *Memoirs: All Rivers Run to the Sea*. New York: Alfred A. Knopf, 1995. Print.
Wiesel, Elie. *Night*. Trans. Marion Wiesel. New York: Hill and Wang, 2006. Print.
Wiesel, Elie. Personal interview. 25 October 2004.
Wiesel, Elie. *Silences et memoires d'hommes: Essais, histoires, dialogues*. Paris: Éditions du Seuil, 1989. Print.
Wiesel, Elie. *The Town Beyond the Wall*. Trans. Stephen Becker. New York: Schocken Books, 1982. Print.
Wiesel, Elie. *The Trial of God (as it was held on February 25, 1649, in Shamgorod)*. Trans. Marion Wiesel. New York: Schocken Books, 1986. Print.
Wiesel, Elie. *Un di velt hot geshvign*. Buenos Ayres: Tsentral-Farband fun Poylishe Yidn in Argentine, 1956. Print.
Wiesel, Elie. "Why Memory?" *Washington Post*, 5 Oct. 2006. Web. 7 Oct. 2006. <http://www.washingtonpost.com/wp-dyn/content/article/2006/10/05/AR2006100501336>.
Wiesel, Elie, and Josy Eisenberg. *Job ou Dieu dans la tempête*. Paris: Fayard-Verdier, 1986. Print.
Wiesel, Elie, and Philippe-Michaël de Saint-Cheron. *Evil and Exile*. Trans. Jon Rothschild. Notre Dame: U of Notre Dame P, 1990. Print.

# PRACTICAL ETHICS

"As one rabbinic sage opined, 'Do you know who can protest against His decree and say to Him, "Why do you do such a thing?"' He who observes the commandments'" (Numbers Rabbah 14:6 quoted in Braiterman 32).

# Chapter 1: "Thou shalt not kill"

In 1968 Primo Levi wrote, "the commandment 'Thou shalt not kill' has been turned upside down [in Auschwitz]" (*Black* 28). In *A Jew Today* Elie Wiesel explained, "The very first war, the one between Cain and Abel, taught us that he who kills another kills himself. That is why 'Thou shalt not kill' is one of the Ten Commandments" (160–61). Wiesel's Rabbi in *Le Serment de Kolvillag* cautions, "L'être humain sanctifie la vie en la célébrant, en luttant contre ce qui l'appauvrit. Le suicide est un meutre. Qui se tue, tue" ["Human beings sanctify life by celebrating it, by fighting against what impoverishes it. Suicide is a murder. Whoever kills himself, kills"] (135). Further, Wiesel notes that "[a]ccording to the Talmud, to humiliate someone in public is to shed his blood" (*Legends* 92). Humiliating him takes away his dignity and does indeed wound him profoundly (*Et où vas-tu?* 181). Judaism promotes human life to the fullest extent, and authentic Christianity, as an offshoot of Judaism, maintains this fundamental belief.

The Nazis, however, succeeded in destroying Jewish life partly because of their intense propaganda efforts to portray Jews as dangerous parasites, less than human, sucking the blood out of the human race, whose most superior strain, so they believed, was so-called Aryan Germans. Between 1933 and 1945 European Jews lost their citizenship, property, professional standing, freedom, and, for many, eventually their lives because of this intentional dehumanization. Once excluded from the human race, they could be exterminated like vermin.

It is clear that both Levi and Wiesel have integrated the biblical fundamental affirmation of human life into their most profound thinking and feeling, for their responses to the denial of honoring and protecting human life are strong. Wiesel has stated, "as surely as the victims are a problem for the Jews, *the killers are a problem for the Christians*" (Brown 171). "The sincere Christian knows that what died in Auschwitz was not the Jewish people but Christianity" (Brown 171). Most of the Nazis were at least nominal Christians who also should have valued human life as much as the Jews; for reasons known only to them they negated this commandment by becoming organized murderers under Hitler's reign. Wiesel explains, "'I believe,'. . . 'that the Christians betrayed the Christ more than the Jews did.' Jews, not Christians, have more nearly followed in the path of Jesus as patient sufferers. Jews were reviled and hated and finally crucified by collective madness in the Holocaust. Christians, on the other hand, have more closely followed in the path of Judas as betrayers of Jesus' teaching" (Estess 76).

Wiesel's strong words to Christians have not prevented him from maintaining deep friendships with authentic believers such as François Mauriac, who encouraged him to write his memoir *Night* and who penned its preface, plus Jean-Marie Cardinal Lustiger, archbishop of Paris (*Memoirs* 271). Wiesel has also carefully studied the New Testament and shows great sympathy for Jesus who must be weeping because of what His followers have done. Wiesel includes a sympathetic picture of "Yeoshua" in *A Beggar in Jerusalem*; Shlomo, one of his crazy beggars, remarks: "'May I tell you about my meeting with Yeoshua? Do you remember him? The innocent preacher who had only one word on his lips: love. Poor man. I saw him the day he was crucified. Not far from here'" (56). Shlomo continues his fantastic tale by relating what he addressed to Yeoshua: "'You think you are suffering [on the cross] for my sake and for my brothers', yet we are the ones who will be made to suffer for you, because of you'" (56). Shlomo's subsequent description of how Jews suffer persecution for Yeoshua's sake ultimately causes Yeoshua to "burst into tears of despair" (56); he proclaims vehemently: "'No, no! This is not how it will be! You are wrong, you must be! This is not how I foresee the reign of my spirit! I want my heritage to be a gift of compassion and hope, not a punishment in blood!'" (56–57). Shlomo ends up weeping for both Yeoshua and the Jewish people (57).

Wiesel's sympathetic treatment of Jesus, even though rendered via an insane beggar in this novel, is echoed by the author's response to Mauriac: "I'm not blaming Jesus [for the crimes committed by baptized Nazi killers and torturers]. He was crucified by the Romans, and now it is Christians who torment him by committing evil in his name" (*Memoirs* 269). Wiesel's respect for Christians is understandable since his focus is always on ethical truth, whoever proclaims it: "I have more in common with an authentic and tolerant Christian than with a Jew who is neither authentic nor tolerant," he states (*A Jew Today* 11).

## Chapter 1

Peter J. Haas sheds some light on how to analyze an ethic gone awry:

> [T]o get at the basic convictions and beliefs held by members of a society about the good life, we must first see how members of that society talk to each other about the good life. This is not only a matter of seeing what people claim they should or should not do. It is, more importantly, a matter of seeing how people explain their decisions and what values and beliefs these explanations assume others already accept as self-evident. It means adducing the precise connotations conjured up by words such as good, evil, warrant, sin, intent, act and the like. It means also describing how these words function in relation to each other in the speakers' and hearers' minds. In short, it means describing the linguistic universe in which a culture's moral discourse takes place. ("Toward a Semiotic" 62)

The "good" affirmed in the commandment to not kill became indeed "turned upside down," to repeat Levi's words, so that killing Jews was "good" and protecting Jews was "evil." This inversion of fundamental Jewish and Christian values became "self-evident" to many in Germany and elsewhere in Europe. Diverse scholars have explored many reasons for this radical transformation of values among which are some non-Jews' jealousy of what was perceived to be Jewish financial, professional, and artistic success; their greed to possess Jewish farms, homes, and businesses; their dislike of Jewish customs, organizations, and perceived "international networks"; their fear of perceived Jewish Bolshevik conquests, and their vitriolic anti-Semitism dating from the Middle Ages.

Abraham Joshua Heschel provides an even deeper analysis of the cultural world views held by Europeans of this era when he emphasizes "a basic difference between the Greek and biblical conception of man" (107). Medieval and modern western European Christianity was of course heavily influenced by a Platonic conception of the "good" linked strongly to the "true" and the "beautiful." Hitler and his followers were able to inject revised definitions of these terms into their milieu and therefore create a "moral discourse," to use Haas's term, different from biblical and Greco-Roman teachings. Heschel explains, "Here is a basic difference between the Greek and the biblical conception of man. To the Greek mind, man is above all a rational being; rationality makes him compatible with the cosmos. To the biblical mind, man is above all a commanded being, a being of whom demands may be made. The central problem is not: What is being? But rather: What is required of me?" (107). Nazi ideology made the irrationality of anti-Semitism "rational," and it implemented a sophisticated bureaucratic apparatus to put this pseudo-rationalism into action, while simultaneously transforming legitimate understandings of obedience to God's commands into unreflective, unconditional obedience to Hitler. This new "truth" became a diabolical "good."

Heschel describes a believer's appropriate responses to God: "*I am commanded—therefore I am*. There is a built-in *sense of indebtedness in the consciousness of man*, an awareness of *owing gratitude*, or being *called upon* at certain moments to reciprocate, to answer, to live in a way which is compatible with the grandeur and mystery of living" (111). Authentic understanding of "Thou shalt not kill" promotes life— obedience to God out of gratitude for the precious gift of life. Nazi moral discourse advocated the killing of Jews in obedience to Hitler as necessary for protecting and enhancing the lives of the so-called Aryan peoples at the expense of those outside of that category. Adolf Hitler and his followers "place[d] anti-Judaism at the center and use[d] this as the hub into which all other intellectual trends were fitted as spokes" (Haas, *Morality* 51). The result was a Nazi system "[s]o internally consistent. . . that it developed an aura of self-evident truth" (Haas, *Morality* 99).

Propaganda appeared early, even before Hitler's rise to power, with hurtful but initially seemingly harmless cartoons of Jews as dangerous predators on German society. A postcard from around 1920 entitled "Gefesselte Germania" (*Wannsee-Konferenz* 25) pictures a beautiful woman similar to a Grecian goddess bound with ropes, hence immobilized, with a crown at her feet (representing the *Kaiserreich* destroyed by Germany's defeat in World War I) next to a sword that closely resembles a Christian cross. Two unnamed but obviously intended to represent Jewish men stand beside her. The bald, well dressed first man looks up at this statuesque feminine figure with a joyful, knowing smile. The second man, bearded and wearing a hat in her presence, drops coins into the money bag he is holding. This small cultural artifact suggests that, along with revising the Greco-Roman understandings of the "good" and the "true," anti-Semitic persons with power were also co-opting the "beautiful," embodied in this suffering "Germania."

Elie Wiesel's response to a question about why "madness" appears so often in his texts now becomes more comprehensible: "mainly because rationalism is a failure and a betrayal" (Abrahamson,

*Against II* 79). The inversion of meanings for the "good," the "true," and the "beautiful" betrayed the Jews and led to their tragic near destruction. Wiesel summarizes, "In truth, Auschwitz signifies not only the failure of two thousand years of Christian civilization, but also the defeat of the intellect that wants to find a meaning—with a capital M—in history" (*Legends* 183). He admits that his works are more influenced by Kabbalah than rationalism, which demonstrated its failure at Auschwitz. He concedes that the Shoah's "deep significance" "transcends reason" (*Conversations* 152).

Polish sociologist Zygmunt Bauman echoes Wiesel's concerns about "reason" when he states, "Reason is, by definition, rule-guided; acting reasonably means following certain rules. Freedom, the trade mark of a moral self, came to be measured by the strictness with which the rules were followed. By the end of the day, the moral person has been unhooked from the bonds of autonomous emotions only to be put in the harness of heteronomous rules. The search that starts from the disbelief in the self's moral *capacity* ends up in the denial of the self's *right* to moral judgment" (69). Those who helped some Jews survive during the Holocaust were "outlaws," acting against the "heteronomous rules" of a German society that had reformulated the definitions of the "good," the "true," the "beautiful," and "freedom." Nazis who followed the "rules" with "strictness" and efficiency received commendations, promotions, increased salaries, and often other perquisites. "Outlaws" such as Otto Jogmin often acted from an ethic that preceded the Nazi redefinitions. When asked why he protected Jews in his home at Wielandstrasse 18 in Berlin-Charlottenburg, he replied simply, "meine Mutter war eben so ein Mensch, war der—so mitleidig war, nicht wahr, da konnte ich einfach nicht anders, ging nicht, ging nichts anderes" ["My mother was just such a 'Mensch,' she was—was so compassionate, you know, that I simply could not do otherwise, could not—it could not have been any other way"] (*Wannsee-Konferenz* 137).

Bauman affirms that "[m]orality is not safe in the hands of reason. . . . Reason cannot help the moral self without depriving the self of what makes the self moral: that unfounded, non-rational, unarguable, no-excuses-given and non-calculable urge to stretch toward the other to caress, to be for, to live for, happen what may" (247). Bauman has been influenced by Emmanuel Levinas who was tutored in Paris after the War by Shoushanie, a Lithuanian whose Yiddish name was Mordechai Rosenbaum (*Memoirs* 129), and who was also

Wiesel's spiritual guide there between 1946 and 1948 (de Saint Cheron 123). Wiesel and Levinas at that time did not yet know each other and hence were unaware of each other's studies with this peripatetic, eccentric brilliant Jewish philosopher (*Conversations* 151), but their views on responsible love for "the other" are similar and may have resulted from those early days of instruction received from Shoushanie. Wiesel affirms that Levinas is the only disciple of Shoushanie who succeeded in transforming the work of this mysterious, peripatetic sage into a "système de valeurs, en système d'idées" ["system of values and ideas"] (Malka 37). Levinas himself gratefully states, "M. Chouchani. Tout ce que je publie aujourd'hui sur le Talmud, je le lui dois" ["Mister Chouchani. All that I publish today on the Talmud I owe to him"] (Malka 111). Wiesel acknowledges, "Levinas and I knew each other well; we were very close. . . . The difference between Levinas and me is that Levinas is no Kabbalist; he is a rationalist" (*Conversations* 151), rooted in "an anti-Kabbalist movement of eastern Europe, . . . Lithuanian rationalism" (*Conversations* 152). Bauman exceeds Levinas's "rationalism" to affirm unconditional care for the other beyond what is "reasonable."

Although never connected to the sage Shoushanie, Primo Levi also acknowledges the irrationality but absolute necessity of love, even though it can coexist with brutality: "Pietà e brutalità possono coesistere, nello stesso individuo e nello stesso momento, contro ogni logica; e del resto, la pietà stessa sfugge alla logica" ["Compassion and brutality can coexist in the same individual and at the same moment, contrary to all logic; and besides, compassion itself escapes all logic"] (*I sommersi e i salvati* I.692). Haas ultimately concludes that "the Holocaust was not the incarnation of evil but instead reflected the human power to reconceive good and evil and then to shape society in the light of the new conception" (*Morality* 9).

Wiesel shows the failure of a seemingly "reasonable" act—the killing of an enemy officer—in *Dawn*, his brief *récit* following *Night*. Here Elisha, as a novice in a small terrorist group, must shoot pointblank the kidnapped British officer John Dawson as an act of retribution for the British occupiers' arrest and execution in Palestine of one of the band's key members. His task is made all the harder because he likes Dawson who tells him that he reminds him of his son in England. At the end of the novel, when Elisha finally does shoot Dawson, he recognizes that he has truly killed himself, at least morally (102). This is Wiesel's clear statement against violence, including violence as an act of revenge (Wiesel, *Evil* 126–27). Outside of the realm of fiction he affirms, "Suffering is often unjust, but it never justifies murder" (*A Jew Today* 106).

This affirmation is echoed in his later novel, *The Fifth Son*, when the son of a Holocaust survivor arranges to assassinate a German businessman receiving philanthropic awards who previously had been a feared sadistic Nazi killer. The novel's Rebbe Zvi-Hersh explains, "the Biblical verse prohibits assassination. It can never be justified" (178). Nevertheless, Reuven's son born after World War II confronts Richard Lander ("the Angel") face to face: "Should I inform him that I was his judge and he my prisoner?" (201). Unlike Elisha in *Dawn*, this son decides not to kill Herr Direktor Wolfgang Berger: "Once the words had been exchanged, I could leave. The *Angel* no longer provoked in me either hatred or thirst for revenge. I had disturbed the pattern of his existence, renewed his memory, spoiled his future joys, that was enough for me" (202).

Wiesel shows through Katriel, one of his key characters in *A Beggar in Jerusalem*, that even an Israeli warrior suffers deeply from having to kill to protect his homeland. David, Katriel's new friend, discovers him alone, trembling "with rage, with hatred perhaps" (182) after bloody combat. Katriel exclaims, "'Yes, I have killed! You want to know whom? And how many times? I don't know myself! I shall never know! And it's of no importance. I've killed and nothing is important any more. . . . Leave me alone! You consider yourself innocent [not having killed], and you understand nothing about innocence, and neither do I'" (182). By the close of the novel Katriel has either been killed in subsequent battles or is missing in action, his fate still undetermined. His transformation from both a loving son who studies Torah with his widowed father and a caring husband and father into an extremely upset warrior shows both the seriousness of killing, even when participating in military actions, and the disastrous results of it for both the killer as well as, of course, the killed.

In this novel Wiesel also includes the words of a wise Jewish father speaking to his son as they are led to a ditch next to which the Germans will soon shoot them: "Whoever kills, becomes God. Whoever kills, kills God. Each murder is a suicide, with the Eternal eternally the victim" (208). This puzzling statement can be clarified by noting Wiesel's understanding that "God. . . is in every human being, and every human being is born of His being" (*Evil and Exile* 32).

Hence, if one person kills another, for whatever reasons, he or she is also killing God within this other. Only God has the right to destroy a part of His creation; therefore the killer exceeds his human limits and "becomes God." Further, since all humans share God's presence within themselves, to kill the God within the other is essentially to kill oneself as well. Wiesel understands the destruction of human life to be of paramount ethical importance.

Primo Levi seems to share that important value. He remarked that he has never even been able to raise a hand against another: "Je ne me suis jamais battu avec personne, par exemple, même enfant, je n'ai jamais réussi à faire le coup de poing avec personne" ["I never got into a fight with anyone, for example, even as a child, I never succeeded in raising a fist to anyone"] (Amsallem 261). Although he joined an underground resistance group in northern Italy after the German invasion of September 1943, he later commented to his biographer Ian Thomson, "'I was a young bourgeois pacifist and I'd rather have died than shoot anyone'" (124). His colleague at arms, Aldo Piacenza, remarked to Thomson, "'Primo kept asking me why men had to kill each other, he seemed astounded by the world's malignancy'" (131). This astonishment was horrifyingly confirmed when two partisans were shot by Sergeant-Major Berto because of their "drunken rampage" in St. Vincent during the night of December 8, 1943: "Partisan justice was undeniably rough justice," Thomson explains, adding: "All the books Levi had read on the glorious Risorgimento, the fine ideas in his head, were meaningless in the light of this appalling incident. Two band members had been executed by a *fellow partisan*. Where was the glory in that? The killings had robbed the Resistance of its slender romantic allure" (134). Levi commemorated these two teenagers in 1952 in his poem "Epitaph" (Thomson 223). Much later, however, he included in *If Not Now, When?* (*Se non ora, quando?*) the shooting of "a Russian partisan who had drunkenly revealed secrets to the enemy" (Thomson 385).

It would be inappropriate to conclude this chapter without discussing Primo Levi's death outside of his apartment beside the interior granite stairwell of 75 Corso Re Umberto. The police concluded that it was a suicide, as is carefully documented by Ian Thomson in his biography of Levi (5). Briefly, "[t]he body had fallen fifteen metres head-first down the stairwell of the building and struck the marble floor at the foot of the lift shaft. Death was instantaneous" (1). A declaration of suicide was first made by Dr. Roberto Mandas, the doctor summoned by the police to view the body at the scene of the accident: '"Confirmed hereby the decease of Primo Levi as the likely result of suicide'" (4). Although Levi's wife, upon returning home from grocery shopping and discovering him dead on the floor by the stairs and elevator cage, at first spoke of his acute depression ('"I feared it, everybody feared it. Primo was tired of life. . . [sic] We did our best never to leave him alone, ever. Just one moment was enough'" [4]), nevertheless she later denied that he had committed suicide. Others have joined her in that denial.

Diego Gambetta in 1999 chronicles additional facts relevant to Levi's death, which strongly suggest that it was an accident resulting perhaps from an episode of dizziness that occurred as Levi leaned over the top of a low railing (three feet and two inches high) looking for the concierge who had a few minutes before delivered his mail (Postscriptum, April 21, 2005, "Primo Levi's Last Moments"). Carole Angier notes that "[t]he height of the banisters [is] 96 centimetres high. Primo was about 170 cm (about five foot five) tall" (722). On the Thursday before this fatal Saturday he had already scheduled an appointment with Dr. Giorgio Luzzati for the following week because of Levi's own concern about his fatigue and dizzy spells (Gambetta, "Primo Levi's Plunge"). Nobel laureate in medicine and close friend Rita Levi Montalcini received a phone call from Levi on Friday, April 10, during which "he sounded in much better spirits" (Angier 718); shortly after his death on Saturday, April 11, 1987, she shrewdly remarked that "[i]f Levi wanted to kill himself he, a chemical engineer by profession, would have known better ways than jumping into a narrow stairwell with the risk of remaining paralyzed" (Gambetta, "Primo Levi's Last Moments"). David Mendel, a British physician with whom Levi corresponded, aptly noted that "Primo could, had he wished, have taken an overdose of his medicine" (Gambetta, "Primo Levi's Last Moments"). Jonathan Druker protests that "[w]e should not succumb to that mental laziness or rely on easy stereotypes of the Holocaust survivor to convince ourselves that a suicide is logical and appropriate when a whole life and a multitude of words in black and white shout their denial" (229).

Levi's son, who lived in the same building in the other apartment next door to that of his parents' and also overlooking the landing, had left with a visiting friend earlier that morning. Angier notes that Levi "seemed to Renzo and his friend completely normal and serene" (723). It seems out of character for the caring Levi to shock his wife, who would be returning momentarily from shopping, and also his son, who had already come back to the building, with his mutilated fallen body. Levi knew from past experience what the result of a fall from the fourth floor of a building would entail, for he described such a shattering drop in *Il sistema periodico* (*The Periodic Table*) when the rope broke on the hoist, thus sending the "cappa d'aspirazione" ("ventilation hood") on a downward fall ending in a definitive crash: "Mentre Emilio ed io assistevamo dal cortile alla funerea cerimonia, la cappa uscí solenne dalla finestra, si librò ponderosa, si stagliò contro il cielo grigio di via Massena, venne abilmente agganciata alla catena del parranco, e la catena gemette e si spezzò. La cappa piombò per quattro piani ai nostri piedi, e si ridusse in schegge di legno e vetro" ["While Emilio and I attended the funeral ceremony in the courtyard, the mounted ventilation hood exited solemnly from the window, balanced itself heavily, was silhouetted against the gray sky of via Massena, became skillfully joined to the chain of the hoist, and the chain groaned and broke. The ventilation hood plunged four floors down to our feet, and was reduced to shards of wood and glass"] (I.607). Angier reports, "Renzo came down, and was the first [of the family] to see his father" (724).

Further, although in 1986, unlike Italo Calvino, "he had instructed his wife what to do with his papers after his death" (Thomson 455), he left no suicide note. He had, however, prepared a will, "a perfectly normal one, leaving his estate to his children, with the use of it during her lifetime to his wife" (Angier 724). He also gave no indication to the nurse caring for his elderly mother in his home or the concierge who cheerily handed him his mail at his door around ten o'clock (Angier 723), a few minutes before the fall, that he was distraught. Gambetta concludes, "Indeed, the facts known to us arguably suggest an accident more strongly than they indicate suicide" ("Primo Levi's Last Moments").

Why, then, did many, including Elie Wiesel ("Why Memory?"), immediately conclude that Levi had committed suicide? Wiesel spoke on the telephone with Levi on April 8, the Wednesday preceding his Saturday fall. During that conversation Levi sounded so depressed to Wiesel that he invited him to come to New York and to stay in his home until he felt better. Levi's response had been a sorrowful "too late" (Anissimov 404; Angier 717). Levi had indeed been depressed by his elderly mother's and mother-in-law's deteriorating mental and physical conditions, his fear of being unable to write anymore, his abhorrence of publications and oral statements made by Holocaust deniers, and the aftereffects of his prostate operation twenty days before his fall (Gambetta "Primo Levi's Last Moments"), but these problems do not necessarily have to result in an outcome of suicide.

Levi's biographer Carole Angier, however, after carefully documenting his final days and presenting evidence that speaks both for and against his fall being an act of suicide, concludes the following:

> He went to the phone [that fateful Saturday morning after having received his mail from the concierge] and called Dr. [Renzo] Gozzi [his psychiatrist]: we know that, '*Non ne posso più*,' he said, 'I can't go on.' Wait, Gozzi said, I'm coming. But he couldn't wait. He called [his mother's private duty] nurse, and told her to answer the phone; we know that too. In case someone might call and stop him in the last second? Because he just needed to get out, and really thought he might walk downstairs? He opened the door, and found himself outside.
>
> It wasn't the light and air he had dreamed of, but it was a deep void.
>
> One last time the thought knocked at his brain, and found the place waiting there. I think he looked for Lucia to stop him. He leaned and looked, but she wasn't there; and he let go. (731)

Angier's construction above includes two facts: Levi's call to his psychiatrist and his request to his mother's nurse to answer the phone while he stepped out. The rest is imagined. Angier herself has recorded numerous times in her lengthy tome that the same words he uttered to his psychiatrist had already often been stated to his friends, without suicide as a consequence. For example, in March, a few weeks earlier, "Euge rang from Milan. Primo said, 'I can't do anything any more. I can't go on.' Giorgio Vaccarino rang, and Primo repeated the same things: 'My mind doesn't work. I can't go on.' They all encouraged him, told him it would pass, and thought it would" (Angier 712). Ian Thomson notes that Levi had asked Piero Fassino, "the secretary of Turin's Communist Party," "to call him again on the morning of Saturday 11 April" (494), so he *was* expecting at least one call.

Levi and Wiesel were both aware of the many concentration camp survivor/writers who had already killed themselves: Jean Améry, Paul Celan, and Tadeus Borowski, among others. Gambetta astutely notes that "in the little he wrote about it, Levi never argued in favor of suicide. When discussing the other writer-survivors who committed suicide—not only Améry but also Paul Celan—he shows no special empathy or understanding for what they did. He says only that suicide is a philosophical act, and reveals that he thought about it both before and after but not while in the camp" ("Primo Levi's Last Moments").

"Thou shalt not kill": if Levi's death was indeed an accident and not a suicide, then perhaps the greatest injustice of all has been inflicted upon him since the charge of killing an exceptionally ethical "Mensch" has been leveled against him when he no longer has the possibility of defending himself against it.

# Works Cited

Abrahamson, Irving, ed. *Against Silence: The Voice and Vision of Elie Wiesel. Vol. II.* New York: Holocaust Library, 1985. Print.

Amsallem, Daniela. *Primo Levi au miroir de son oeuvre: Le témoin, L'écrivain, Le chimiste.* Lyon: Editions du Cosmogone, 2001. Print.

Angier, Carole. *The Double Bond: Primo Levi a Biography.* New York: Farrar, Straus and Giroux, 2002. Print.

Anissimov, Myriam. *Primo Levi: Tragedy of an Optimist.* Trans. Steve Cox. London: Aurum Press, 1998. Print.

Bauman, Zygmunt. *Postmodern Ethics.* Oxford: Blackwell, 1993. Print.

Braiterman, Zachary. *(God) after Auschwitz: Tradition and Change in Post-Holocaust Jewish Thought.* Princeton: Princeton UP, 1998. Print.

Brown, Robert McAfee. *Elie Wiesel: Messenger to All Humanity.* Notre Dame: U of Notre Dame P, 1982. Print.

Druker, Jonathan. "Reading Suicide into the Works of Primo Levi." *The Legacy of Primo Levi.* Ed. Stanislao G. Pugliese. New York: Palgrave Macmillan, 2005. 221–29. Print.

Estess, Ted L. *Elie Wiesel.* New York: F. Ungar Publishing Company, 1980. Print.

Gambetta, Diego. "Primo Levi's Last Moments." *Boston Review* (Summer 1999). Web. 31 Aug. 2009. <http://www.bostonreview.net/BR24.3/gambetta.html>.

Gambetta, Diego. "Primo Levi's Plunge: A Case against Suicide." *New York Times* 7 Aug. 1999: A15. Print.

Haas, Peter J. *Morality after Auschwitz: The Radical Challenge of the Nazi Ethic.* Philadelphia: Fortress Press, 1988. Print.

Haas, Peter J. "Toward a Semiotic Study of Jewish Moral Discourse: The Case Of Responsa." *Semeia* 34 (1985): 59–83. Print.

Heschel, Abraham J. *Who Is Man?* Stanford, CA: Stanford UP, 1965. Print.

Levi, Primo. *The Black Hole of Auschwitz.* Ed. Marco Belpoliti. Trans. Sharon Wood. Malden, MA: Polity Press, 2005. Print.

Levi, Primo. "Epitaph." *Primo Levi: Collected Poems.* Trans. Ruth Feldman and Brian Swann. London: Faber and Faber, 1988. 21. Print.

Levi, Primo. *If Not Now, When?* Trans. William Weaver. New York: Penguin Books, 1995. Print.

Levi, Primo. *The Periodic Table.* Trans. Raymond Rosenthal. New York: Alfred A. Knopf, 1996. Print.

Levi, Primo. *Se non ora, quando? Opere II.* Torino: Einaudi, 1988. 183–517. Print.

Levi, Primo. *Il sistema periodico. Opere I.* Torino: Einaudi, 1987. 428–649. Print.

Levi, Primo. *I sommersi e i salvati. Opere I.* Torino: Einaudi, 1987. 651–822. Print.

Malka, Salomon. *Monsieur Chouchani: L'énigme d'un maître du XXe siècle, Entretiens avec Elie Wiesel suivis d'une enquête.* Paris: Editions Jean-Claude Lattès, 1994. Print.

Saint Cheron, Philippe M. de. *Elie Wiesel: Pèlerin de la mémoire.* Paris: Plon, 1994. Print.

Thomson, Ian. *Primo Levi: A Life.* New York: Metropolitan Books Henry Holt and Company, 2002. Print.

*Die Wannsee-Konferenz und der Volkermord an den europaischen Juden: Katalog der standigen Ausstellung.* Berlin: Haus der Wannsee-Konferenz, Gedenk- und Bildungsstätte, 2008. Print.

Wiesel, Elie. *A Beggar in Jerusalem.* Trans. Lily Edelman and the Author. New York: Schocken Books, 1970. Print.

Wiesel, Elie. *Conversations.* Ed. Robert Franciosi. Jackson: U of Mississippi P, 2002. Print.

Wiesel, Elie. *Dawn.* Trans. Frances Frenaye. New York: Bantam Books, 1982. Print.

Wiesel, Elie. *Et où vas-tu?* Paris: Éditions du Seuil, 2004. Print.

Wiesel, Elie. *The Fifth Son.* Trans. Marion Wiesel. New York: Warner Books, 1985. Print.

Wiesel, Elie. *A Jew Today.* Trans. Marion Wiesel. New York: Random House, 1978. Print.

Wiesel, Elie. *Legends of Our Time.* New York: Holt, Rinehart and Winston, 1968. Print.

Wiesel, Elie. *Memoirs: All Rivers Run to the Sea.* New York: Alfred A. Knopf, 1995. Print.

Wiesel, Elie. *Night.* Trans. Marion Wiesel. New York: Hill and Wang, 2006. Print.

Wiesel, Elie. *Le Serment de Kolvillag.* Paris: Éditions du Seuil, 1973. Print.

Wiesel, Elie. "Why Memory?" *Washington Post,* 5 Oct. 2006. Web. 7 Oct. 2006. <http://www.washingtonpost.com/wp-dyn/content/article/2006/10/05/AR2006100 501336>.

Wiesel, Elie, and Philippe-Michaël de Saint-Cheron. *Evil and Exile.* Trans. Jon Rothschild. Notre Dame: U of Notre Dame P, 1990. Print.

# Chapter 2: "Thou shalt not commit adultery"

Elie Wiesel confesses that his personal timidity around women "often hobbled my love stories. Friendship is a more simple feeling" (*Conversations* 138). As a child and a seriously practicing Hasid, he "did not dare to look at women" (*Conversations* 131). As an adult, he refuses to write about "sexually obsessed" characters (*Memoirs* 67).

He seems to have mastered what Zygmunt Bauman terms '"successful love'": "the respect for the mystery in the beloved, cultivation of difference, suppression of possessive urges, refusal to smother the autonomy of the beloved with the bulldozer of domination—preserve and replenish the sublime, the unknown, the recondite, the tremendous in the partner, thus keeping alive both the moral and the aesthetic value of the partnership" (181). Wiesel's wife is an accomplished translator, a cultured, caring person who engages in her own good works via their Elie Wiesel Foundation for Humanity in New York which they both created with the funds awarded to him for the Nobel Peace Prize (*And the Sea Is Never Full* 369). She often chooses not to accompany him on his many speaking trips, despite his stating in his *Memoirs* how very much he needs her wisdom and counsel, and she is much less religious than he who scrupulously observes the Sabbath and Jewish holidays (*And the Sea Is Never Full* 11). Nevertheless his love for her and pride in her have endured throughout more than forty years of their marriage without outside incidents tarnishing that joy. He affirms, "Marion, my wife, my ally, my confidante, it is she who often prevents me from making mistakes. It is to her that I owe the wisdom that enables me to follow a certain path. And she has remained young, which I am no longer" (*And the Sea Is Never Full* 406).

In his *Memoirs* he proudly speaks of her Zionist efforts: "In the corridors I might have encountered a young Jewish girl from Vienna, beautiful and daring, who transported documents and provided a hiding place for guns: my future wife [Marion]" (167). After their first meeting in the mid 1960s, he acknowledges, "I wasn't sure what I found most striking about her: the delicacy of her features, the brilliance of her words, or the breadth of her knowledge of art, music, and the theater" (*Memoirs* 338).

His awe of her talents has not diminished over the years. In his second volume of memoirs, he writes in 1996, decades after their wedding in Jerusalem in 1969 (*And the Sea Is Never Full* 7), "I owe much to Marion. She knows how to suggest, to correct, to critically evaluate texts and decisions" (*And the Sea Is Never Full* 6). For example, he frankly confesses his dependence on her regarding his decisions relevant to the new Holocaust Memorial Council for which President Jimmy Carter asked him to be chairman of its founding committee: "Marion. Je ne fais rien, je ne décide rien sans elle ni sans lui demander son avis" ["Marion. I do nothing, I decide nothing without her nor without asking her opinion"] (. . . *Et la mer* 319). When she did not accompany him with a delegation to Poland appointed by President Bill Clinton, he lamented, "I miss Marion. I need her advice, her support. But she refused to join me. She has never liked ceremonies" (*And the Sea Is Never Full* 196). However, when she did accompany him to the U.S.S.R. shortly after he was awarded the Nobel Prize for Peace in 1986, he followed her lucid, practical advice after he had failed to evoke any positive response from Russian officials when he tried to intervene for Andrei Sakharov, *their* Nobel Prize winner, and other political dissidents:

> With her usual logic, Marion advises me to take a direct approach: 'Why don't you ask to meet him [Mikhail Gorbachev]?' I stare at her; did I hear her right? 'Meet him? To whom, do you think, should I submit such a request?' As always her answer is clear and simple. 'Write him.' Fine—I'll write him a letter. And then what? 'Then you give it to Andrei [the young official in charge of our security]. He'll know what to do.' It sounds so simple when Marion says it that I feel disarmed. Anyway, I have nothing to lose. (*And the Sea Is Never Full* 262)

Wiesel follows her advice, and an emissary from Gorbachev does indeed soon arrive at their hotel offering the Wiesels a meeting with him (*And the Sea Is Never Full* 266).

Among the books which he has dedicated to her are *A Beggar in Jerusalem*, *The Forgotten*, and *Memoirs: All Rivers Run to the Sea*. She has also translated many of his texts into English: *And the Sea Is Never Full: Memoirs, 1969—*, *The Fifth Son*, *A Jew Today*, *Twilight*, *Souls on Fire*, *Night*, *The Trial of God*, and others. He admiringly writes in the

"Preface to the New Translation" of *Night*: "Marion, my wife, . . . knows my voice and how to transmit it better than anyone else" (xiii).

Wiesel also acknowledges that, in addition to her professional expertise, she has helped him to mature personally and ethically over the years. For example, she aided him in overcoming his fear of having children: "I was convinced that a cruel and indifferent world did not deserve our children. . . . It was Marion who persuaded me otherwise. It was wrong to give the killers one more victory. The long line from which I sprang must not end with me. She was right" (*And the Sea Is Never Full* 43).

Together they have also organized and hosted important international conferences such as the successful "The Anatomy of Hate" symposium in Norway (. . . *Et la mer* 45) and elsewhere—"the United States, the Middle East, and Europe" (*And the Sea Is Never Full* 369). Wiesel remarks appropriately proudly:

> As for the artistic aspect of the event, Marion heads the special team that has taken on the intricate and subtle preparations of the concert that, traditionally, becomes the highlight of our conferences. Audrey Hepburn, delicate and supremely gracious, and Gregory Peck, grave and regal, act as masters of ceremonies [in Oslo]. The orchestra is conducted by Lukas Foss. On the program, some of the most outstanding performers of our time: the flutist James Galway, the soprano Frederica von Stade, the bass Simon Estes. (*And the Sea Is Never Full* 375)

Primo Levi was also married to his Lucia for just short of forty years. He and the beautiful, intelligent Lucia Morpurgo were wed on September 8, 1947, at the Town Hall in Turin followed by a "religious blessing" at her home (Thomson 236). Biographer Carole Angier notes, "Lucia Morpurgo. . . . was a year younger than Primo, slender, blonde, and attractive. . . . The family was Jewish, but not at all religious; and less culturally Jewish even than Primo's" (453). The racial laws of 1938 barred Lucia from admission to the university, and so she studied privately with sculptor Roberto Terracini; she could again follow her goal of delving into art history at the university in 1946, after the war (Angier 454).

A second biographer, Ian Thomson, describes her as follows:

> Lucia was interested in music, painting, could happily recite Dante (and did). She came from Perugia, and was said by many to have a faint provincial air of prudishness and propriety. She could also be difficult and jealous. But if the twenty-six-year-old Primo was sexually innocent, so too

was Lucia. 'I was her first man (and she my first woman).' With her aquiline nose and long pale neck, Lucia was beautiful. And, crucially, she listened to Levi at a time when he needed desperately to talk. Lucia was his counselor and confidante. And she was able to listen longer than most because none of her immediate family had perished in the camps. (211–12)

In *Il sistema periodico* (*The Periodic Table*) Primo Levi describes his joy as a result of falling in love with her in February 1946. Amidst his efforts to solve a difficult paint problem (the spoilage of many cans because of an imbalance of ingredients), as described in "Chromo," he inserts that over the week-end he fell in love:

> . . . il destino mi riserbasse un dono diverso ed unico: l'incontro con una donna, giovane e di carne e d'ossa, calda contro il mio fianco attraverso i cappotti, allegra in mezzo alla nebbia umida dei viali, paziente sapiente e sicura mentre camminavamo per le strade ancora fiancheggiate di macerie. In poche ore sapemmo di appartenerci, non per un incontro, ma per la vita, come infatti è stato. In poche ore mi ero sentito nuovo e pieno di potenze nuove, lavato e guarito dal lungo male, pronto finalmente ad entrare nella vita con gioia e vigore; altrettanto guarito era ad un tratto il mondo intorno a me, ed esorcizzato il nome e il viso della donna che era discesa agli inferi con me [Vanda Maestro] e non ne era tornata [. . . destiny reserved for me a different and unique gift: the meeting with a woman, young and of flesh and bones, warm against my side through our overcoats, cheerful amidst the humid fog of the avenues, patient, wise, and secure while we walked through the streets still flanked with debris (from the war bombings). In a few hours we knew that we belonged to each other, not for an encounter but for life, as in fact it has been. In a few hours I felt myself new and full of new strength, washed and healed of a long illness, ready finally to enter into life with joy and vigor; equally was healed suddenly the world around me, and the name and the face of the woman who had descended into hell with me and had not returned was exorcized]. (572)

Lucia was artistic and sensitive, a caring teacher of both children and adults seeking an education after work hours at night. Gifted and intelligent herself, she is portrayed by some of Levi's biographers as "frightened of the 'brilliant ones', Levi's cerebral women friends: Bianca Guidetta Serra, Ada Della Torre, Nicoletta Neri, Tina Rieser" (Thomson 315; Angier 522). These historians of Levi's life also note that she suffered from living her entire married life with Levi's mother at 75 Corso Re Umberto, thus never having had charge of her (and his) own home (Thomson 315, 523).

Levi believed that a strong family was foundational to society (Thomson 317), and he criticized his daughter's living with a leftist at age nineteen during the politically turbulent 1960s (Thomson 317). However, he was not immune to cultivating close friendships with beautiful, intelligent women such as Franca Mussa Ivaldi, a fellow tourist on his week long trip to Israel (Thomson 319). When he was criticized by "Turin's Jewish community" "the flirtation was quietly ended" (Thomson 319–20).

He was more cautious with Edith Bruck, a Hungarian who had endured Auschwitz as a child (Thomson 344). "If Bruck tried to envelop Levi in her arms (she had the motherly tendency), he flinched away red-faced. . . . Levi always preferred strictly asexual relationships with women" (344). Indeed, he wrote a commendatory preface for her *Due stanze vuote* [*Two Empty Rooms*] rather than engage in intimate relationships with this attractive survivor, fifteen years younger than he (Speelman 474). He encouraged her in her writing of books, as he also did Liliana Millu, another Auschwitz survivor, for whom he wrote the following in his preface to her *Il fumo di Birkenau* [*The Smoke of Birkenau*]:

> Leur [the women's] état etait bien plus mauvais que celui des hommes, pour diverses raisons: elles étaient physiquement moins aptes à resister aux travaux, plus difficiles et plus humiliants que ceux des hommes; la pensée de leur famille les torturait; la présence obsédante des crématoires, les cheminées au milieu du camp des femmes, que l'on ne pouvait pas faire semblant de ne pas voir et qui contaminaient de leur odeur infecte leurs jours et leurs nuits, leurs moments de répit et d'illusion, leurs rêves et leur timide espoir [Their condition was much worse than that of the men, for a variety of reasons: they were physically less capable of enduring the heavy work projects, more difficult and more humiliating than those of the men; the thought of their family tortured them; the obsessive presence of the crematoriums, the chimneys in the midst of the women's camp, that no one could pretend to not see and which contaminated with their noxious odor their days and their nights, their moments of respite and of illusion, their dreams and their timid hope]. (Quoted in Speelman 478)

Thus Levi felt deep compassion for female concentration camp survivors like Edith Bruck and Liliana Millu, and he was pleased to encourage them in their writing about their experiences, but his relationships with them remained friendly and platonic.

He shows similar compassion for his wife who cared for their sick children at night while he pleaded working the next day as an excuse for avoiding this self-sacrificing obligation: "my wife has spent many nights in it [the spare room in their apartment] attending [our children] when they were sick; I never did, with the ironclad alibi of work at the factory and the Olympian selfishness of all husbands" ("My House" 13). He seems to have understood well the "male ego."

His love for Lucia deepened as their care for their elderly ill mothers increased. In 1983 Levi wrote in English to a psychiatrist, Ruth Hoffman, an immigrant from central Europe practicing in London:

> For some months I have not been well. . . . I suffer from a depression which began insidiously after the wave of success with *If Not Now, When?* and was aggravated in December owing to my mother's illness. She is 88 and lives with my wife and I [sic]. Her illness has left her in need of every kind of help and above all she is seriously depressed herself. Her depression only adds to (or multiplies with!) my own, which is interwoven with a sense of guilt toward my wife, who is wonderful, expert, efficient and attentive, while I am inept, distracted, and useless in the house—except for shopping. (Thomson 410)

Levi's admiration and appreciation of Lucia are evident here, and this glimpse at the challenges they both faced in their personal lives is striking. Lucia somehow continued to function well and lovingly amidst two very depressed individuals, her mother-in-law and her husband, even while also caring for her own mother who was blind and debilitated (Angier 602, 730).

Gaia Servadio, an Italian writer and journalist working in London, also recalls Levi's tender care for Lucia when they were on a speaking tour promoting his works: "Levi said he had courted Lucia by bike and he seemed boyishly proud of his bicycle courtship. 'My impression was of a very tender relationship,' remembered Servadio. During the meal Levi often turned, smiling, to Lucia; here was a couple who had come through hard times together—and who were happier, as always, when away from 75 Corso Re Umberto" (Thomson 460).

Lucia is absent from most of Levi's writings, but he does honor her with a fourteen-line poem entitled the date of her birthday, "12 July 1980," when she was sixty years old; it concludes: "They [these lines] are my rough way of saying how dear you are,/ And that I wouldn't be in this world without you" (*Primo Levi: Collected Poems* 42).

Given the dedication of Elie Wiesel and Primo Levi to their wives and families, the question arises whether or not they can describe in their fiction incidents of infidelity or even sexual violence, having not experienced these themselves. As noted above, Wiesel says that he refuses to write about "sexually obsessed" characters (*Memoirs* 67), but in his angriest novel, *The Accident* (also translated into English as *Day*), first published in French in 1961 before he met Marion and awarded the Prix Rivarol in 1962 (de Saint Cheron 190), he includes a brutal scene between Kathleen, a young American, and her upset concentration camp survivor lover, the first person narrator, which strikes hard in its stylistic brevity, even in translation:

> "I'll prove to you that I'm not a saint," I muttered angrily.
> Without a word I started to undress her. She didn't resist. When she was naked, she sat down again as before. Her head resting on her knees, she looked at me in anguish as I too undressed. Now there were two lines around her mouth. I could see fear in her eyes. I was pleased; she was afraid of me, and that was good. Those who, like me, have left their souls in hell, are here only to frighten others by being their mirrors.
> "I am going to take you," I told her in a harsh, almost hostile voice. "But I don't love you."
> I thought: she must know. I'm not a saint at all. I'll make love without any commitments. A saint commits his whole being with every act.
> She undid her hair, which fell to her shoulders. Her breast rose and fell irregularly.
> "What if I fall in love with you?" she asked with studied naiveté.
> "Small chance! You'll hate me rather."
> Her face became a little sadder, a little more distressed. "I'm afraid you're right."
> Somewhere, above the city, there was a hint of dawn in the foggy world.
> "Look at me," I said.
> "I'm looking at you."
> "What do you see?"
> "A saint," she answered.
> I laughed again. There we were, both naked, and one of us was a saint? It was grotesque! I took her brutally, trying to hurt her. She bit her lips and didn't cry out. We stayed together until late that afternoon. (34)

This scene, bordering on rape, expresses hateful love, if such an oxymoron can be imagined, the confusion the angry survivor feels about himself and his lover when she altruistically and even passionately tries both to honor him by calling him a "saint" and to love him by surrendering herself to him physically and emotionally. It is not a trite scene created for sexual sensationalism; instead, it expresses vividly the damage in all areas—physical, emotional, spiritual, and sexual—done to the Shoah victim. In short, Wiesel is quite capable of portraying sexuality poignantly and meaningfully even without biographically having experienced such a scene.

Primo Levi's rendering of illicit sexuality surpasses Wiesel's description above because his calm, good hero, the watchmender of *If Not Now, When?* (*Se non ora, quando?* 1982), Mendel, steals Line away from his friend Leonid, resulting in this unbalanced partisan's suicidal mission because of this loss and betrayal. Mendel has befriended Leonid because he feels great compassion for him:

> Leonid's silences oppressed him. Instinctively, he liked Leonid, who seemed one of those men you can trust; but this passivity was irksome. When a watch is dusty, that's a sign it's very old, or else the case has come loose; and then you have to take it completely apart and clean it, piece by piece, with light gasoline. Leonid wasn't old; so it was his case that had some crevices in it. What kind of gasoline would be needed to clean Leonid's works? (46)

One night desire for a woman overcomes Mendel: "It was an adolescent's desire, without shape, soft and warm and white: he tried to describe it to himself and failed. Desire for a bed, and a woman's body in the bed; desire to dissolve inside another, a woman, and to be one flesh with her, a double flesh isolated in the world, away from roads, weapons, fears, and memories of the slaughter" (191–92). He cannot resist seeking Line, Leonid's lover:

> Beside Line, Leonid was sleeping, and the two were wrapped in the same blanket; . . . . Mendel helped Line unwrap herself from the blanket without waking Leonid. Together they climbed to the loft: . . . They lay down, and Mendel undressed Line, removing her army clothing. . . . Mendel undressed, and immediately Line clung to him as if to wrestle. . . . I am the woman of no one, and by resisting I bind you to me. . . . Nobody's and everybody's, like Rahab of Jericho: Mendel perceived this and felt stabbed, as at the last moment he tore himself from her. The effort was so lacerating that Mendel sobbed aloud, in the dark silence of the mill. (191–94)

The next day, the band of partisans moves on: "Mendel marched in silence, and didn't feel pleased to be Mendel" (195).

Line is an attractive, fiery Russian, Marxist, Zionist feminist (131), imbued with, no doubt, *The Communist Manifesto* of 1848 which critiques "bourgeois" marriage: "The bourgeois family will vanish as a matter of course when its complement vanishes, and both will vanish with the vanishing of capital" (Marx 37). "Our bourgeois, not content with having the wives and daughters of their proletarians at their disposal, not to speak of common prostitutes, take the greatest pleasure in seducing each others' wives" (39). "Communists. . . . desire to introduce, in substitution for a hypocritically concealed, an openly legalized community of women" (39). Line has no problem leaving Leonid for Mendel. However, she will also move on to other lovers, while Mendel remains alone yet again, having already lost his wife Rivke back in his village when it was overrun by Nazis (20, 28, 111). "Line separated from Mendel. It was sad, like all partings, but it didn't surprise anyone" (257).

Leonid dies because of their love affair, playing the role of the hero to a fatal degree:

> Mendel flattened himself on the ground, heard the bullets whistling in midair above his head, and out of the corner of his eye he saw Leonid jump to his feet. "Get down," he whispered, trying to restrain him: but Leonid eluded him, jumped over the hedge, fired a round in replay, and plunged, head down, in the direction of the door. From the house came a single, isolated shot, and Leonid fell across the threshold. (223)

Later Mendel tells Line sorrowfully, "'It wasn't the German who killed Leonid, and not Gedaleh, either. . . . [but the] two of us'" (230).

In his commentary on Numbers 14:33, Robert Alter notes that "[w]horing is of course a standard biblical metaphor for sinfulness—especially for betrayal (modeled on sexual betrayal)" (753). Levi's Mendel has "whored" and knows it. He reflects that he has indeed "covet[ed] my neighbor's woman" (317). This incident again shows the influence that the Decalogue and the Torah have had on Levi. Despite the violence of Wiesel's scene depicted above, Kathleen and the narrator are both single, free to commit themselves to each other, even if "grotesquely," to use Wiesel's descriptor. Mendel has stolen Line away from his friend, even though they are not officially, in a "bourgeois" manner, married. The result is his friend's suicidal mission in combat. Paradoxically, Wiesel the Hasid seems much more secular in his writing about sexuality in *The Accident* than Levi the agnostic in the award winning *If Not Now, When?* (Premio Campiello and Premio Viareggio). "Thou shalt not commit adultery" is related to promoting life, as noted in Chapter 1, and to not stealing, as will be shown in Chapter 3. Patrick D. Miller notes that "the Commandments are not simply distinct rules but actually highly interconnected modes of living that interact constantly with one another" (233). If "Thou shalt not commit adultery" limits sexual partners to monogamous marriages, it does so because it is an important, essential thread woven into the tapestry of Jewish ethics.

# Works Cited

Alter, Robert. *The Five Books of Moses: A Translation with Commentary.* New York: W. W. Norton & Company, 2004. Print.
Angier, Carole. *The Double Bond: Primo Levi a Biography.* New York: Farrar, Straus and Giroux, 2002. Print.
Bauman, Zygmunt. *Postmodern Ethics.* Oxford: Blackwell, 1993. Print.
Bruck, Edith. *Due stanze vuote.* Venise: Marsilio, 1974. Print.
Elie Wiesel Foundation for Humanity. <http://www.eliewieselfoundation.org>.
Levi, Primo. *If Not Now, When?* Trans. William Weaver. New York: Penguin Books, 1995. Print.
Levi, Primo. "My House." *Other People's Trades.* Trans. Raymond Rosenthal. New York: Summit Books, 1989. 11–15. Print.
Levi, Primo. *The Periodic Table.* Trans. Raymond Rosenthal. New York: Alfred A. Knopf, 1996. Print.
Levi, Primo. *Se non ora, quando? Opere II.* Torino: Einaudi, 1988. 183–517. Print.
Levi, Primo. *Il sistema periodico. Opere I.* Torino: Einaudi, 1987. 428–649. Print.
Levi, Primo. "12 July 1980." *Primo Levi: Collected Poems.* Trans. Ruth Feldman and Brian Swann. London: Faber and Faber, 1988. 42. Print.
Marx, Karl, and Frederick Engels. *Manifesto of the Communist Party.* Trans. Samuel Moore. Chicago: Charles H. Kerr Publishing Company, 1998. Print.
Miller, Patrick D. *The Ten Commandments.* Louisville, Kentucky: Westminster John Knox Press, 2009. Print.
Millu, Liliana. *Il fumo di Birkenau.* Florence: Giuntina, 1986. Print.
Saint Cheron, Philippe M. de. *Elie Wiesel pèlerin de la mémoire.* Paris: Plon, 1994. Print.
Speelman, Raniero. "Les Compagnons de Levi, d'autres témoins italiens de la Shoah." *Primo Levi à l'oeuvre: La Réception de l'oeuvre de Primo Levi dans le monde.* Ed. Philippe Mesnard et Yannis Thanassekos. Paris: Éditions Kimé, 2008. 467–82. Print.
Thomson, Ian. *Primo Levi: A Life.* New York: Metropolitan Books Henry Holt and Company, 2002. Print.
Wiesel, Elie. *The Accident.* Trans. Anne Borchardt. New York: Bantam Books, 1982. Print.
Wiesel, Elie. *And the Sea Is Never Full: Memoirs, 1969—.* Trans. Marion Wiesel. New York: Alfred A. Knopf, 1999. Print.
Wiesel, Elie. *A Beggar in Jerusalem.* Trans. Lily Edelman and the Author. New York: Schocken Books, 1970. Print.
Wiesel, Elie. *Conversations.* Ed. Robert Franciosi. Jackson: U of Mississippi P, 2002. Print.
Wiesel, Elie. *. . . Et la mer n'est pas remplie: Mémoires 2.* Paris: Éditions du Seuil, 1996. Print.
Wiesel, Elie. *The Fifth Son.* Trans. Marion Wiesel. New York: Warner Books, 1985. Print.
Wiesel, Elie. *The Forgotten.* Trans. Stephen Becker. New York: Schocken Books, 1992. Print.

Wiesel, Elie. *A Jew Today*. Trans. Marion Wiesel. New York: Random House, 1978. Print.

Wiesel, Elie. *Memoirs: All Rivers Run to the Sea*. New York: Alfred A. Knopf, 1995. Print.

Wiesel, Elie. *Night*. Trans. Marion Wiesel. New York: Hill and Wang, 2006. Print.

Wiesel, Elie. *Souls on Fire: Portraits and Legends of Hasidic Masters*. Trans. Marion Wiesel. New York: A Touchstone Book, 1993. Print.

Wiesel, Elie. *The Trial of God (as it was held on February 25, 1649, in Shamgorod)*. Trans. Marion Wiesel. New York: Schocken Books, 1986. Print.

Wiesel, Elie. *Twilight*. Trans. Marion Wiesel. New York: Schocken Books, 1988. Print.

# Chapter 3: "Thou shalt not steal"

Shoah survivors generally do not speak of stealing in the ghettos and concentration camps; their term for it is "organizing": "One had to organize or scheme—be it day or night—in order to survive perhaps a little longer, sometimes only an extra day or just a few hours" (Edelheit 368). Primo Levi describes the consequences of theft at Auschwitz in *If This Is a Man*:

> theft in Buna, punished by the civilian authorities, is allowed and encouraged by the SS; theft in the camp, severely repressed by the SS, is considered a normal exchange operation by the civilians; theft among prisoners is generally punished, but the punishment strikes the thief and the victim with equal gravity. The reader is now invited to consider what "good" and "evil", "just" and "unjust" could possibly mean in the camp; let everybody judge, on the basis of the picture I have outlined and of the examples given above, how much of our ordinary moral world could survive on this side of the barbed wire. (*Se questo è un uomo* 87, quoted in Cicioni 31)

Levi chose his own good (stealing necessities from both I. G. Farben's Buna and the SS's Auschwitz) (Thomson 162) and his own evil (never stealing from another prisoner). He explains, "'survival without giving up anything of one's own moral world was granted only to very few superior individuals made of the stuff of martyrs and saints'" (*Se questo è un uomo* 94, quoted in Cicioni 37). Wiesel never stole despite his father's and his great needs. He states in "Io e Primo Levi," "Io non ho mai mangiato più della porzione che ricevevo" (205) ["I never ate more than the portion which I received"]. Does this make him one of Levi's "saints"? The vehement reaction of Wiesel's protagonist in *The Accident* to being called a "saint" (as noted in Chapter 2) suggests that he himself would also reject this designation. (Ironically, David Mendel has suggested that Levi himself comes close to sainthood: "[h]e was an exceptionally good man. We don't have saints in our religion, but he was as near to one as we do have" 73.)

Wiesel explains in his *Memoirs* how he did nothing extraordinary to survive—he never "organized": "Logically, I shouldn't have survived. Sickly, timid, fearful, and lacking all resourcefulness, I never did anything to stay alive. I never volunteered for anything, never jostled anyone to get a tin of soup. Coward that I was, I preferred to eat less and to let myself be devoured by hunger rather than expose myself to blows. I was less afraid of death than of physical suffering" (79–80).

The difference between their ages and levels of education reveals itself vividly in their varied reactions to "organizing"—Wiesel, arriving at Auschwitz at age fifteen, steeped in Hasidic studies, kept as low a profile as possible while Levi, having been awarded by the University of Turin his diploma in chemistry with highest honors, volunteered for an oral chemistry examination and succeeded in being recruited to work in I. G. Farben's chemical laboratory. Among all of his twenty-one chapters named for chemical elements in *Il sistema periodico* (*The Periodic Table*), only one is set at Auschwitz: "Cerio." Levi writes, "rubavo per mangiare. Se non si comincia da bambini, imparare a rubare non è facile; mi erano occorsi diversi mesi per reprimere i comandamenti morali e per acquisire le tecniche necessarie. . . . Rubavo tutto, salvo il pane dei miei compagni" ["I stole in order to eat. If one does not begin as a child, to learn to steal is not easy; I needed several months to repress the moral commandments and to acquire the necessary techniques. . . . I stole everything, except the bread of my companions"] (*Il sistema periodica* I.559). Levi's clear statement that he "stole" ("rubavo") rather than "organized" shows the continued impact of "Thou shalt not steal."

"Cerio" describes his theft of small sticks of "iron-cerium" from the Buna lab, which could be trimmed into many lighter flints, each lighter worth one daily bread ration when sold on the Auschwitz black market. This theft guaranteed that he and Alberto, with whom he shared everything—the sticks, their shaping, and their selling—could have enough to eat until the Russians, heard at a distance from Auschwitz, liberated the camp. Unfortunately Alberto perished on his forced march (also shared with Wiesel and his father) to Buchenwald and Mauthausen. Levi's scarlet fever and quarantine in the hospital ward at Auschwitz saved him from that death march so that he did indeed survive to greet the Russian liberators.

Both Levi and Wiesel focused on being ethical human beings. According to Jack Kolbert, the ethical behavior of Wiesel, whose maternal tongue is Yiddish, manifests itself with him being a true "Mensch," "someone endowed with honesty, fairness, justice, integrity, respect for the sanctity of human life, and with compassion for the underdog" (147). A Mensch maintains his own personal dignity by making ethical choices that reflect truthfulness, justice, and love; hence he affirms the dignity of others while living out his own integrity in his relationships with them. Wiesel describes one such Mensch at Auschwitz: "We loved him [this visionary friend in the camps] because he responded to every appeal for help, he set his face against evil, he clung to his humanity in a world where humanity was denied—and he took very little credit for it. He wanted no thanks" (*Legends* 56). Levi had to juggle and prioritize the virtues of a Mensch in order to justify his thefts: personal survival and love for Alberto took precedence over the honest exchanges that Levi knew in civilian life before and after Auschwitz.

The challenge of making right ethical choices in an inhumanly oppressive environment is communicated in Levi's poem "The Survivor" ("Il superstite"): "Non ho usurpato il pane di nessuno,/ Nessuno è morto in vece mia. Nessuno" ["I haven't usurped anyone's bread./ No one died in my place. No one"] (*Opere II*: 581). The question, though, remains whether a survivor can be absolutely sure of this? Levi confesses in *The Drowned and the Saved*, "I might be alive in the place of another, at the expense of another; I might have usurped, that is, in fact killed" (82). He is exquisitely ethically sensitive to the possibility that the greatest theft of all may be stealing another's life.

Wiesel thought that Levi was too hard on himself when he felt guilt for having survived Auschwitz: "His theory of a 'gray zone' in which every inmate was guilty—some more, some less, directly or indirectly, simply for having survived—well, all this seems to me simplistic and unfair. By speaking of the 'relativity' of their innocence, he was attenuating the guilt of the killers. Only the criminals are guilty, I told him; to compare the victims in any way with the torturers was to dilute or even deny the killers' responsibility for their actions" (*And the Sea Is Never Full* 347). Massimo Giulani believes that Wiesel misunderstood Levi's "gray zone" theory postulated in his final work, *The Drowned and the Saved*: "[Levi] never said nor wrote simply that, in the 'gray zone,' every inmate was guilty just for having survived. . . . This is a clear distortion of his thought" (Giulani 3). Regardless of where guilt is assigned, Levi's sensitivity to the possibility of having "usurped" another inmate's life reflects his honoring the dignity of every human being.

Wiesel reveals moments in his memoirs when he, too, mourns those who might have replaced him in *Selektionen* and at other times. For example, as late as April 10, 1945, Germans were evacuating Jews from Buchenwald. Liberated by the Americans on April 11, 1945 (*And the Sea Is Never Full* 216), Wiesel explains, "That day [April 10] I stayed behind. Someone else took my place. Since then I have often wondered who left because I stayed behind. I will never know him, but I know I owe him my life" (*Memoirs* 96). The pervasive threat of death and the fire, fumes, and ashes from the crematoriums which verified its daily reality heightened the awareness of both survivors that they were privileged to live yet another day and that, by doing so, they might be stealing life from others. The Nazi system was designed to psychologically entrap good people in this circular cage of environmental morbidity.

As a manager and businessman long after his Auschwitz days, Levi continued to refuse to steal. Ian Thomson notes, "even in Italy the kickback and bribery culture known as *la bustarella* ('the little envelope') offended Levi. In business he was a man of unbending rectitude, and he disappointed his patrons in Moscow's Soyuzchimexport (the foreign-trade organization that dealt with SIVA) by refusing to accept bribes" (324).

Thoroughly sensitive, then, to how they might have been thieves, both Wiesel and Levi were distressed by the "thieves of time": "My friend and companion Primo Levi called these malevolent critics and commentators 'thieves of time. . . . who infiltrate themselves through keyholes and cracks and cart out our memories without leaving a trace'" (Wiesel, *Wise Men* 334). These are the intellectuals who appropriate aspects of the Shoah experience for their own personal advantage or artistic use without honoring the seriousness of the subject and the full truth of its survivors' memories and experiences. Such misuse of this genocide angers these two key artists who have been "there" and who know that such representations distort the truth of their experiences. Wiesel wrote in his original Yiddish draft of *Night* (*Un di velt hot geshvign*) the following concluding thoughts which now appear in the first volume of his memoirs in French (but not in their English translation):

> Maintenant, dix ans après Buchenwald, je me rends compte que le monde oublie. L'Allemagne est un Etat souverain. L'armée allemande a ressuscité. Ilse Koch, la femme sadique de Buchenwald, est mère de famille, et heureuse. Des criminels de guerre se promènent dans les rues de Hambourg

et Munich. Le passé est effacé, enterré. Allemands et antisémites déclarent au monde que l'histoire de six millions de victimes juives n'est qu'un mythe, et le monde, dans sa naïveté, y croira, sinon aujourd'hui, demain ou après-demain [Now, ten years after Buchenwald, I realize that the world forgets. Germany is a sovereign state. The German army has resurrected. Ilse Koch, the sadistic woman of Buchenwald, is a mother of children, and happy. Some war criminals walk around the streets of Hambourg and Munich. The past is erased, buried. Germans and anti-Semites declare to the world that the history of six million Jewish victims is only a myth, and the world, in its naivete, believes it, if not today, then tomorrow or the day after tomorrow]. (*Tous les fleuves* 455)

He adds, "Ce que j'ai dit, en 1955, sur l'oubli, l'indifférence et les néfastes ambitions des négationnistes, je pourrais le répéter, sans y toucher, aujourd'hui, en 1994" ["What I said in 1955 about the forgetfulness, indifference, and evil ambitions of the Holocaust deniers I could repeat, without changing a thing, today in 1994"] (*Tous les fleuves* 456).

Belgian scholar Albert Mingelgrün has carefully summarized some disturbing works of European and American literary art appearing in the decades after Wiesel's comment in 1955; these texts *have* dangerously distorted the events of the Shoah. Mingelgrün groups them in a genre that he calls "livres-prétextes" ("pretext books"), for they assume facts and themes from this historical tragedy and reformulate them in ways related to the production of science fiction or detective novels. Philip K. Dick's *Le maître du Haut Château* [*The Man in the High Castle*], Norman Spinrad's *Rêve de fer* [*The Iron Dream*], Antoine Volodine's *Alto Solo*, and Maurice G. Dantec's *Les racines du mal* [*Roots of Evil*] all reveal what most survivors would consider distortions of their trauma.

In Dick's novel, which originally appeared in 1962, Germany and Japan have conquered the United States and split its geographical territory between them. Rumors about Jewish control of international funds and decadent art still circulate, and the powers that be fear Hawthorne Abendsen, sequestered in the High Castle in the Rocky Mountains, and hence seek his life, for he regrets that Roosevelt's successor did not pursue a more fervent anti-Nazi strategy (Mingelgrün 18). Here can be observed the hypothetical "what if" approach of science fiction (What if the Allies had lost to Germany and Japan?) and the detective story's search for the criminal rebel who defies the regime in power. Shoah survivors could legitimately ask if such a novel is necessary. Even those who would not go so far as

Wiesel does in considering the Holocaust to be an irrational "mystical" event might still find Dick's trivialization of it offensive.

In Spinrad's *Rêve de fer* a decade later (1972), the reader understands that the novel is really written by Adolf Hitler whose original title for it is *Le Seigneur du Svastika* [*The Lord of the Swastika*]. Spinrad describes "la Grande République de Heldon" [the Great Republic of Heldon] whose inhabitants embody the pure human genotype. The protagonist Feric Jaggar gains adherents of "pure men" and extinguishes those weaker (Mingelgrün 19). Thus Nazi racial ideology, to the horror of Jews and others who detest its lies, has surfaced again. It is understandable why survivors like Levi and Wiesel wonder if anything has been learned from their and others' horrific experiences during World War II.

Volodine's *Alto Solo* (1991) is almost a continuation of Spinrad's distorted dystopia. Mobs on the rampage in search of victims, scapegoating, and emotional discourses given by a certain "Zagoebel" (a reincarnation of Goebbels?), affirmed by fanatical cries of approval from the crowd (Mingelgrün 19), all echo nightmarish events of the 1930s and 1940s.

Dantec's *Les racines du mal* (1995) imagines some Nazi systems to be at work in contemporary society. Andreas Schaltzmann believes that the Nazis have hidden power over France. Transit camps and other facilities really disguise concentration camps, and he becomes a resistance fighter against those behind these zones of cruelty (Mingelgrün 19–20). Again, a real survivor of the Shoah would have to wonder why revive traumatic memories and attempt to integrate them into European life fifty years after the liberation of the concentration camps? Is this a muddled attempt to be "avant-garde" with risqué material? If so, is it worth retraumatizing the survivors and thrilling with false knowledge those born after World War II? Levi and Wiesel have spent their lives verbally and in writing witnessing to the truth of their experiences in the world of concentration camps, but many addicted to popular culture rather than serious survivor literature will formulate their ideas about the Shoah from bizarre novels such as these.

A recent extremely strange novel, Amélie Nothomb's *Acide sulfurique: Roman* [*Sulfuric Acid: A Novel*] (2005), may surpass in offensiveness all of those mentioned above, for it dares both to present a concentration camp as the setting for a shockingly popular "reality" television show ("Concentration") and to place "Pietro Livi," whom Mingelgrün identifies as Primo Levi (Lechat 39), in the heart of it, in love with "Pannonique," the camp's beautiful, courageous heroine. It is frightening to read how this program so successfully captivates its television spectators, since real persons are abducted from the streets, placed in the camp, and tortured by blows, starvation, insults, and back breaking work assignments, while omnipresent cameras roll on, recording their daily suffering. Hired actors who serve as *Kapos* select prisoners daily to be killed. The television spectators are drawn to CKZ 114 (Pannonique) because of her graceful, quiet, audacious steadfastness as well as her occasional critical remarks addressed to them directly into the camera (109, 178–79), usually a technical faux pas in film-making.

Unlike the original concentration camps, however, men and women on this show work together as a small unit and are housed together in the same crude barracks. This housing arrangement permits the quiet romance between EPJ 327 (Pietro Livi) and CKZ 114 to develop. Livi resembles the real Levi in his compassion for others, deep wisdom, and sensitivity, but, unlike Levi, he does not actively resist this odd "social construction of reality" since perhaps this would detract, in the Belgian author's plan, from the acute heroism of CKZ 114 who daily fights off the lesbian approaches of Kapo Zdena and shares with her unit the chocolate bars this aggressor surreptitiously drops into her uniform pocket. Eventually CKZ 114's strained relationship with Zdena will lead to the latter liberating the camp, bearing in hand Molotov cocktails apparently consisting of sulfuric acid.

I was drawn to this novel because I wanted to see if Nothomb would dare to represent Levi shamefully eighteen years after his death in 1987 and I wondered if any goodness could come out of such a bizarre text. Her Livi is too passive for my taste, but at least he is consistently a person of integrity, worthy of the heroine's love. Curiously, he seems to be a combination of both Levi and Wiesel. He is described to be in his thirties (30) and is a professor (38), like Wiesel, not a chemist, like Levi. He lives partially because of his love for Pannonique ("Sans vous, je serais mort" ["Without you, I would be dead"]) (46), but the philosophical discussions which he has with her alone and with the members of their unit around their meager dinner table are totally unrealistic (63–65). The novel's camp is liberated after six months (139, 184), the television ratings having elevated themselves to the culminating evening performance when every citizen watches the show (175). The historical reality was that one was fortunate at Auschwitz to survive for the first three months and beyond, even if in a totally weakened, degraded, and often mentally confused condition.

Nothomb provides the interior monologue of her heroine which shows Levi's agnosticism: the existence of such a camp proves the lack of existence of God (68). Unlike Levi, however, Pannonique herself decides to become "Dieu, principe de grandeur et d'amour" ["God, principle of greatness and love"] (70). Of course, the fictional lover Livi worries about her endangering her life (111) as she boldly speaks to the cameras, demanding that the spectators change their channels or turn off their televisions (81, 109). Their platonic love affair is envied by Kapo Zdena, who seriously considers placing Livi on the list of those to be killed, but she refrains from doing so when she realizes that she can learn something from him about the power of words, the very force which attracts Pannonique to him (101). Livi's mastery of words and asexual relationship do indeed echo the real Levi's relationships with brilliant women besides his wife Lucia.

If any good comes out of this novel, it is an emphasis on personal authenticity, the solid base underneath Livi's skill with words. Even the brutal, dense Kapo Zdena realizes that Livi and Pannonique are not "des êtres vides" ["empty beings"] but real people (102). Kapo Zdena's only consolation is that everyone else she knows is "vides"; she resolves to figure out how she can stop being such a nullity (102).

Nothomb does not clearly state what being a real human being entails, although one assumes that her characters Livi and Pannonique embody that authenticity. Psychiatrist Murray Bowen supplies a definition that fits what this novelist seems to be communicating:

> The solid self says, 'This is who I am, what I believe, what I stand for, and what I will do or will not do,' in a given situation. The solid self is made up of clearly defined beliefs, opinions, convictions, and life principles. . . . The pseudo-self is composed of a vast assortment of principles, beliefs, philosophies, and knowledge acquired because it is required or considered right by the group. (365)

Thus the insane "pseudo-selves" of the organizers and the participants, outside of the victims themselves, as well as those of the television spectators provide a negation of all that is worthy in a "solid self" or human being who is not "vide." If anything positive emerges from Nothomb's shocking text, it is this humanistic emphasis which is verified by Livi himself finally speaking to the cameras after the spectators have voted—a new privilege granted to them in order to avoid having the television ratings decline—to execute Pannonique:

> "Vous avez besoin qu'elle [Pannonique] disparaisse parce qu'elle est votre contraire: elle est aussi pleine que vous êtes vides! Si vous n'étiez pas de tels néants, vous ne trouveriez pas intolérable l'existence de celle qui a de la substance! Une émission telle que 'Concentration' est le miroir de votre vie et c'est par narcissisme que vous êtes si nombreux à la regarder!" ["You need for her to disappear because she is your opposite: she is as full as you are empty! If you were not such nullities, you would not find intolerable the existence of her who has substance! A program like 'Concentration' is the mirror of your life, and it is narcissism that makes you so numerous in watching it!"]. (180–81)

Significantly, Livi stops his harangue at the television cameras because he senses that no one is listening to him (181). It is interesting to note that Primo Levi himself described those at Auschwitz who had lost everything—home, habits, clothes, loved ones, in fact everything (*Se questo è un uomo* I.20–21)—as being "vuoti" ["empty"] the Italian equivalent of the French "vides." In this postmodern setting of a televised concentration camp, the spectators are "vides" while at least two of the victims are solid, authentic human beings.

I am unsure that this emphasis on becoming authentic human beings, like Pannonique and Livi, is worth the trouble of reading 193 pages of a text that revives the Shoah in a shocking, superficial way. At least it is not overtly anti-Semitic—none of the characters are designated as Jews—but using the Holocaust scenario as the cruel setting of a reality show pushes trivialization of this tragedy to the extreme. As Mingelgrün remarks, "On est là dans une pornographie avérée et dans le divertissement trivial" ["One finds oneself immersed in a confirmed pornography and in trivial entertainment"] (Lechat 39).

Historian Gavin I. Langmuir cautions against embedding longstanding prejudices of an "in group" against an "out group" into "cultural media":

> Finally, in addition to the already socially significant xenophobia and the chimerical rumors, both kinds of chimerical accusations [those specifically made by the "ingroup" against the "outgroup" and those which blossom

into a "conspiracy" theory] come to be used in literature, art, and other cultural media, where their function of symbolizing social and psychic menaces makes them peculiarly valuable. Thereby, they become deeply rooted in the culture, an almost unavoidable element in social indoctrination, and an influence on social policy. The essential inferiority produced by the self-fulfilling prophecy has acquired monstrous lineaments. The monster may in fact be a combination of the chinks in the social armor protecting the members of the ingroup and of the psychic cleavages within individual members, but for many in the ingroup those threatening fissures leading from cosmos to chaos will have been reassuringly located, localized, externalized, and concretized so that they may be attacked directly, immediately, and brutally. (349–50)

It is hard to say if popular novels such as the few described above could indeed radically influence the public psyche, but the authors who write them, the "thieves of time," are taking that risk, whatever their personal reasons behind the production of such texts. Levi and Wiesel are also novelists, but their fictional treatments of the deep truths which they have gained from their horrific experiences of torture and loss add to veracities about humanity rather than distorting them. Appropriation of Holocaust material for art should be done with delicacy and respect for its victims, not for sensationalism, strange psychic projections, or profit. Wiesel believes that the victims' "suffering is being transformed into farce and entertainment in films, plays, docudramas, and musicals" (*Wise Men* 334). He continues, "Only those who were there know what it meant to be there. . . . In many academic and literary circles, a kind of taboo has been broken. Now everything goes. Nothing is off-limits any more. What used to be sacred is being commercialized, trivialized" (*Wise Men* 335).

At the farthest extreme of the "thieves of time" are the negationists who deny that such a genocide has even occurred. Wiesel and Levi view these deniers as trying to kill already dead Jews yet a second time by both removing them from memory and affirming that they had never been murdered by the Nazis—hence committing a fatal double theft of their lives. Wiesel expresses the disgust and weariness that Holocaust survivor writers experience when having to reaffirm the facts: "it is humiliating to have to combat the Holocaust deniers by reiterating that the tragedy did indeed occur, that our parents and grandparents were in fact murdered. At some point in their lives, every writer who has written about the Holocaust has had to defend himself against this sort of accusation, which leaves one feeling smeared and powerless. Yet it is crucial to denounce such malevolence, whose most dangerous and perverse effect would be to make people shrink from speaking of the Holocaust" (*Memoirs* 333).

"Thou shalt not steal": Levi and Wiesel worried about stealing from others at Auschwitz; would that the avant-garde Holocaust thieves and deniers were as conscientious.

# Works Cited

Bowen, Murray. *Family Therapy in Clinical Practice*. Northvale, New Jersey: Aronson. 1998. Print.
Cicioni, Mirna. *Primo Levi: Bridges of Knowledge*. Oxford: Berg, 1995. Print.
Dantec, Maurice G. *Les racines du mal*. Paris: Gallimard, 1995. Print.
Dick, Philip K. *Le maître du Haut Château*. Trans. Jacques Parsons. Paris: Club du Livre d'Anticipation, coll. *J'ai lu*, no. 567, 1970. Print.
Edelheit, Abraham J., and Herschel Edelheit. *History of the Holocaust: A Handbook and Dictionary*. Boulder: Westview Press, 1994. Print.
Giuliani, Massimo. *A Centaur in Auschwitz: Reflections on Primo Levi's Thinking*. Lanham, Maryland: Lexington Books, 2003. Print.
Kolbert, Jack. *The Worlds of Elie Wiesel: An Overview of His Career and His Major Themes*. Selinsgrove: Susquehanna UP, 2001. Print.
Langmuir, Gavin I. *Toward a Definition of Antisemitism*. Berkeley: U of California P, 1996. Print.
Lechat, Benoît, et al. "De Degrelle aux *Bienveillantes*, Jonathan Littell et l'écriture de la Shoah." Bruxelles: *La Revue nouvelle* (juillet-août 2008): 36–44. Print.
Levi, Primo. *The Drowned and the Saved*. Trans. Raymond Rosenthal. New York: Vintage International, 1989. Print.
Levi, Primo. *If This Is a Man*. Trans. Stuart Woolf. New York: First Collier Books Trade Edition, 1993. Print.
Levi, Primo. *The Periodic Table*. Trans. Raymond Rosenthal. New York: Alfred A. Knopf, 1996. Print.
Levi, Primo. *Se questo è un uomo*. *Opere I*. Torino: Einaudi, 1987. 1–212. Print.
Levi, Primo. *Il sistema periodica*. *Opere I*. Torino: Einaudi, 1987. 428–649. Print.
Levi, Primo. "Il superstite." *Opere II*. Torino: Einaudi, 1987. 581. Print.
Levi, Primo. "The Survivor." *Primo Levi: Collected Poems*. Trans. Ruth Feldman and Brian Swann. London: Faber and Faber, 1988. 64. Print.
Mendel, David. "Primo Levi and the Jews." *The Legacy of Primo Levi*. Ed. Stanislao G. Pugliese. New York: Palgrave Macmillan, 2005. 61–73. Print.
Mingelgrün, Albert. "La figure du bourreau Nazi au tournant du XXe siècle: Quelques variations littéraires." *Revue pluridisciplinaire de la foundation Auschwitz* 102 (janvier-mars 2009): 17–27. Print.
Nothomb, Amélie. *Acide sulfurique: Roman*. Paris: Albin Michel, 2005. Print.
Spinrad, Norman. *Rêve de fer*. Trans. Jean-Michel Boissier. Paris: Pocket, coll. *Folio SF*, no. 239, 1992. Print.
Thomson, Ian. *Primo Levi: A Life*. New York: Metropolitan Books Henry Holt and Company, 2002. Print.
Volodine, Antoine. *Alto Solo*. Paris: Minuit, 1991. Print.
Wiesel, Elie. *The Accident*. Trans. Anne Borchardt. New York: Bantam Books, 1982. Print.
Wiesel, Elie. *And the Sea Is Never Full: Memoirs, 1969—*. Trans. Marion Wiesel. New York: Alfred A. Knopf, 1999. Print.
Wiesel, Elie. "Io e Primo Levi." *Nuova Antologia* 127 (1992): 204–08. Print.
Wiesel, Elie. *Legends of Our Time*. New York: Holt, Rinehart and Winston, 1968. Print.

Wiesel, Elie. *Memoirs: All Rivers Run to the Sea*. New York: Alfred A. Knopf, 1995. Print.
Wiesel, Elie. *Night*. Trans. Marion Wiesel. New York: Hill and Wang, 2006. Print.
Wiesel, Elie. *Tous les fleuves vont à la mer: Mémoires I*. Paris: Éditions du Seuil, 1994. Print.
Wiesel, Elie. *Un di velt hot geshvign*. Buenos Ayres: Tsentral-Farband fun Poylishe Yidnin Argentine, 1956. Print.
Wiesel, Elie. *Wise Men and Their Tales—Portraits of Biblical, Talmudic, and Hasidic Masters*. New York: Schocken Books, 2003. Print.

# Chapter 4: "Thou shalt not bear false witness against thy neighbour"

Elie Wiesel affirms, "Je suis libre non parce que d'autres ne le sont pas, mais parce que d'autres le sont. Autrement dit: tant qu'il y a quelque part un homme ou une femme privés de liberté, la mienne n'est pas entier" ["I am free not because others are not, but because others are. Otherwise stated: as long as there is somewhere a man or a woman deprived of liberty, mine is not complete"] (*Et où vas-tu?* 181). Like Primo Levi, he was also a slave at Auschwitz, and he, too, knew that he could not liberate himself on his own. He and other prisoners trusted that somehow the word about the horror they were experiencing would leak out to the Allies and that these would aid in liberating those suffering behind barbed wire.

However, when members of the underground, like Jan Karski, did indeed inform dignitaries in England and America about the Jewish suffering they had witnessed (Karski, *Story* 384, 387–88), even before Levi and Wiesel had arrived in Auschwitz, they were not fully believed. Wiesel writes about Karski's frustrated efforts: "It was not his fault that his voice had encountered walls of incomprehension, if not indifference to what was being done to the Jews of Europe. His interlocutors refused to accept his testimony. 'I don't believe you,' responded [Supreme Court Justice] Felix Frankfurter when Karski told him of the death camps. And seeing Karski's bewilderment, the judge added, 'I didn't say you weren't telling the truth. I only said I'm not capable of believing you.'" ("A Survivor Remembers" 71). Karski was thought to be "bearing false witness" because what he related as truthfully as possible seemed unbelievable and probably unbearable to be fully accepted as truth.

Hence, the Allies never bombed the train tracks leading to Auschwitz, about which Wiesel has still not ceased to complain, while, as Levi notes, "they abundantly bombed the contiguous industrial area" (*The Mirror Maker* 166), and they did little to alleviate Jewish suffering during World War II. Karski regrets that Claude

Lanzmann omitted in his *Shoah* (the one Holocaust film of which Wiesel unconditionally approves ["A Survivor Remembers" 68; *And the Sea Is Never Full* 122]) his testimony to dignitaries about the tragedies he had seen:

> The time devoted to my account and the construction of *Shoah* forced Lanzmann to omit the section of the interview that I felt was the most important part of my Jewish mission at the end of 1942. . . . For me the central point of my interview was that, having made my way to the West, I described the tragedy and demands of the Jews to four members of the British War Cabinet, including Anthony Eden, President Roosevelt and three key members of the American government, the Apostolic Delegate in Washington, Jewish leaders in the United States, distinguished writers and political commentators such as Walter Lippmann, and George Sokolsky. None of these matters could be discussed by anyone else. After all, this would have demonstrated how the Allied governments, which alone were capable of providing assistance to the Jews, left the Jews to their own fate. ("*Shoah*" 174)

Like Karski, acutely aware of how truth can be ignored or distorted so that "false witnesses" are regarded as speakers of truth, and vice versa, Wiesel informs himself about post-Auschwitz atrocities and "bears witness" regarding these as well as, of course, those of the Shoah. He knows that people who suffer acutely and unjustly usually cannot liberate themselves.

Ethicist John K. Roth affirms, "In unprecedented ways, the Holocaust shows us what is evil and what is good, what is right and what is wrong" (Rittner 184). Centuries of Christian anti-Semitism were evil; lies told by false witnesses against Jews were wrong. The horrific outcome that is the Shoah speaks for itself. In order to prevent future tragedies truth must prevail, a truth that liberates those most vulnerable to the oppression caused by lies.

Both Primo Levi and Elie Wiesel have studied historical events leading up to and occurring during World War II, and they have carefully listened to and encouraged survivors to record their experiences. Both gifted authors use their keen minds, horrific experiences, and intense compassion to courageously "bear true witness" about the Holocaust, thus countering those who try to deny its monumental reality. On occasion they have verified with each other events that they remember happening during their tragic sojourns at Auschwitz. Wiesel recalls:

> When we turned our gaze inward we saw the same universe. The selections, the *kommandos*, the 'roll calls' in the icy wind, the hanging of the young boy, a member of the underground—yes, he [Levi] remembered it all as I did. Sometimes he would question me about a sentence of mine he had read somewhere; I told him I was a bad interpreter of my writings. I did better commenting on his. (*And the Sea Is Never Full* 346)

Both also often use a neutral tone when telling their tales, that of the expert witness before a jury. They understand that such objective narration lends credence to their testimonies. Wiesel applies to himself the dictum he posits for prophets: "Exaggeration is forbidden and risky. To exaggerate truth is to distort it. It is thus incumbent upon the prophet to reject excess" (*Wise Men* 179). Levi identifies more with the precise objectivity of the scientific observer. His biographer Ian Thomson notes regarding Levi's composition of *If This Is a Man*, "as Levi wrote the book, his hardest task was to contain his anger. If he gave way to grief or moral outrage it would tarnish his credibility as a witness. . . . Likewise it was Levi's intention that the reader should be sole judge and jury of the crime he was describing" (226). Although Wiesel's and Levi's motivations for their understandings of the need for precision and accuracy may differ somewhat, their narrative outcomes nevertheless are similar: horrific facts are often presented calmly and clearly, all window dressing put aside.

Levi expresses his disdain even for survivors who exaggerate the horrors of the camps; he describes one such narrator: "Il a été vraiment deporté au camp, mais il écrit des livres désastreux! Il sont vraiment mauvais, parce qu'ils ont le but précis d'accumuler violence sur violence, dégoût sur dégoût, abomination sur abomination. Ce sont des romans noirs, en substance, beaucoup plus que des témoignages. Et ils sont également faux" ["He has really been a deportee from the camps, but he writes some disastrous books! They are really bad, because they have the clear goal of accumulating violence on violence, disgust on disgust, abomination on abomination. They are *romans noirs*, in substance, much more than testimonies. And they are equally false"] (Amsallem 272).

Wiesel writes in his "Preface to the New Translation" by Marion Wiesel of *Night*, "Only those who experienced Auschwitz know what it was. Others will never know. But would they at least understand?" (ix). In an attempt to "at least understand," the following is a comparison and contrast of Wiesel's and Levi's personal perceptions and writing styles via an examination of passages from Wiesel's *Night* and Levi's *Survival in Auschwitz* (entitled *If This Is a Man* in its original British English translation), their key memoirs, relevant to some of the topics they claim to have shared when they "turned [their] gaze inward" and together recalled brutal experiences at Auschwitz— "selections, the *kommandos*, the 'roll calls' in the icy wind, the hanging of the young boy, a member of the underground" (*And the Sea Is Never Full* 346).

Writing his memoir originally ten years after the War, and unacquainted yet with Levi, Wiesel echoes his Italian title, *Se questo è un uomo* [*If This Is a Man*]: "In a few seconds, we had ceased to be men" (*Night* 37). This frightening realization occurred during the night of his family's arrival in Auschwitz, after he had been separated from his mother and sisters; having been almost forced into a burning pit filled with babies dumped from a truck (*Night* 32–34), the fifteen-year-old Wiesel moved on with his father through the usual sequence of stripping, being shaved, running to barracks, disinfection, showering, and finally having odd and ill fitting pieces of clothing thrown at him (*Night* 35–36). This occurred in May 1944 while in *Survival in Auschwitz* Levi describes the same dehumanizing process upon his arrival at Auschwitz in February 1944 when the weather was bitterly cold and he ran naked over ground covered with snow, ice, and muddy slush. Wiesel continues, "The three 'veteran' prisoners, needles in hand, tattoed numbers on our left arms. I became A-7713. From then on, I had no other name" (*Night* 42). Levi's left arm had already declared him to be 174517 (*Survival* 27) three months previously. Levi more graphically describes his own transformation into a creature less than human:

> When we finish [showering, having clothes thrown at them], everyone remains in his own corner and we do not dare lift our eyes to look at one another. There is nowhere to look in a mirror, but our appearance stands in front of us, reflected in a hundred livid faces, in a hundred miserable and sordid puppets. We are transformed into the phantoms glimpsed yesterday evening [unloading luggage from the freight car in which Levi had just arrived].
>
> Then for the first time we became aware that our language lacks words to express this offense, the demolition of a man. (*Survival* 26)

Wiesel's and Levi's witnesses to their first nights in Auschwitz are in agreement, although Levi, despite being the scientist of few words and his disclaimer that "our language lacks words to express this offence," is much more eloquent about this cruel process of dehumanization than is Wiesel. Levi acknowledges that he wanted to accent certain "interwoven themes: the effort to understand 'how it could have happened'; the almost scientific study of human behavior (of others and myself) in those extreme conditions; the daily and painful comparison with the life outside; the reawakening (sometimes desired, sometimes unconscious and spontaneous) of literary memories of Dante's *Inferno*. But I would like here [in 1982] to emphasize one among these themes: the call to the Bible" (Levi, "Beyond Survival" 13). This surprising "call to the Bible" in Levi's early text, long before he began serious studies of it and its commentaries, will be discussed below, following the continued comparison of events (and reactions to these) which Levi and Wiesel experienced during the months between May 1944, when Wiesel arrived, and January 1945, when Wiesel departed for Buchenwald.

After only a few weeks, Wiesel acknowledges his further dehumanization: "The bread, the soup—those were my entire life. I was nothing but a body. Perhaps even less: a famished stomach" (*Night* 52). Levi also notes how quickly the incredible focus on hunger—waking and sleeping—took hold of him: "A fortnight after my arrival I already had the prescribed hunger, that chronic hunger unknown to free men, which makes one dream at night, and settles in all the limbs of one's body. . . . already my own body is no longer mine: my belly is swollen, my limbs emaciated" (*Survival* 37). Again, Levi takes time to describe his condition of suffering from hunger in more detail than does Wiesel. He is the scientist documenting all of the relevant facts of the situation while Wiesel is the Hasidic child turned into an adult survivor overnight, trying to understand what happened to him (and others).

Similarly, Levi carefully portrays his surroundings at Auschwitz, including the infamous *Appellplatz*, more graphically than does Wiesel: "In the middle of the Lager is the roll-call square, enormous, where we collect in the morning to form the work-squads and in the evening to be counted. Facing the roll-call square there is a bed of grass, carefully mown, where the gallows are erected when necessary" (*Survival* 33). Levi writes about "the 'roll calls' in the icy wind" whose memory he shares with Wiesel: "In the morning while we wait endlessly lined up in the roll-call square for the time to leave for work, while every breath of wind penetrates our clothes and runs in violent shivers over our defenceless bodies, and everything is grey around us, and we are grey" (*Survival* 71).

Levi admits to having witnessed at least thirteen hangings in the *Appellplatz* at Auschwitz (*Survival* 148), and so, although not mentioning the specific hanging of Wiesel's "young boy from Warsaw" (*Night* 61) in *Survival in Auschwitz*, he surely could not have avoided witnessing this horrific scene. Wiesel describes it:

> Two SS were headed toward the solitary confinement cell. They came back, the condemned man between them. He was a young boy from Warsaw. An inmate with three years in concentration camps behind him. He was tall and strong, a giant compared to me.
>
> His back was to the gallows, his face turned toward the judge, the head of the camp. He was pale but seemed more solemn than frightened. His manacled hands did not tremble. His eyes were coolly assessing the hundreds of SS guards, the thousands of prisoners surrounding him. (62–63)

Levi notes that "those whom hunger had not yet reduced to a definitive inertia often profited from the moments of general panic [caused by the Allies' aerial bombardments of Buna] to undertake doubly rash expeditions (since, besides the direct risk of the raid, theft carried out in conditions of emergency was punished by hanging) to the factory kitchens or the stores" (*Survival* 118). The "young boy from Warsaw's" crime was stealing during an air raid, and his final words are recorded by Wiesel: "'Long live liberty! My curse on Germany! My curse! My—'" (62). Wiesel continues, "Then the entire camp, block after block, filed past the hanged boy and stared at his extinguished eyes, the tongue hanging from his gaping mouth. The Kapos forced everyone to look him squarely in the face" (62–63). Wiesel comments, "I watched other hangings. I never saw a single victim weep. These withered bodies had long forgotten the bitter taste of tears" (63). It is typical of his compact writing style not to elaborate on the lack of tears exhibited by both those being hung and the spectators forced to watch them.

His next words, however, a sentence fragment ("Except once." 63), proceed to tell the tragic tale of how he and the other prisoners "were weeping" (*Night* 64) over the child who took seemingly forever to die by hanging because he was too small to pull the rope tightly enough, like an adult could; hence he struggled wretchedly "for more than half an hour" (*Night* 65) between life and death. "That night," Wiesel concludes, "the soup tasted of corpses" (*Night* 65).

Levi provides yet another gruesome story of hanging, this time the execution of probably a member of the *Sonderkommando* who had dared to participate in a revolt within Auschwitz that resulted in one of the crematoriums at Birkenau being blown up. Levi explains:

> The man who is to die in front of us today in some way took part in the revolt. They said he had contacts with the rebels of Birkenau, that he carried arms into our camp, that he was plotting a simultaneous mutiny among us. He is to die today before our very eyes: and perhaps the Germans do not understand that this solitary death, this man's death which has been reserved for him, will bring him glory, not infamy. . . . everybody heard the cry of the doomed man, it pierced through the old thick barriers of inertia and submissiveness, it struck the living core of man in each of us: '*Kameraden, ich bin der Letz!*' [sic] (Comrades, I am the last one!) (*Survival* 149)

Both Levi and Wiesel experienced the horrible October 1944 selection performed quickly by the infamous Dr. Mengele. Somehow both Wiesel and his father escaped, but "[t]hose whose numbers had been noted were standing apart abandoned by the whole world. Some were silently weeping" (*Night* 72). Levi also avoided death at this time, and we shall discuss in Chapter 6 his rejection of prayer, despite his acute terror at this moment. His sorrow for those who were selected for the gas chambers is evident: "Does Kuhn [an old man thanking God for not having been selected] not see Beppo the Greek in the bunk next to him, Beppo who is twenty years old and is going to the gas chamber the day after tomorrow and knows it and lies there looking fixedly at the light without saying anything and without even thinking any more?" (*Survival* 129–30).

Although still subject to selections in Auschwitz's meager infirmary, both Wiesel and Levi found temporary relief there from the hardships and the bitter toil of their daily lives as slave laborers. Wiesel writes, "Actually, being in the infirmary was not bad at all: we were entitled to good bread, a thicker soup. No more bell, no more roll call, no more work. From time to time I was able to send a piece of bread to my father" (*Night* 78). Again, unlike Wiesel, Levi describes the *Krankenbau* in more detail: "Ka-Be is the abbreviation of Krankenbau, the infirmary. There are eight huts, exactly like the others in the camp, but separated by a wire fence. They permanently hold a tenth of the population of the camp, but there are few who stay there longer than two weeks and none more than two months: within these limits they are held to die or be cured" (*Survival* 45–46).

Wiesel suffered from a swollen infected foot in January 1945 which required painful surgery without anesthesia (*Night* 79). Only a few days after this surgery and while only partially healed (*Night* 80–82), he chose to accompany his father on the excruciating forced march to Gleiwitz with the ultimate destination of Buchenwald, Germany. Levi was in another part of the infirmary at the same time, in the section for those with contagious diseases since he suffered from scarlet fever. He chose to remain there and was liberated on January 18, 1945, by the Russians approaching from the east, two days after Wiesel and his father had departed on their terrible forced march which is recorded in the last thirty-five pages of *Night*.

On arriving at Buchenwald exhausted and near death, Wiesel notes, "Very close to us stood the tall chimney of the crematorium's furnace. It no longer impressed us. It barely drew our attention" (*Night* 104). Like Levi, he was now a veteran concentration camp survivor at only sixteen years of age in comparison to Levi's twenty-five years of life experience. Wiesel's father died on January 29, 1945 (*Night* 112), and it is from this date on that he identifies himself as a "*Muselmann*" until the American army liberated Buchenwald on April 11, 1945 (*Night* 113). (Levi succinctly defines a "*Muselmann*" as "the weak, the inept, those doomed to selection" [*Survival* 88]).

Despite being a "*Muselmann*," Wiesel mentions in *Night* seriously considering suicide only once, and that was as an alternative to being forced into the pit of burning babies on the night of his arrival. He tells his father, "'I'll run into the electrified barbed wire. That would be easier than a slow death in the flames'" (33). The older, humanistic Levi considers suicide to be the one existential choice left for the beaten down prisoner: "Or it is raining, windy and you have the usual hunger, and then you think that if you really had to, if you really felt nothing in your heart but suffering and tedium—as sometimes happens, when you really seem to lie on the bottom—well, even in that case, at any moment you want you could always go and touch the electric wire-fence, or throw yourself under the shunting trains, and then it would stop raining" (*Survival* 131). Later he remarks, "I am not even alive enough to know how to kill myself" (144).

Curiously, Levi even linked obscure writing to suicide. Amidst her detailed analysis of days and events during Levi's last months of life many decades after the Auschwitz experience, when he was acutely depressed, Carole Angier remarks, "When he was well he was still interested, engaged, amused. And he disapproved of suicide. Suicide was like obscure writing: a flight from the world, and from people; a betrayal of the aims of life, which was his only religion, and of our responsibility not to spread despair" (714). Levi's "only religion" echoes Wiesel's understanding of the core emphasis on life in Judaism. Wiesel affirms:

> Or, dans le judaisme, nous rejetons la souffrance, nous ne faisons pas de la souffrance une religion, nous ne faisons pas de la souffrance un système de valeurs, nous la combattons. 'Tu choisiras la vie', tu choisiras les vivants, tu choisiras ceux qui veulent vivre. Donc la Torah, c'est la vie, l'arbre de la vie, c'est toujours centré sur la vie, et la souffrance est contre la vie [Moreover, in Judaism, we reject suffering, we do not make of suffering a religion, we do not make of suffering a system of values, we fight it. 'You shall choose life', you shall choose the living, you shall choose those who want to live. Thus the Torah, it is life, the tree of life, it is always centered on life, and suffering is against life]. (Malka 41–42)

Levi's early memoir, *Se questo è un uomo,* first published in 1947 by De Silva and then printed with additions to it by Einaudi in 1958, manifests more biblical allusions than one might expect to find in the writings of a confirmed agnostic. Levi himself notes these in his essay "Beyond Survival" of 1982 where he speaks of the prayers of the Gattegno women in the transit camp of Fossoli on the night before their deportation to Auschwitz: the women "unloosened their hair, took off their shoes, placed the *yortsayt* candles on the ground and lit them according to the customs of their fathers, and sat on the bare soil in a circle for the lamentations, praying and weeping all the night" (13–14). These women were lamenting their and their loved ones' deaths before they occurred.

Levi continues, "The biblical theme and tone often return during the months of imprisonment. From time to time there arises the intuition of a destiny decided, beyond man, by an incomprehensible God" (14). Further, he notes, "The theme of the confusion of languages as a punishment of the insolence of men recurs insistently. But here the mythical event is transformed: the insolence is that of Hitler's Germany, forcing her slaves of a hundred languages to build her rash towers. And for this, she will be punished" (14). He also affirms that, although "full of ambivalence," nevertheless the theme of salvation weaves its way into his memoir: "Today I think that if for no other reason than that an Auschwitz existed, no one in our age should speak of Providence. But without doubt in that hour [after the

Germans had vacated Auschwitz] the memory of biblical salvations in times of extreme adversity passed like a wind through all our minds" (14).

Paradoxically, then, Levi, the agnostic, seems to have been imbued with biblical stories and themes even before his arrival at Auschwitz and chose to compose his memoir of his concentration camp experiences embracing these themes of faith, while Wiesel, the Hasidic believer, began to feel a new, unknown until then, anger at God Who seemed to have abandoned His people at Auschwitz, thus breaking His covenant with them. One finds in Wiesel's *Night*, first published in French in 1958, this revealing passage:

> Someone began to recite Kaddish, the prayer for the dead. I don't know whether, during the history of the Jewish people, men have ever before recited Kaddish for themselves.
> "*Yisgadal, veyiskadash, shmey raba.* . . May His name be celebrated and sanctified. . ." whispered my father.
> For the first time, I felt anger rising within me. Why should I sanctify His name? The Almighty, the eternal and terrible Master of the Universe, chose to be silent. What was there to thank Him for? (33)

Levi is in awe of the Gattegno women praying for the dead before they have died, indeed the night before their deportation (Levi, *Survival* 16), while Wiesel, having just arrived at Auschwitz, is infuriated by the Kaddish. His anger is intensified as shown in the brutal, poetic prose of this frequently excerpted citation from *Night*:

> Never shall I forget that smoke.
> Never shall I forget the small faces of the children whose bodies I saw transformed into smoke under a silent sky.
> Never shall I forget those flames that consumed my faith forever.
> Never shall I forget the nocturnal silence that deprived me for all eternity of the desire to live.
> Never shall I forget those moments that murdered my God and my soul and turned my dreams to ashes.
> Never shall I forget those things, even were I condemned to live as long as God Himself.
> Never. (34)

Wiesel has obviously resurrected his charred faith, but it can never embrace his childish innocence before his deportation. Although he and his father continued to pray each morning, he also acknowledges, "Some of the men spoke of God: His mysterious ways, the sins of the Jewish people, and the redemption to come. As for me, I had ceased to pray. I concurred with Job! I was not denying His existence, but I doubted His absolute justice" (45). He now has much wisdom when, as an elderly professor, he teaches about Job to his students.

How to celebrate Rosh Hashanah in the Fall of 1944 at Auschwitz raised even more questions for the young Wiesel: "What are You, my God? I thought angrily. How do You compare to this stricken mass gathered to affirm to you their faith, their anger, their defiance? What does Your grandeur mean, Master of the Universe, in the face of all this cowardice, this decay, and this misery? Why do you go on troubling these poor people's wounded minds, their ailing bodies?" (66). These bitter, angry questions reflect again an ongoing belief in God, but one penetrated by disillusionment and frustration which only increases as the sacred prayers commence:

> Blessed be God's name?
> Why, but why would I bless Him? Every fiber in me rebelled. Because He caused thousands of children to burn in His mass graves? Because He kept six crematoria working day and night, including Sabbath and the Holy Days? Because in His great might, He had created Auschwitz, Birkenau, Buna, and so many other factories of Death? How could I say to Him: Blessed be Thou, Almighty, Master of the Universe, who chose us among all nations to be tortured day and night, to watch as our fathers, our mothers, our brothers end up in the furnaces? Praised be Thy Holy Name, for having chosen us to be slaughtered on Thine altar? (67)

Shortly thereafter, by Yom Kippur of 1944, Wiesel remarks, "Deep inside me, I felt a great void opening" (69). His childhood faith in a just and loving God was destroyed. It has taken him a lifetime to build a more complex belief in a mysterious, indefinable God, One Whose ordinances Wiesel follows but Whose ways are beyond his comprehension.

Many lies were told about Jews since the first century of the Christian era, as has been carefully traced by Rosemary Radford Ruether in *Faith and Fratricide*, Gavin I. Langmuir in *Toward a Definition of Antisemitism* and *History, Religion, and Antisemitism*, and other historians. Additional untruths have been forwarded since the conclusion of World War II by Holocaust deniers and negationists around the world. Those who remained indifferent to the anti-Semitic mendacities which contributed to the Shoah and those who give any credence to the negationist lies following it place themselves in violation of "Thou shalt not bear false witness against thy neighbor." As noted in the previous chapter, such "false witness" can lead to the theft, a second time, of Jewish victims' lives.

Primo Levi and Elie Wiesel have borne a true witness to the tragic events that occurred during the Shoah and the lives that were destroyed because of these atrocities. Their Auschwitz testimonies, although narrated in distinct styles and from two different points of view, Levi's being the more detailed, Wiesel's the more concise, Levi's approaching a faith in God, Wiesel's departing from it, are basically in agreement. They indeed have borne a true witness for their neighbors and against their enemies; their testimonies deserve to be heeded.

# Works Cited

Amsallem, Daniela. *Primo Levi au miroir de son oeuvre: Le témoin, L'écrivain, Le chimiste.* Lyon: Editions du Cosmogone, 2001. Print.
Angier, Carole. *The Double Bond: Primo Levi a Biography.* New York: Farrar, Straus and Giroux, 2002. Print.
Karski, Jan. "Shoah." *Claude Lanzmann's Shoah: Key Essays.* Ed. Stuart Liebman. New York: Oxford UP, 2007. 171–74. Print.
Karski, Jan. *Story of a Secret State.* Boston: Houghton Mifflin, 1944. Print.
Langmuir, Gavin I. *History, Religion, and Antisemitism.* Berkeley: U of California P, 1990. Print.
Langmuir, Gavin I. *Toward a Definition of Antisemitism.* Berkeley: U of California P, 1996. Print.
Lanzmann, Claude, dir. *Shoah.* Les Films Aleph, 1985. New Yorker Films Artwork, 2003. Film.
Levi, Primo. "Beyond Survival." Trans. Gail Soffer. *Prooftexts* 4.1 (January 1984): 9–21. Print.
Levi, Primo. *If This Is a Man.* Trans. Stuart Woolf. New York: First Collier Books Trade Edition, 1993. Print.
Levi, Primo. *The Mirror Maker: Stories and Essays.* Trans. Raymond Rosenthal. New York: Schocken Books, 1989. Print.
Levi, Primo. *Se questo è un uomo. Opere I.* Torino: Einaudi, 1987. 1–212. Print.
Levi, Primo. *Survival in Auschwitz: The Nazi Assault on Humanity.* Trans. Stuart Woolf. New York: A Touchstone Book Simon & Schuster, 1996. Print.
Malka, Salomon. *Monsieur Chouchani: L'énigme d'un maître du XXe siècle, Entretiens avec Elie Wiesel suivis d'une enquête.* Paris: Éditions Jean-Claude Lattès, 1994. Print.
Rittner, Carol, and John K. Roth, ed. *"Good News" after Auschwitz? Christian Faith within a Post-Holocaust World.* Macon, GA: Mercer UP, 2001. Print.
Ruether, Rosemary Radford. *Faith and Fratricide: The Theological Roots of Anti-Semitism.* New York: The Seabury Press, 1974. Print.
Thomson, Ian. *Primo Levi: A Life.* New York: Metropolitan Books Henry Holt and Company, 2002. Print.
Wiesel, Elie. *And the Sea Is Never Full: Memoirs, 1969–.* Trans. Marion Wiesel. New York: Alfred A. Knopf, 1999. Print.
Wiesel, Elie. *Et où vas-tu?* Paris: Éditions du Seuil, 2004. Print.
Wiesel, Elie. *Night.* Trans. Marion Wiesel. New York: Hill and Wang, 2006. Print.
Wiesel, Elie. "A Survivor Remembers Other Survivors of *Shoah.*" *Claude Lanzmann's Shoah: Key Essays.* Ed. Stuart Liebman. New York: Oxford UP, 2007. 67–72. Print.
Wiesel, Elie. *Wise Men and Their Tales—Portraits of Biblical, Talmudic, and Hasidic Masters.* New York: Schocken Books, 2003. Print.

# Chapter 5: "Thou shalt not covet thy neighbour's house"

Primo Levi has observed the human need for a "home" of some kind: "la facoltà umana di scavarsi une nicchia, di secernere un guscio, di erigersi intorno una tenue barriera di difesa, anche in circonstanze apparentemente disperate, è stupefacente [I.53] (the human capacity to carve out a niche, to secrete a protective shell, to build around themselves a flimsy defensive wall, even in the most apparently desperate circumstances, is astonishing)" (quoted in Gordon, *Primo Levi's* 205). Although a computer analysis of twelve of Levi's texts reveals that "casa" ["home"] "was one of 752 words found to appear in all 12 texts of the corpus analysed" (J. Nystedt quoted in Gordon, "How Much" 41), his love of "home" is perhaps communicated most eloquently in his essay "La mia casa" where he describes his attachment to the apartment at 75 Corso Re Umberto where he was born and which he inhabited most of his life, barring his sojourn in Auschwitz.

Rather than "covet[ing] his neighbour's house," he confirms that there is no place else where he would prefer to live ("La mia casa" III.587): "per trasferirmi in un'abitazione piú bella, piú moderna e piú comoda, soffrirei come un esule, o come una pianta che venga trapiantata in un terreno a cui non è avvezza" ["to move to a more beautiful, modern, and comfortable dwelling I would suffer like an exile, or like a plant transplanted on to a terrain to which it was not accustomed"] ("La mia casa" III.588). His home on the third floor (or the fourth floor according to American standards) provided him with a comfortable office overlooking the busy traffic, streetcars, and chestnut trees below. His home also contained family mementoes such as his father's umbrella stand, an old horseshoe once found by his uncle Corrado—whether it brought luck to the household or not remains a question—and a key whose lock has long been forgotten ("La mia casa" III.588–89). He lovingly describes the back room overlooking a private courtyard and the various transformations it has undergone according to the needs of his growing family, including those it sheltered when Turin suffered aerial bombardment by the Allies during World War II ("La mia casa" III.589). His meditative musings about his beloved home conclude with a reaffirmation of the impossibility of living elsewhere: "Abito a casa mia come abito all'interno della mia pelle: so di pelli piú belle, piú ampie, piú resistenti, piú pittoresche, ma mi sembrerebbe innaturale cambirale con la mia" ["I live in my home as I live in my skin: I know about more beautiful, ample, resistant, picturesque skins, but it would seem unnatural to me to exchange them for mine"] ("La mia casa" III.591).

Robert S. C. Gordon has noted that Levi often juxtaposes the recurring theme of home with Jewish deportation and exile, particularly that "antiethical, valueless, alien 'other place' or 'no-place' of the Lager" ("How Much" 41). Levi is also extremely sensitive to the wounding that occurs when "home" is lost: "Si immagini ora un uomo a cui, insieme con le persone amate, vengano tolti la sua casa, le sui abitudini, i suoi abiti, tutto infine, letteralmente tutto quanto possiede: sarà un uomo vuoto. . . [I.20–21] . . . . (And now imagine a man who, along with his dearest, is deprived of his home, his habits, his clothes, in short of literally everything he possesses: he will be a shell of a man. . . )" (Gordon, *Primo Levi's* 207). Levi's sensitivity reveals itself when in 1985 he writes sadly about the homeless he observes on the streets of New York:

> i non accettati, i poveri diavoli. Uomini e donne, bianchi e neri (ma i neri sono in maggioranza), in stracci o vestite con proprietà, se ne stanno seduti a terra o appoggiati ai muri; non chiedono nulla; guardano nel vuoto; fumano o masticano gomma in silenzio; alcuni dormono fra i piedi dei passanti, sotto un tetto de cartone ondulato, altri frugano nei bidoni delle immondizie [the unaccepted, the poor people. Men and women, white and black (but the black are in the majority), in rags or suitable clothes, seated on the ground or leaning against walls; they ask for nothing; they look into empty space; they smoke or chew gum silently; some sleep among the feet of those passing by, under a tent of corrugated cardboard, others sort through the garbage cans.]. ("Tra le vette" III.939).

His description of New York's homeless includes phrases that echo those used to describe the *Muselmänner*, "the irreversibly exhausted, worn out prisoner[s] close to death" (Levi, *Drowned* 98), of Auschwitz: "non chiedono nulla; guardano nel vuoto; . . . alcuni dormono fra i piedi dei passanti." The repetition of these phrases suggests Levi's trauma experienced in Auschwitz and his amazement to discover those who resembled the disintegrating *Muselmänner* in the heart of Manhattan, supposedly the center of democracy and artistic sophistication.

Although Elie Wiesel spent nights with the *clochards* in Paris when he had no money to pay the rent for his humble room, except for his sojourns in Auschwitz and Buchenwald, he was never reduced to being totally homeless. Nevertheless, having lost his parents, grandparents, and younger sister during the Shoah, he arrived in France as a sixteen-year-old orphan, not knowing French at that time and hence not understanding the invitation to become a French citizen offered on the train exiting from Germany to France. Following his usual concentration camp behavior, he was too afraid to raise his hand as many others did (*Memoirs* 109). Hence he remained painfully *apatride*, without a passport and a country, hence a "nobody" to French immigration and police officers, until he finally gained citizenship in the United States in 1961 (*Memoirs* 301). "Stateless persons were regarded not only as noncitizens but as somewhat subhuman as well," he notes (*Memoirs* 240).

He received clothes, food, and, most important of all to him, religious books at his orphanage outside of Paris. Gradually he learned French, found some employment as a tutor of Jewish studies to children of Jewish French families, took some courses in psychology at the Sorbonne, and eventually became a journalist. Curiously, he chose to embrace the ascetic life that living out of a suitcase provides: "Vagabond par goût et par profession, déraciné, je ne possédais qu'une machine à écrire et une valise" [Vagabond by choice and by profession, uprooted, I possessed only a typewriter and a suitcase"] (*Tous les fleuves* 356), he remarks, when describing his years as a young journalist in Paris. Wiesel in a sense parallels some of Levi's wise wanderers "who carry with them, snail-like, their home-forged wisdom, their craft on their backs" like Faussone, the hero of *La chiave a stella* (*The Monkey's Wrench*) (Gordon, "How Much" 64).

Although Wiesel has verbally, both by speaking and by writing, fought for the rights of the undocumented from El Salvador and Guatemala to receive political asylum or "sanctuary" in the United States (*And the Sea Is Never Full* 94), hence a "home," he truly finds home to be in one's heart: "Every human being is a sanctuary, for God resides there. And nobody has the right to violate it" (*And the Sea Is*

*Never Full* 94). This understanding of home parallels Primo Levi's as demonstrated when he describes himself on the long odyssey home to Turin after the War (*La Tregua*) (*The Truce* or *The Reawakening*) and that of Mendel, his watchmender hero of *Se non ora, quando?* (*If Not Now, When?*). Both Levi and his fictional creation, deprived of their homes, must establish a "home" in their hearts as they keep traveling hopefully seeking their homes, Levi's real home in Turin on Corso Re Umberto and Mendel's fantasized home in Palestine. Unlike Wiesel, however, both Levi and Mendel question whether "God resides" in that inner sanctuary.

Levi's journey chronicled in *The Reawakening* shows him slowly coming alive to his body and surrounding nature, as he battles recurring illnesses, ongoing hunger, even when fed satisfactorily, and numerous slow train rides and sojourns in transit camps. His focus on getting back to Turin never pales, although he omits calling on God to help him get there, even in his moments of greatest fatigue and frustration. (After having refused prayer during the October 1944 *Selektion* at Auschwitz, as will be discussed in Chapter 6, why should he consider it in less dangerous circumstances?) After several months of journeying he finally recognizes that he may really reach his destination:

> We looked at each other, almost bewildered. We had resisted, after all; we had won. After the year of Lager, of anguish and patience, after the wave of death that followed the liberation, after the cold and hunger, the contempt and the haughty company of the Greek, after the illness and misery of Katowice, after the senseless journeys which had made us feel condemned to orbit for eternity in Russian space, like useless spent stars, after the idleness and bitter nostalgia of Starye Dorogi, we were rising once more, travelling upwards, on the journey home. Time, after two years of paralysis, had regained vigour and value, was once more working for us, and this put an end to the torpor of the long summer, to the threat of the approaching winter, and made us impatient, hungry for the days and miles ahead. (182)

Levi had been liberated by the Russians in January of 1945, but he did not arrive "home" until October 19. He notes at the beginning of his journey that, as the threat from Auschwitz and its tormentors receded, the "pain of exile, of my distant home, of loneliness" (18) increased. He vividly describes the unwelcome realization that, at the close of his imprisonment and enslavement, he is "like an athlete who arrives at his goal, and who, in the act of falling spent to the ground, is brutally hauled to his feet, and forced to start running again, in the

## Chapter 5

dark, towards another goal of unknown distance" (40). He notices that some of his fellow Italians in Poland create love relationships with Polish women that mimic a real home (86), but he does not envy them. Levi feels confirmed in his objective on May 8, 1945, Victory in Europe day, when the Germans surrendered to the Allies: "[f]rom that day, in fact, our homes were no longer forbidden us, no war front now separated us from them, no concrete obstacle, only red tape" (90).

After suffering yet one more illness, he "felt an imperious need to take possession of [his] body again, to re-establish a contact, by now broken for almost two years, with trees and grass" (106). He notices how other people are seeking their homes, too: Sore and her sister, originally from Minsk, Russia, are trying to travel home, sharing a small suitcase and void of money (114). Some nomads have encamped at Zhmerinka, a village, "and their home was an enormous cart" (119) which he compares to his freight car. From July 15 to September 15 he lived at Starye Dorogi in the Red House (144), suffering from acute nostalgia while always longing for home. Here he rediscovers the beauty of nature (152). Finally, he "reached Turin . . . my house was still standing, all my family was alive, no one was expecting me. I was swollen, bearded and in rags, and had difficulty in making myself recognized" (207), but he ultimately was warmly welcomed home.

Home, however, was invaded frequently at night by his horrible nightmares: "I am alone in the centre of a grey and turbid nothing, and now, I know what this thing means, and I also know that I have always known it; I am in the Lager once more, and nothing is true outside the Lager. All the rest was a brief pause, a deception of the senses, a dream; my family, nature in flow, my home" (207). This frightening dream invades the "sanctuary" which "nobody has the right to violate" (Wiesel, *And the Sea Is Never Full* 94). Perhaps to exorcise this dream Levi wrote a novel whose seed idea he mentions at the close of *The Reawakening*:

> A new truck [freight car] was travelling with us towards Italy at the end of our train, crammed with young Jews, boys and girls, coming from all the countries of Eastern Europe. None of them seemed more than twenty years old, but they were extremely self-confident and resolute people; they were young Zionists on their way to Israel, travelling where they were able to, and finding a path where they could. A ship was waiting for them at Bari; they had purchased their truck, and it had proved the simplest thing in the

world to attach it to our train; they had not asked anybody's permission, but had hooked it on, and that was that. I was amazed, but they laughed at my amazement: 'Hitler's dead, isn't he?' replied their leader, with his intense hawk-like glance. They felt immensely free and strong, lords of the world and of their destinies. (205)

Thus Levi created Mendel and his partisan friends who fight all over central Europe during the war and eventually ride a freight car, just as described above, into Milan (*If Not Now, When?* 328).

*If Not Now, When?* (*Se non ora, quando?*) was published in 1982, five years before Levi's death, and was preceded by many months of research into real bands of Jewish partisans and fervent young Zionist groups (*If Not Now, When?* 347–49). The fictional, likable Mendel is twenty-eight years old as the novel opens, and he has lost his wife, home, and village to the Nazis. He joins with others in a similar state and learns how to shoot and kill people (111), both contrary to his nature and profession as a watchmender. He is good at fixing broken equipment, although a '"locomotive isn't a clock"' (174), and others respect him for his calmness and goodness. (It is significant that, in lieu of a rabbi, he is asked to marry Piotr and Black Rokhele when she becomes pregnant, 261–63.) Like Levi, his goodness stems from an innate love of others, not from God: "so far it didn't seem that the Lord had bothered much about saving him and his family" (*If Not Now, When?* 46).

Mendel and others seek what Leonid describes well: '"You play the hero, but you want what I want: a house, a bed, a woman, a life that has some meaning, a family, a village that's your village"' (54). An "ordinary" life like this truly represents home for those who cannot return to their previous homes. Always hoping for Zion, Mendel and Gedaleh, the partisan band's leader, share the same goals: "survive, do the maximum damage to the Germans, and go to Palestine" (160). Gedaleh later explains to a peasant farmer, '"We're tired of war and walking, we're homesick for the tasks of peacetime"' (209). He adds, '"we'll go to Palestine, and we'll try to build the house we've lost, and to start living again the way all other people live"' (215). It is significant that neither Levi himself nor Mendel nor the other members of the partisan band "covet" the homes of others. Their goal remains homes of their own in the "promised land."

Mendel reflects the limitations of bearing his home within himself. On the one hand, he ruminates, "Where is my house? It is in no place. It's in the knapsack I carry on my back, it's in the shot-down Heinkel, it's at Novoselki, it's in the camp of Turov and in Edek's camp, it's beyond the sea, in fairy-tale land, where milk and honey flow" (271). On the other hand, "I don't know what I want or where I am, and perhaps I don't even know who I am anymore. Last night I dreamed somebody was asking me that, and I didn't know the answer" (230). Levi the rationalist is haunted by his nightmare of the Lager while Mendel, the novel's quiet hero, confesses that his dream reveals his poor comprehension of who he is becoming outside of his original home and village. Such confusion may well characterize many survivors.

Wiesel's real home had been in Sighet, Hungary or Romania, depending on when each regime had gained political control over its fate. In his *Memoirs* he speaks fondly of happy memories acquired in this home: his father's grocery store at the front of the house, his grandfather Dodye Feig's joyful visits (*And the Sea Is Never Full* 25), his mother's serene care for him and their home. None of these could ever be replicated, and so in Paris as a young man he did not even try to recreate a "home." However, he was more than the "shell of a man" which Levi states will be the consequence of not having a real home anymore. Wiesel's mysticism emphasized "asceticism"; hence he found some contentment in living simply with very few material possessions beyond what could be placed in his one suitcase. His second piece of luggage, his typewriter, of course, was a necessity for his profession of journalist, memoirist, and novelist.

Although he lived simply and ascetically, he at least did not succumb to the tension that Levi felt from trying to function well in two very different professions after having experienced "snakes in [his] path." Levi's autobiographical, passive narrator explains to Faussone, the rigger, in another novel, *The Monkey's Wrench* (*La chiave a stella*): "In distant times I, too, had got involved with gods quarreling among themselves; I, too, [like Tiresias] had encountered snakes in my path, and that encounter had changed my condition, giving me a strange power of speech. But since then, being a chemist in the world's eyes, and feeling, on the contrary, a writer's blood in my veins, I felt as if I had two souls in my body, and that's too many" (52).

As a poorly paid journalist Wiesel wrote on his portable typewriter in Yiddish the first draft of what would be condensed into *Night* while he travelled on a boat, at first unbeknownst to him, with European Jewish refugees who had departed from Israel seeking asylum in Brazil (*Memoirs* 239–42). These refugees, having tried life in Palestine, had found it to be too challenging (241). They could have been Mendel's band disillusioned with Palestine, "the fairy-tale land," once they had finally arrived. Wiesel the memoirist, however, is too absorbed in his writing to at first recognize their presence. He describes his passionate commitment to finishing his task before the boat landed:

> I spent most of the voyage in my cabin working. I was writing my account of the concentration camp years—in Yiddish. I wrote feverishly, breathlessly, without rereading. I wrote to testify, to stop the dead from dying, to justify my own survival. I wrote to speak to those who were gone. As long as I spoke to them, they would live on, at least in my memory. My vow of silence would soon be fulfilled; next year [1955] would mark the tenth anniversary of my liberation. I was going to have to open the gates of memory, to break the silence while safeguarding it. The pages piled up on my bed. I slept fitfully, never participating in the ship's activities, constantly pounding away on my little portable [typewriter], oblivious of my fellow passengers, fearing only that we would arrive in São Paulo too soon. (239–40)

Wiesel was ignorant of the emotional storm awaiting him: absorbed in his memoirs, he was unaware of the nearly forty Israeli emigrants who had crossed the Atlantic Ocean in third class accommodations. Upon arrival they were denied permission to disembark. Hence, Wiesel and the emigrants sailed for days from port to port, "pariahs rejected everywhere" (240), while Wiesel gradually became "a sort of spokesman for the exiles" (241). Having written several news dispatches that eventually were reprinted in the American Jewish press (241), he happily ended this odyssey when the refugees were finally allowed to land in São Paulo, "taken in charge by a Jewish charity" (241). He also surrendered there his only copy of his Yiddish memoir to Mark Turkov, a Jewish publisher, who was instrumental in its publication (*Un di velt hot geshvign*) well before the much shorter French version *La Nuit* (*Night*) appeared in 1958 (241). Although transient and bearing two stories within him, the European/Israeli emigrants' and his own, he was still less divided than Levi as he daily pursued both of his vocations as chemist and writer.

In the early 1990s Wiesel eventually did return to his home in Sighet, now Romania. Later he learned that "the Romanian government has decided to turn [his] house into a museum"; rather than "coveting" his own house, he promised its current inhabitants that "as long as they are not offered other decent lodgings, they can stay on in their home—or rather in mine" (*And the Sea Is Never Full* 293). In July 1995 he returned again with his son Elisha and nephew Steve (*And the Sea Is Never Full* 293). He writes of this visit poetically as if he were directly addressing his father who had been brutally murdered at Buchenwald fifty years before:

> For a few hours I speak to two young visitors who bear your name, Father. I show them their grandparents' room. I stroll with them in the courtyard, in the little garden where Tsipouka [Wiesel's youngest sister who was killed the night of his family's arrival at Auschwitz] liked to play. I can still see the sun's rays making her hair glisten like gold. I see her and, as always when I think of her, my eyes fill with tears. I must hide my face, hide inside my face.
> We halt in front of my Grandmother Nissel's house. The window where long ago she waited for a small schoolboy on Fridays, to offer him a special roll, is closed. Seeing Tsipouka, she would smile. And my little sister would smile back. Right now I would so like to be able to speak of my grandmother with her black scarf on her head. And of the little girl with golden hair . . . [sic] but I cannot. My heart is pounding. Could I have returned to Sighet to die? (407–08)

Even returning to the house where he was born and raised in Sighet and to his beloved grandmother's home, Elie Wiesel cannot recapture the homes that these once had been because his loved ones no longer live there. They live inside him as well as in his writings, factual and fictional. He has no desire to "covet" anyone's home because he does indeed carry his *real* home, his beloved family, within him.

Perhaps this is why Wiesel's first four fictional texts present houses or enclosures, not "homes." In *Dawn* (*L'Aube*, 1960), a *récit*, his first fictional text after his memoir *Night*, the reader meets Elisha: "Elisha is my name. At the time of this story I was eighteen years old. Gad had recruited me for the Movement and brought me to Palestine. He had made me into a terrorist" (11). Elisha, of course, must live somewhere in Palestine:

> As I stepped off the ship at Haifa two comrades picked me up in their car and took me to a two-storey house somewhere between Ramat-Gan and Tel Aviv. This house was ostensibly occupied by a professor of languages, to justify the comings and goings of a large number of young people who were actually, like myself, apprentices of a school of terrorist techniques. The cellar served as a dungeon where we kept prisoners, hostages, and those of our comrades who were wanted by the police. (25).

A real "home" does not include prisoners in the cellar. Elisha, however, has no other. At the end he will shoot the British hostage, John Dawson, indeed, hidden in the cellar.

Eliezer, the protagonist of the novel *The Accident* (*Le Jour*, 1961), which won the Prix Rivarol in 1963, finds home in a full body plaster cast in a hospital bed after he is hit by a taxi as he crosses a street in New York one evening when he is out with his girlfriend Kathleen. Although he prefers dark solitude, here he has no choice about who visits him—doctors, nurses, friends, journalist colleagues, and others. He reflects bitterly, "The ten weeks I spent in a world of plaster had made me richer. I learned that man lives differently, depending on whether he is in a horizontal or vertical position. The shadows on the walls, on the faces, are not the same" (79). When he finally is discharged from his hospital, he learns that Kathleen will take care of him, since he cannot yet put weight on his feet, and that he must deal with the secret that only his Hungarian survivor friend, the artist Gyula, discerns: the accident was really a suicide attempt. He thinks that to go on living he must lie:

> Kathleen will be happy, I decided. I'll learn to lie well and she'll be happy. It's absurd: lies can give birth to true happiness. Happiness will, as long as it lasts, seem real. The living like lies, the way they like to acquire friendships. The dead don't like them. Grandmother would not accept being told less than the truth. Next time, I promise you, Grandmother, I'll be careful. I won't miss the train [to heaven] again. (87).

This brief novel ends with the reader uncertain about whether Eliezer is going "home" to live or to try to die again. It shows poignantly how the survivor remains in the realm of the dead even years after being liberated from it at Auschwitz.

In *The Town Beyond the Wall* (*La Ville de la chance*, 1962), which also was awarded the Prix Rivarol in 1964, Michael's home is a Communist prison where he ends up after having returned to his hometown in Romania, now behind the Iron Curtain. The daring search for his family's home, and the confrontation with the silent bystander who had watched them be deported to a concentration camp, results in his imprisonment by a new regime, this time not Nazis but Marxists. Michael is tortured by having to stand hours on end, one day after another, without relief; his tormentors want to know who escorted him from the west across the frontier to the Communist controlled east and why he is there. Most of the novel is filled with Michael's random thoughts and recollections as he stands at the wall, a torment called "Prayers" by his persecutors. At the end of the "Second Prayer," the second section of this strange fragmented text, the narrator relates:

> Finally the spokesman for all the "whys" fell silent. A great silence spread through the temple [the prison]. The door opened. Two guards came to take the prisoner to the toilet.
> Michael walked cautiously and with great difficulty; an immense weight crushed down on his shoulders. I have no more legs, he thought; I have only two crutches.
> His teeth chattered. (98)

After the close of the third day of Prayer, Michael must be carried out by two guards (130). In his cell he meets gentle Menachem, "a very handsome Jew, with the moving face of a Byzantine Christ, [who] was murmuring prayers" (133), and they become friends. Michael is heartbroken when Menachem is taken away (168). He is left in the cell with a bully ("the Impatient One") and an autistic, motionless introvert ("the Silent One") (168). Awakened one night when the bully attacks the introvert, Michael succeeds in separating them, thus saving "the Silent One's" physical life, although not touching his hidden inner life. Urged on by the voice of Pedro in his mind—Pedro who had escorted him to this town and about whom he refused to provide the Communists any information—Michael decides to "save" the bully's victim: "He changed corners [in the cell] immediately; now he was living where Menachem had lived" (172). Michael has a new home—this action of trying to heal another, despite his own frailty and frustration, and this movement, finally, into a "home," where a loving friend had once lived, is the most positive motion that any of Wiesel's characters have made so far in these beginning fictional works. Michael finds a welcoming "home" in the corner of his absent friend; he never "covets" this home but rather begins to share its warmth with the introvert in much worse shape even than he.

"Home" in *The Gates of the Forest* (*Les Portes de la forêt*, 1964) is at first Gregor's cave where he is hiding from the Nazis, reconciled to the fact that his father will never return to this home (5). After hearing a frightening stranger in the forest outside his door finally speak Yiddish, Gregor reveals a welcoming spirit similar to Michael's described above; he hospitably declares: '"Whoever you are, wherever you come from, come here. I have a safe hiding place with room enough for both of us'" (7). Gregor (actually his Jewish name is Gavriel which means "man of God") will have his problems in this novel, but it is already evident that the Wieselian protagonist has evolved into someone who can care deeply for others, even providing a "home"—a major step of growth beyond the anger of Elisha the terrorist, the depression of Eliezer the failed suicide, and the misery of Michael the prisoner. As I have shown in *Is God Man's Friend? Theodicy and Friendship in Elie Wiesel's Novels*, friendship brings healing to Wiesel and his characters; with deep inner healing comes home in its truest sense.

Marion Wiesel succeeded over the years in creating beautiful, warm homes for her formerly peripatetic husband (*And the Sea Is Never Full* 73). Significantly, a picture of his home in Sighet occupies a prominent place on the wall of his home study: "Before me, always, is the photograph of the house in which I was born. . . . With all that has happened to me, it is essential for me to remember that place" (Wiesel, *And the Sea Is Never Full* 4). He continues, "In my study you will find no medals, no diplomas. But over the table where I work there hangs a single photograph. It shows my parents' home in Sighet. When I look up, that is what I see. And it seems to be telling me: 'Do not forget where you came from.'" (*And the Sea Is Never Full* 404). He now prefers "home" much more to travels (*And the Sea Is Never Full* 6, 154; . . . *Et la mer* 49, 257).

# Works Cited

Gordon, Robert. '"How Much Home Does a Person Need?' Primo Levi and the Ethics of Home." *Primo Levi: The Austere Humanist.* Ed. Joseph Farrell. Bern: Peter Lang, 2004. 37–65. Print.

Gordon, Robert S. C. *Primo Levi's Ordinary Virtues: From Testimony to Ethics.* Oxford: Oxford UP, 2001. Print.

Lambert, Carole J. *Is God Man's Friend? Theodicy and Friendship in Elie Wiesel's Novels.* New York: Peter Lang, 2006. Print.

Levi, Primo. *La chiave a stella. Opere II.* Torino: Einaudi, 1988. 3–181. Print.

Levi, Primo. *The Drowned and the Saved.* Trans. Raymond Rosenthal. New York: Vintage International, 1989. Print.

Levi, Primo. *If Not Now, When?* Trans. William Weaver. New York: Penguin Books, 1995. Print.

Levi, Primo. "La mia casa." *Opere III.* Torino: Einaudi, 1990. 587–91. Print.

Levi, Primo. *The Monkey's Wrench.* Trans. William Weaver. New York: Penguin Books, 1987. Print.

Levi, Primo. *The Reawakening.* Trans. Stuart Woolf. New York: A Touchstone Book, 1995. Print.

Levi, Primo. *Se non ora, quando? Opere II.* Torino: Einaudi, 1988. 183–517. Print.

Levi, Primo. "Tra le vette di Manhattan." *Opere III.* Torino: Einaudi, 1990. 936–39. Print.

Levi, Primo. *La tregua. Opere I.* Torino: Einaudi, 1987. 213–425. Print.

Levi, Primo. *The Truce.* Trans. Stuart Woolf. London: Bodley Head, 1965. Print.

Wiesel, Elie. *The Accident.* Trans. Anne Borchardt. New York: Bantam Books, 1982. Print.

Wiesel, Elie. *And the Sea Is Never Full: Memoirs, 1969—.* Trans. Marion Wiesel. New York: Alfred A. Knopf, 1999. Print.

Wiesel, Elie. *L'Aube.* Paris: Édition du Seuil, 1960. Print.

Wiesel, Elie. *Dawn.* Trans. Frances Frenaye. New York: Bantam Books, 1982. Print.

Wiesel, Elie. *. . . Et la mer n'est pas remplie: Mémoires 2.* Paris: Éditions du Seuil, 1996. Print.

Wiesel, Elie. *The Gates of the Forest.* Trans. Frances Frenaye. New York: Schocken Books, 1982. Print.

Wiesel, Elie. *Le Jour.* Paris: Éditions du Seuil, 1961. Print.

Wiesel, Elie. *Memoirs: All Rivers Run to the Sea.* New York: Alfred A. Knopf, 1995. Print.

Wiesel, Elie. *Night.* Trans. Marion Wiesel. New York: Hill and Wang, 2006. Print.

Wiesel, Elie. *La Nuit.* Paris: Les Éditions de Minuit, 1958. Print.

Wiesel, Elie. *Les Portes de la forêt.* Paris: Éditions du Seuil, 1964. Print.

Wiesel, Elie. *Tous les fleuves vont à la mer: Mémoires I.* Paris: Éditions du Seuil, 1994. Print.

Wiesel, Elie. *The Town Beyond the Wall.* Trans. Stephen Becker. New York: Schocken Books, 1982. Print.

Wiesel, Elie. *Un di velt hot geshvign.* Buenos Ayres: Tsentral-Farband fun Poylishe Yidn in Argentine, 1956. Print.

Wiesel, Elie. *La Ville de la chance.* Paris: Éditions du Seuil, 1962. Print.

# ESSENTIAL SPIRITUALITY

"But where was Kadosh Barukhú, 'the Saint, Blessed be He': he who breaks the slaves' chains and submerges the Egyptians' chariots? He who dictated the Law to Moses, and inspired the liberators Ezra and Nehemiah, no longer inspired anyone; the sky above us was silent and empty" (Levi, *The Periodic Table* 55–56).

# Chapter 6: "I am the LORD thy God.... Thou shalt have no other gods before me"

Primo Levi is often called an Enlightenment thinker, a rationalist who studied human beings as carefully as the chemicals he used in his laboratory. Resentful of the Fascist "spirituality" which overlay most of his education in the humanities in 1930s Turin, Italy, he turned to the natural sciences—biology, chemistry, and physics—where material truth could be verified without Fascist "spiritual" commentary. Massimo Giuliani notes, "Fascism did like subjectivity, esteemed spirituality (so easy to associate with the 'fascist mystics' that was taught from the elementary school), [and] celebrated the eternal values of ancient Roman civilization" (20). Levi sought concrete truth; he remarked to Tullio Regge, "'I had hoped to go very far. . . to the point of possessing the universe, to understanding the why of things. But now [after working at the paint factory SIVA for sixteen years] I know you can't'" (Thomson 291).

Levi is also known for the high ethics that permeate his memoirs, essays, novels, and science fiction stories, particularly the virtues of love and justice. Even so, ethics pertain more to the disciplines of philosophy and theology than to scientific inquiry. If anything, a Darwinian theory of the survival of the fittest may assert itself in the sciences, but this paradigm is counter to Levi's demonstrated care for others, the weakest, and especially those lost in the Holocaust. Levi's stand for the victims of the Nazis and his desire that their oppressors assume the guilt for the atrocities committed against these oppressed stem from some source beyond scientific rationalism. Wiesel notes, "If Darwin, the scientist, for example, had not reduced man to the state of an animal, maybe people would have thought twice before killing human beings. Even Darwin wasn't the first. If the Church hadn't seen the Jews as subhuman, maybe the Germans would have thought twice too. The Holocaust could not have happened had there not been this combination of factors" (*Conversations* 50).

In addition to Darwinism and Christian anti-Semitism, Levi also attributed responsibility for the Holocaust to Friedrich Nietzsche who had lived in Turin. Ian Thomson believes that Levi's chapter title "This Side of Good and Evil" in *If This Is a Man* (*Se questo è un uomo*) parodies Nietzsche's *Beyond Good and Evil*: "The philosopher's assault on western morality and scorning of Judaeo-Christian compassion for the weak had foreshadowed a moment in the 1940s—Auschwitz—when humanity began to die. . . . Levi knew that Hitler had used his violent Social Darwinism as justification for the extermination of European Jewry" (Thomson 226). Wiesel also is aware of Nietzsche's negative influence on German Nazis: "But if Nietzsche could cry out to the old man in the forest that God is dead, the Jew in me cannot. I have never renounced my faith in God. I have risen against His justice, protested His silence and sometimes His absence, but my anger rises up within faith and not outside it" (*Memoirs* 84). Wiesel, as elsewhere, here again protests God's seeming passivity before the horrendous events of the Shoah, while Levi does not attack God, having given up belief in Him years before during his adolescence; nevertheless, Levi recognizes the injustice of persecuting the weak and innocent with or without God's acknowledgment of it.

Joseph Farrell, although he states starkly that "there is no trace of any theology, no hint of the numinous in Levi, never" (122), still describes Levi's world view as being biblically motivated:

> Primo Levi is a writer of the light, motivated by the *fiat lux* of the Book of Genesis. Even in the darkness in which he was compelled to spend many of his days, both in Auschwitz and in anxious recollection after his release, he held fast to the conviction that darkness is only temporary and man-made, and can be dispelled. There is no cosmic law which compels humanity to inhabit darkness, even if there is no longer any God to irradiate supernatural light. (138)

Hence Levi is not caught up in the enigmatic, horrifying darkness of Kafka's characters, and this search for light helps to explain the depression he experienced when translating Kafka's *The Trial* (*Il Processo*) (*Der Prozess*) (Angier 631). Farrell affirms that Levi maintained "a belief in goodness and justice": "There is something Biblical in his appeal to the 'just man' as the standard of rectitude" (136).

For example, like Wiesel (. . . *Et la mer* 147–48), Levi loved children. Erica Scroppo, his daughter Lisa's friend, recounts a vivid childhood memory that illustrates his championing of the weakest:

> When Lisa put on a simpleton's voice to ask for the salt, her father angrily rebuked her: it was unkind to poke fun at the disabled. Another of the children's games that was promptly banned by Levi involved the torture of imaginary monkeys. . . . he knew how people like to pick on a weakness, and was sensitive to the slightest suggestion of cruelty, even a child's. 'The moment the defenceless are derided,' Levi liked to say, 'is the moment Nazism is born.' (Thomson 263)

Some months after his traditional *bar mitzvah* at age thirteen, Levi stopped praying to the Jewish God he had learned to address in that ceremony. God and "God talk" seemed meaningless to him. He much preferred studying earthly realities such as the rocks he climbed and the friends with whom he climbed them. After the Italian racial laws against Jews were enacted in Italy during his college years, he found heaven to be empty or, at least, God to be silent. During the huge, terrifying *Selektion* at Auschwitz in October 1944, he almost prayed to God to be spared, but then he stopped himself. His prayer would have been inauthentic since he had ignored God since childhood. Subsequently he admitted that if he had prayed then, he would later have been ashamed of himself. He explains:

> Like [Jean] Améry, I too entered the Lager as a nonbeliever, and as a nonbeliever I was liberated and have lived to this day. Actually, the experience of the Lager with its frightful iniquity confirmed me in my non-belief. It prevented, and still prevents me from conceiving of any form of providence or transcendent justice. Why were the moribund packed in cattle cars? Why were the children sent to the gas? I must nevertheless admit that I experienced (and again only once) the temptation to yield, to seek refuge in prayer. This happened in October 1944. (*Drowned* 145)

He continues, "A prayer under these conditions [during the terrifying *Selektion*] would have been not only absurd (what rights could I claim? And from whom?) but blasphemous, obscene, laden with the greatest impiety of which a nonbeliever is capable. I rejected that temptation: I knew that otherwise, were I to survive, I would have to be ashamed of it" (*Drowned* 146). Paradoxically, Levi's refusal to pray to God at this time resulted from a near pious honoring of God and a wholesome desire to be perfectly truthful before Him. He refrained from prayer because he believed a "nonbeliever's" desperate cry for help, after ignoring God most of his adult life, would have been an unworthy, shameful affront to God. This choice would not have been such a meaningful ethical decision for him if he had been a total atheist.

After his liberation from Auschwitz, he became angry if anyone (including Nicolò Dallaporta, one of his favorite university professors and an Orthodox Christian) suggested that God had saved him in order that he might witness on behalf of those who had been murdered by the Germans. "Such an opinion," Levi remarks, "seemed monstrous to me. It pained me as when one touches an exposed nerve, and kindled the doubt I spoke of before: I might be alive in the place of another, at the expense of another; I might have usurped, that is, in fact, killed. The 'saved' of the Lager were not the best, those predestined to do good, the bearers of a message: what I had seen and lived through proved the exact contrary" (*Drowned* 82). If there were a God, he should have been just, and saving some over others, perhaps more deserving, was unjust.

This righteous anger against God, or in opposition to those who tried to give a godly meaningfulness to his survival of the concentration camps, expresses a concept of justice more sophisticated and better thought out than the facile remarks of his believing friends. Levi's personal understanding of love and justice tends to exceed that of many Jews and Christians, yet when asked by Ferdinando Camon if he were a believer, he replied, "No, I never have been. I'd like to be, but I don't succeed" (Camon 67). He recalls that some believers at Auschwitz had tried to evangelize him, but he thought that it would be unjust for him to accept their faith: "But how can you, a nonbeliever, fabricate for yourself or accept on the spot an 'opportune' faith only because it is opportune?" (*Drowned* 146–47). Even his rejection of faith is a consequence of his maintaining high ethical standards. He did not want to be "opportunistic" before God.

Levi does, however, admit to praying in his own way. In a letter a year after their liberation from Auschwitz, he wrote to his friend Jean Samuel in France:

> It is a miracle that I am still alive, in good health, with my family. I have made a vow never to forget that, and I repeat it to myself every day, like a prayer. It is not that I thank Providence, because if there really was a Providence, Auschwitz and Birkenau would never have existed; but this way, from now on I can genuinely enjoy all the little things in life that

usually go unnoticed, and not grumble too much about everyday worries, great or small. (Anissimov 253)

Elie Wiesel remembers lengthy conversations with Levi: their ethics were similar, but their belief in God differed (*Memoirs* 82–83). Wiesel is a Hasid who studies kaballa; Levi was a rationalist who studied the elements of this world, not the next. Both insist upon love and justice in human relationships, and both have acted on these values. Wiesel's sources are the Bible, its commentators, Jewish mysticism and tradition, and his beloved teachers. Levi's main source is his ingrained desire to know the truth about humankind and life. That truth is arrived at by study, experimentation, and experience. Giuliani affirms, "His is a laic ethics, because it makes no appeal to any Transcendence. It has its foundation in reason, and only in human rationality" (39). However, is this entirely true when Levi, along with Wiesel, agrees that not God but "chance" saved them from death in the obscene universe of concentration camps, "chance" and the compassion of friends (Camon 67)? As David Mendel notes, "He felt he survived by Chance, luck, *Muzzel*" (70). Chance and compassion are not usually associated with "human rationality." Levi's ethical actions go beyond what is humanly reasonable.

Levi's and Wiesel's varying spiritualities can be observed in their diverse reactions to the *Shemà*, Judaism's sacred prayer learned early by children, recited daily by orthodox believers, and invoked by martyrs before their death, including many approaching the gas chambers at Auschwitz. Mirna Cicioni reproduces the essential verses (Deuteronomy 6:4–9):

> Hear, O Israel: The Lord our God, the Lord is one. Love the Lord our God with all your heart, and with all your soul, and with all your strength. And these words, which I command you this day, shall be upon your heart, and you shall teach them diligently to your children, and you shall repeat them when you sit in your house, and when you walk by the way, and when you go to bed, and when you rise. And you shall bind them upon your arm, and you shall wear them on your foreheads between your eyes as a reminder. And you shall write them on the door-posts of your house and on your gates. (52)

These verses emphasize the necessity of loving God and remembering Him and His words at all times. Levi has echoed them in an odd way in his untitled poem which prefaces *Se questo è un uomo* (*Survival in Auschwitz*). "Shemà" dates from January 10, 1946, but Levi said that it was already in his head while he was at Auschwitz (Amsallem 226). Massimo Lollini has noted that Levi was wary of his own poetry since he "thought that poetry was connected to the irrational side of his soul" and hence less controlled than his prose (69), which makes this text all the more significant. Levi addresses those who live comfortably and securely in their "warm houses": "Meditate that this came about: / I commend these words to you" (*Survival* 11); "these words" are, however, not the Torah but his memoir describing vividly, as noted in Chapter 4, his horrific experiences in Auschwitz. These are the words which must be "[c]arve[d]" onto the "hearts" of all everywhere. If not, he closes his "Shemà" with a malediction: he wishes that his readers' homes collapse and that "[d]isease render you powerless, / Your offspring avert their faces from you" (*Collected Poems* 9).

Levi's "*Shemà*" replaces God's words with the Shoah and adds a curse on anyone who dares to forget this tragedy. His verses reflect both his rejection of God and his post-Holocaust eccentric spirituality. This is in contrast to Wiesel's strained efforts to assert his faith at Auschwitz II-Birkenau in 1979:

> The next day our delegation went to the death camps—to Treblinka, to Auschwitz. We were a group of five survivors from the same camp, and we remembered the place not as it is now but as it was then: At last we came to a very specific site: where the death chambers and the fires consumed our people one generation ago. As we stood there I did not know what to say, I did not know what to do. A prayer? No prayer should be said, could be said, at that place. Reciting any prayer would have been blasphemy. So we stood there. Then suddenly—unplanned, unconsciously, out of the depths of my being, out of the depths of my memory, I heard myself whispering the ancient prayer, which is not even a prayer: *Shema Yisrael, Adoshem Elokenu, Adoshem Ehad*. Suddenly all my friends took up this whisper. And it was more than a whisper—it was a shout, a shout of defiance, the only one we could have made: *Shema Yisrael*. We are still here, and God is still our God, and He is still the only One. *Shema Yisrael*. Listen Israel. That moment will remain with us for many centuries. (Abrahamson, *Against I* 169)

Thus, Wiesel with great difficulty prays the *Shemà* to assert his faith amidst the ruins of the gas chambers and crematoriums at Auschwitz while Levi removes God and His words as the focal point of remembrance in this prayer, replacing these with the Shoah itself. These treatments of the *Shemà* epitomize their spiritualities. Levi will not speak to God in prayer while Wiesel argues with God in prayer. By maintaining his contact with God, Wiesel fulfills the meaning of his name "Eliezar": "help of God" (Leizman 63) or, as Robert Alter translates it, "my God is aid" (417).

Wiesel recalls his discussions with Levi as their friendship grew: "He refused to understand how I, his former companion of Auschwitz III, could still call himself a believer, for he, Primo, was not and didn't want to be. He had seen too much suffering not to rebel against any religion that sought to impose a meaning upon it. I understood him, and asked him to understand me, for I had seen too much suffering to break with the past and reject the heritage of those who had suffered. . . . I needed God, Primo did not" (*Memoirs* 82–83).

Wiesel summarizes Levi's problem with orthodox belief: "Either God is God, and therefore all powerful and hence guilty of letting the murderers do as they pleased, or His power is limited, in which case he is not God. In other words, if God is God, then He is present everywhere. But if He refuses to show Himself, he becomes immoral and inhuman, the enemy's ally or accomplice" (*Memoirs* 83). This line of reasoning is not too far from Wiesel's own in *Night* when he protests, "If God will not rescue us, then is there a god? If there is and he still will not rescue us, then is he a weakling or a fiend?" (79). The older Wiesel writing his *Memoirs* has obviously decided to continue believing in God despite the horrific mystery of His presence or absence at Auschwitz which began to evoke his rage and questions in 1948 and 1949 (*Conversations* 186). He does, however, in 1978 speak about "the dark side of God" (*A Jew Today* 113). Levi's reasoning remains persuasive, but he, too, cannot ignore God. Mendel, his protagonist in *Se non ora, quando?* (*If Not Now, When?*), who strongly resembles Levi himself (Thomson 390), frequently invokes God, but in an unorthodox way: "Che la guerra finisca, Signore a cui non credo" ["Let the war end, Lord in whom I don't believe"] (*Se non ora, quando?* II.422).

Sociologist Peter L. Berger notes that the "agnostic position is by definition a weak one. The agnostic doesn't radically reject what's believed in religion, as the atheist does. Maybe he even would *like* to believe as the believer does, but the knowledge he's gathered by study and experience restrains him. . . . Doubt is the hallmark of the agnostic. . . . the agnostic lives with and in doubt that is troubled by faith" (108–09). Elie Wiesel has chosen to maintain an orthodox Jewish faith in God that is deeply troubled by questions about His omnipotence, love, justice, and goodness, while Primo Levi refused belief in God after Auschwitz while choosing to live by His commandments, a choice evidenced in his actions rather than in any religious affirmations. Berger acknowledges that there is "a thin line" between the believer "troubled by doubt" and the agnostic "troubled by faith" (109).

This ambiguous attitude is further demonstrated when Levi spoke to Waldensian schoolchildren about anti-Semitism in 1975, for he "define[d] himself as *'una persona in ricerca,'* 'a man in search of a faith'. . . . In fact Levi envied believers—the more so, the older he got—and wished he could believe in god. 'To have a father, a judge, a teacher would be good, calming'" (Thomson 345). Sergio Parussa has suggested that Levi experienced "*teshuva*, which is usually rendered in English with the terms 'return' or 'repentance,'" but "*teshuva* is also a way of regaining the notion of one's own Jewish identity, of the individual and collective sense of belonging to a tradition that may have been previously forsaken" (87). He continues:

> This concept of *teshuva* corresponds to Primo Levi's meaning when he described himself as 'un ebreo di ritorno' (a returning Jew) as someone who had renewed his interest in Judaism only after the promulgation of the Fascist racial laws and the deportation to the concentration camp. His return to Judaism, his literary meditations on Jewish culture, may be described as a secular work of *teshuva*. (87)

Despite their acknowledged differences of opinion about belief in God, both Wiesel and Levi shared similar ethics based on a common concept of what it is to be "human." Levi demonstrates this understanding at the close of *Se questo è un uomo* (*Survival in Auschwitz*) when Towarowski proposes to the other gravely ill prisoners that each give a little bread to Primo, Charles, and Arthur who had found rations, put together a makeshift stove, and cooked a simple meal after the Germans had departed with the "healthy" prisoners on the long, horrible march to Buchenwald in January 1945. Levi states that the sick men in their barracks agreed, as they never would have the day before when they had still been Häftlinge under the Germans' control. Indeed, "[f]u quello il primo gesto umano che avvenne fra noi. Credo che si potrebbe fissare a quel momento l'inizio del processo per cui, noi che non siamo morti, da Häftlinge siamo lentamente rideventati uomini" ["This was the first human sign that happened among us. I believe that I can locate at that moment the beginning of the process through which we, who were not dead, from prisoners slowly became men again"] (*Se Questo* I.167).

Wiesel would probably agree: "Each time a person surprises me by remaining human, by offering a gift, being generous, resisting evil, and surely by fighting evil, I am grateful to God, grateful that I am the contemporary of that person" (Rittner 35). Typically, Levi describes the gratitude of his companions to men (Levi, Charles, and Arthur) while Wiesel is grateful to both God and generous persons. Both writers value friendships—with each other and with others who share their understanding of what it means to be truly human. Sharing this ethic, both sacrificed themselves to help their friends. These moments escape the boundaries of Levi's rationalism and border on Wiesel's mysticism—an irrational care for others that enhances Levi's understanding of a human being's innate dignity and which annuls a Darwinian survival of the fittest. Levi's fear of "spirituality" and "God talk" kept him bound to human beings who affirmed their dignity on earth. Wiesel's religious vocabulary permits him to talk with ease about biblical heroes, Jewish martyrs, and love of God, men, and Torah:

> This is the concept of Hasidism. If there is nothing else to be done, to love one another, *Ahavat Yisrael*, which is one branch of the three *ahavot*, the three loves, the Hasidic cardinal principles. What are they? Number one is *Ahavat Yisrael*: You must love your fellow man. Number two is *Ahavat Hashem*: You must love God. Number three is *Ahavat Torah*: You must love God's Torah. If you accept these three, you cannot go wrong. (Abrahamson, *Against II* 261).

He has also written about love for the stranger, the *ger* (*From the Kingdom* 56), who must not be "absorbed" but rather is encouraged to "maintain his [own] identity and enrich it" (*From the Kingdom* 61). Hence eschewing converting others to Judaism, he acknowledges that in Jewish tradition the stranger may well turn out to be "a prophet in disguise, one of the hidden just men, or even the Messiah" (*From the Kingdom* 63). This emphasis on loving the stranger is a natural consequence of remembering that the Jews were once all strangers in Egypt (*Inside, Stranger* 29).

In his chapter "Zinco" of *Il sistema periodico* (*The Periodic Table*) Levi posits respect for the other and refusal to change him so that a homogeneous "purity" can be obtained. His ethic is similar to Wiesel's honoring the one who is different while his description varies greatly from Wiesel's biblical imagery:

l'elogio della purezza, che protegga dal male come un usbergo; l'elogi dell'impurezza, che dà adito ai mutamenti, cioè alla vita. Scartai la prima, disgustosamente moralistica, e mi attardai a considerare la seconda, che mi era piú congeniale. Perché la ruota giri, perché la vita viva, ci vogliono le impurezze, e le impurezze delle impurezze: anche nel terreno, come è noto, se ha da essere fertile. Ci vuole il dissenso, il diverso, il grano di sale e di senape: il fascismo non li vuole, li vieta, e per questo tu non sei fascista: vuole tutti uguali e tu non sei uguale. Ma neppure la virtú immacolata esiste, o se esiste è detestabile [the elogy of purity, which protects from evil like a shield; the elogy of impurity, which makes possible mutations, therefore life. I rejected the first, disgustingly moralistic, and I stopped to consider the second which was more acceptable to me. Because the wheel turns, because life lives, they want impurities, and impurities from impurities: also in the earth, as it is known, if it is to be fertile. We need dissent, diversity, the grain of salt and mustard: fascism does not want these, forbids them, and for this reason you are not a fascist; it wants everyone equal and you are not equal. But not even immaculate virtue exists, or if it exists it is detestable]. ("Zinco" I.458–59)

Both Wiesel and Levi appreciate "dissent, diversity, . . . salt and mustard" and manifest no desire to redesign the other (or "purify" him or her) for the sake of an "immaculate" unity. Richness results from this diversity, and it must be respected. Both authors know the pain of being considered the "impurity" that troubles a society that favors sterile homogeneity. Levi in 1982 even provides his own commentary of the passage cited above:

> In 1938. . . . [n]ewspapers and magazines composed by the totalitarian [Italian Fascist] regime speak insistently of the Jews as different, as potential (or actual) enemies of Fascism, as noxious 'impurities' in the pure body of the Italian people. The Nuremburg laws are cited as an example to be imitated. The themes of the fanatical propaganda of Dr. Goebbels are taken up: the Jew, reproduced in humorous cartoons with the traditional Semitic features, is at once the capitalist who starves the 'Aryan' peoples, and the blood-thirsty Bolshevik, the destroyer of Western civilization. . . . The young version of myself described by me here [in "Zinc" of *The Periodical Table*] is confusedly proud of being 'an impurity.' (Levi, *Beyond Survival* 11).

Levi's respect for diversity even includes support of certain mystics like, not only Wiesel, but also Alexander Solzhenitsyn. Ian Thomson notes that "Levi was one of the few Italian writers to champion Solzhenitsyn. Most left-leaning Italian intellectuals saw him as a Slav reactionary and mystic" (325). Levi recognized truth in the gifted Russian writer's descriptions of prisons and work camps.

## Chapter 6

Both Wiesel and Levi also share in common a sense of "chance" or "luck" controlling their lives. Wiesel writes, "When was it that I realized I was not in control of my destiny? It was by chance that I had survived, by chance that I had followed one road rather than another. It was by chance that I had become a journalist. Events unfolded outside me and beyond my will. Very often I simply let myself be carried along" (*Memoirs* 276). Levi felt that he survived Auschwitz because of "luck":

> I think I'd undergone a process [in the camps] of maturing, having had the luck to survive. Because it's not a question of strength, but of luck: you can't beat a concentration camp with your own strengths. I'd been lucky: for having been a chemist, for having met a bricklayer who gave me something to eat, for having overcome the language difficulty (this I can claim to have done); I never got sick—I got sick only once, at the end, and this too was lucky, because I missed the evacuation of the camp [which Wiesel and his father were forced to endure]. The others . . . were transferred to Buchenwald and Mauthausen in the middle of winter. (Camon 67).

The humanistic focus which both writers share—that man's task is to do what is just and good on earth, not in heaven, and to alleviate suffering—allows them to speak of "chance" rather than God controlling their lives.

Carole Angier reproduces a brief observation from Levi's friend Gisella who wrote in her 1982–1983 diary: "At the end of the year he says: 'I'm looking for God, but I can't find him'" (655). As a student of kabbala, Wiesel finds God in his study of Torah as well as in personal prayer to God. Daniel Chanan Matt explains that for a kabbalist the "hidden essence of Torah is God. The ultimate purpose of study is direct experience of the divine, who is real Torah; the search for meaning culminates in revelation" (207). Levi felt no obligation to love God or look for Him while studying Torah. Nevertheless, his acts of compassion for others and his love of justice demonstrate an understanding of what is desired by God, according to His Decalogue, and hence what is essential to Jewish ethics.

Perhaps the fundamental elements in Jewish ethics are congruent with what makes sense to a genuine humanist, a vigilant observer of life, and a diligent seeker of truth. In a world rife with cruelty the enactment of these ethics may become more important than acknowledging their Source. Diversity, the juxtaposition of the non-believer and the believer, leads to a richness that culminates in faithful friendship between Levi and Wiesel, and a rich, shared ethic that is open to all.

# Works Cited

Abrahamson, Irving, ed. *Against Silence: The Voice and Vision of Elie Wiesel, Vol. I.* New York: Holocaust Library, 1985. Print.

Abrahamson, Irving, ed. *Against Silence: The Voice and Vision of Elie Wiesel. Vol. II.* New York: Holocaust Library, 1985. Print.

Alter, Robert. *The Five Books of Moses: A Translation with Commentary.* New York: W. W. Norton & Company, 2004. Print.

Amsallem, Daniela. *Primo Levi au miroir de son oeuvre: Le témoin, L'écrivain, Le chimiste.* Lyon: Editions du Cosmogone, 2001. Print.

Angier, Carole. *The Double Bond: Primo Levi a Biography.* New York: Farrar, Straus and Giroux, 2002. Print.

Anissimov, Myriam. *Primo Levi: Tragedy of an Optimist.* Trans. Steve Cox. London: Aurum Press, 1998. Print.

Berger, Peter, and Anton Zijderveld. *In Praise of Doubt: How to Have Convictions without Becoming a Fanatic.* New York: Harper One, 2009. Print.

Camon, Ferdinando. *Conversations with Primo Levi.* Trans. John Shepley. Marlboro, VT: Marlboro Press, 1989. Print.

Cicioni, Mirna. *Primo Levi: Bridges of Knowledge.* Oxford: Berg, 1995. Print.

Farrell, Joseph. "From Darkness to Light: Primo Levi, Man of Letters." *Primo Levi: The Austere Humanist.* Ed. Joseph Farrell. Bern: Peter Lang, 2004. 117–39. Print.

Giulani, Massimo. *A Centaur in Auschwitz: Reflections on Primo Levi's Thinking.* Oxford: Lexington Books, 2003. Print.

Kafka, Franz. *Il Processo (Der Prozess).* Trans. Primo Levi. Torino: Einaudi (coll. "Scrittori tradotti da scrittore"), 1983. Print.

Leizman, Reva B. "The Road Towards Regeneration and Salvation in the Novels of Elie Wiesel." Ph.D. Dissertation (Comparative Literature). Case Western Reserve University. June 1977. Print.

Levi, Primo. "Beyond Survival." Trans. Gail Soffer. *Prooftexts* 4.1 (January 1984): 9–21. Print.

Levi, Primo. *The Drowned and the Saved.* Trans. Raymond Rosenthal. New York: Vintage International, 1989. Print.

Levi, Primo. *If Not Now, When?* Trans. William Weaver. New York: Penguin Books, 1995. Print.

Levi, Primo. *If This Is a Man.* Trans. Stuart Woolf. New York: First Collier Books Trade Edition, 1993. Print.

Levi, Primo. *The Periodic Table.* Trans. Raymond Rosenthal. New York: Alfred A. Knopf, 1996. Print.

Levi, Primo. *Se non ora, quando? Opere II.* Torino: Einaudi, 1988. 183–517. Print.

Levi, Primo. *Se questo è un uomo. Opere I.* Torino: Einaudi, 1987. 1–212. Print.

Levi, Primo. "Shemà." *Collected Poems.* Trans. Ruth Feldman and Brian Swann. London: Faber and Faber, 1988. 9. Print.

Levi, Primo. *Il sistema periodica. Opere I.* Torino: Einaudi, 1987. 428–649. Print.

Levi, Primo. *Survival in Auschwitz: The Nazi Assault on Humanity.* Trans. Stuart Woolf. New York: A Touchstone Book Simon & Schuster, 1996. Print.

Lollini, Massimo. "Primo Levi and the Idea of Autobiography." *Primo Levi: The Austere Humanist*. Ed. Joseph Farrell. Bern: Peter Lang, 2004. 67–89. Print.

Matt, Daniel Chanan. *Zohar: The Book of Enlightenment*. Ramsey, New Jersey: Paulist Press, 1983. Print.

Mendel, David. "Primo Levi and the Jews." *The Legacy of Primo Levi*. Ed. Stanislao G. Pugliese. New York: Palgrave Macmillan, 2005. 61–73. Print.

Nietzsche, Friedrich. *Beyond Good and Evil*. Trans. Walter Kaufmann. New York: Random House, Vintage Books, 1966. Print.

Parussa, Sergio. "A Hybridism of Sounds: Primo Levi between Judaism and Literature." *The Legacy of Primo Levi*. Ed. Stanislao G. Pugliese. New York: Palgrave Macmillan, 2005. 87–94. Print.

Rittner, Carol. "An Interview with Elie Wiesel." *Elie Wiesel: Between Memory And Hope*. Ed. Carol Rittner. New York: New York UP, 1990. 30–41. Print.

Thomson, Ian. *Primo Levi: A Life*. New York: Metropolitan Books Henry Holt and Company, 2002. Print.

Wiesel, Elie. *Conversations*. Ed. Robert Franciosi. Jackson: U of Mississippi P, 2002. Print.

Wiesel, Elie. . . . *Et la mer n'est pas remplie: Mémoires 2*. Paris: Éditions du Seuil, 1996. Print.

Wiesel, Elie. *From the Kingdom of Memory: Reminiscences*. New York: Summit Books, 1990. Print.

Wiesel, Elie. *Inside a Library;* and *The Stranger in the Bible*. Cincinnati: Hebrew Union College—Jewish Institute of Religion, 1981. Print.

Wiesel, Elie. *A Jew Today*. Trans. Marion Wiesel. New York: Random House, 1978. Print.

Wiesel, Elie. *Memoirs: All Rivers Run to the Sea*. New York: Alfred A. Knopf, 1995. Print.

Wiesel, Elie. *Night*. Trans. Marion Wiesel. New York: Hill and Wang, 2006. Print.

# Chapter 7: "Thou shalt not make unto thee any graven image"

Although Primo Levi intentionally chose humanistic rationalism over religious, mystical spirituality, he did not hesitate to use mythological or fantastic characters in his writings. The centaur is one such character. Carole Angier affirms that this image describes both the writer himself and "mankind as a whole, that 'tangle of flesh and mind, of divine inspiration and dust'" (501). The centaur is a Greco-Roman classical figure, not a biblical creation, fitting for Levi's formation in the humanities as a youth—five years of Greek studies and eight years of Latin (Cavaglion 7). Did he make the centaur, or "mankind as a whole," a god before God? Or, did he subtly acknowledge that this '"tangle of flesh and mind'" was indeed somehow divinely created—that a creative living force existed in "mankind"?

Another of Levi's biographers, Ian Thomson, also emphasizes the equating of Levi with a centaur:

> In . . . 'Quaestio de Centauris' . . . he imagines himself as a 260-year-old half man, half horse. This equine whimsy marks the beginning of an enduring, even obsessive attempt on Levi's part to present himself as two halves or twin poles. Levi was not the only Italian literary figure engaged in two careers, but he alone tried to create a grand personal mythology out of this cloven state; in countless interviews he remarked on the tension in his life between the [paint] factory and the typewriter, writing and the family. . . . Interestingly, centaurs themselves have dual personalities: on the one hand, wise teachers; on the other, lustful, drunken womanizers. Perhaps Levi wished to identify with the side of the half man, half horse that he was not. (*Primo* 298–99)

Thomson calls Levi's referring to himself as a "centaur" a "mythology," but it is doubtful that Trachi, the centaur featured in "Quaestio de Centauris," really is meant to personify Levi. The first person narrator of this tale is a young man, not the centaur, who enjoys listening to Trachi's wisdom. When Trachi falls in love with Teresa De Simone, a local neighbor, and the narrator himself yields to her seduction and makes love to her, Trachi seems to go insane. He rampages around the neighborhood, selecting and raping female horses until he is last seen by some fishermen vigorously swimming toward the Levant ("Questio de Centauris" III.130). The story is more about the damage done by the betrayal of two (human) friends than about the sexual prowess of a centaur. The betrayal shifts the centaur's focus from "wise teacher" to "lustful... womanizer" which was never a part of Levi's character. Significantly, the youthful narrator feels great shame at having betrayed his companion of many years and enormous regret at having lost him.

Thomson also mentions Levi's "long-held fascination with the world of spells and magic" (*Primo* 220). For example, Levi surprised his colleagues at SIVA, his paint factory, "by his ability to read [Tarot] cards" (Thomson, *Primo* 250), and he was pleased to meet "Turin's white-magician Gustavo Rol, the undisputed psychic star of 1970s Italy.... Rol reanimated the interest Levi had always had in the paranormal, and which his table-rapping father Cesare had first instilled in him" (Thomson, *Primo* 347). If Levi were not an orthodox believer, like Wiesel, he at least had an interest in spiritualistic topics like Tarot cards and white-magicians.

Moreover, Wiesel has also been fascinated by the occult. He relates in his *Memoirs* that as a child he read Hebrew, Aramaic, and Hungarian texts that informed him about "[a]strology, magic, morphology, hypnotism, graphology, parapsychology, alchemy" (34). He admits, "In short, I became entranced by what lay beyond reality" (34). Nevertheless, he concludes, "Fifty years later I can reveal the truth: It doesn't work, and I say that from experience. Countless times I tried to thwart Hitler, visiting myriad evils and maladies upon him" (34).

Wiesel evolved into a committed Hasid while Levi remained a troubled agnostic, but one who emanated a kind of spiritual aura. Thomson notes that "[l]ike many people, [Simone Lakmaker] had found his presence 'oddly spiritual'. (Indeed, this perceived 'spirituality' was becoming part of Levi's personality. An electrical expert at Bayer, Hans Schlegel, had noted in 1974 that Levi's eyes were faintly almond-shaped and looked 'holy'.)" (*Primo* 447). When asked by Lakmaker if he believed in God, however, Levi affirmed his unbelief, qualified by '"I believe in fellow man'" (*Primo* 447). His generous humanism always predominated over any spiritual leanings, but did it equate with making a "graven image" out of humankind?

Elie Wiesel comments that the Talmud insists "on warning us against self-indulgence and, above all, self-adoration, which is compared to idolatry. . . . True humility is judging oneself with severity and judging others with understanding" (*Wise Men* 218). Elsewhere he notes that a proud person is an idolator, for his sense of superiority over others makes him "l'esclave de sa propre idole qui est lui-même" ["the slave of his own idol which is himself"] (*Et où vas-tu?* 41). He concludes, "Nul ne doit être dieu, ni pour l'autre ni pour soi-même" [No one should be god, neither for another nor for himself"] (*Et où vas-tu?* 85–86).

However, in an interview with me he also enigmatically affirmed that "spiritual and humanistic are the same" (Personal interview). Since he believes that God is in all human beings, then perhaps spiritual and humanistic do become synonomous. In *A Beggar in Jerusalem* he includes the rabbi's blessing on the protagonist David as a child, a blessing specifically requested by his mother: '"Let him love God but only through man: that would satisfy me"' (68). This again suggests that loving man equates with loving God—humanistic and spiritual again veer into each other.

Psychologists also affirm that a healthy love of self is necessary for a balanced love of others. Primo Levi told his biographer Ian Thomson that '"[i]t was only after my humanity had been obliterated,' after I had written *If This Is a Man*, that I felt a true 'man' again—a man in the sense of the title of that book'" (Thomson, "Writing" 154). Such self-recognition and affirmation do not equate with self-idolatry and do empower him who had experienced "obliteration" to reach beyond himself to help others. Levi had already experienced before the Shoah the absence of God and the need to affirm himself in order to survive on earth without Him. He mentions in "Potassio" of *Il sistema periodico* (*The Periodic Table*) that he and other Jewish youth gathered to study the Bible in order to find again "la giustizia e l'ingiustizia e la forza che abbatte l'ingiustizia: a riconscere in Assuero e in Nabucodonosor i nuovi oppressori. Ma dov'era Kadosh Barukhú, 'il Santo, Benedetto sia Egli', colui che spezza le catene degli schiavi e sommerge i carri degli Egizi? Colui che aveva dettato la Legge a Mosè, ed ispirato i liberatori Ezra e Neemia, non ispirava piú nessuno, il cielo sopra noi era silenzioso e vuoto" ["justice and injustice and the strength that overthrows injustice: to recognize in Ahasuerus and in Nebuchadnezzar the new oppressors. But where was God, 'the Holy One, Blessed be He,' he who breaks the chains of the slaves and submerges the chariots of the Egyptians? He who had dictated the Law to Moses, and inspired the liberators Ezra and Nehemiah, no longer inspired anyone, the sky above us was silent and empty"] (*Il sistema periodico* I.475–76). This silence of God motivated Levi to depend on himself for survival, and Auschwitz only increased that self-respect and self-reliance. It cannot be equated with self-centered egotism, however, because it embraced others, such as Alberto in Auschwitz, beyond himself.

Wiesel relates loving others to loving God; does Levi's love for others actually indicate a hidden (from him) love for God?

Levi and Wiesel have experienced the cruelty of those who have neither fear of nor love for God and who take themselves to be gods: "Hitler était tenu pour un dieu par son peuple mais, en dessous, il y avait des milliers de petits Hitler à tous les échelons de la nation" [Hitler was taken for a god by his people, but, below him, there were millions of little Hitlers at every level of the nation"] (Wiesel *Et où vas-tu?* 86). Hence, idolatry may proliferate itself dangerously at the expense of those called upon to be the idolators' worshippers, but it is absent from those who love God while loving human beings and affirming the dignity that Hitler and his subordinates annihilated.

Both Levi and Wiesel feared exerting power over others and hence turning into unloving "*Kapos.*" Thomson describes Levi's difficulties as manager at SIVA, Rico Accati's paint factory. Levi "seemed unable to discipline workers—even if it was for the workers' own good [such as enforcing safety measures]—or to take a firm stand on hiring and firing. . . . the more orders [Levi] gave at SIVA, the more he felt uncomfortably like an Auschwitz *Kapo*" (*Primo* 339). These tensions contributed to his decision to retire early from SIVA and devote more of his time to his writing.

Wiesel also describes himself as totally ineffective at giving orders. This stems from a childhood incident when he was too ardent a commander over other youth. He relates:

> During the time Sighet was under Hungarian rule, schoolchildren had to do compulsory service in the Leventes, a kind of scout movement under the supervision of the army and the Ministry of Education. We had to perform various tasks, such as digging trenches at army bases, helping firefighters, or clearing snowbound streets. One day—it was a Friday—I was assigned to

head a team. Exempted from the task of wielding a shovel, I was supposed to oversee, command, and shout—very loudly. I took my role seriously, rushing from group to group berating laggards: Hurry up, the snow has to be cleared by nightfall, before Shabbat! Suddenly I found myself face to face with the grandson of the Borsher Rebbe. He was a close friend of mine. We often studied together, and prayed at the same times. He stared at me with an expression not so much of disapproval as of sadness and surprise. Was I going to harangue him too, make him feel my power, my authority? When my eyes met his, I was overcome by remorse. I began to stammer excuses, at which point our commander appeared on the scene. Realizing that I was not cut out for this job, he shook me and screamed, 'Next time, you fool, you'll sweat blood like everyone else.' [Je préférais cela: I preferred that (*Tous les fleuves* 440).] Out of the corner of my eye I saw my friend smiling. I would later see men of all ages who, in extreme situations, brutally exercised their power over their fellow inmates. . . . Ultimately, the only power to which man should aspire is that which he exercises over himself. (*Memoirs* 311)

Wiesel's fear of and even disdain for exerting authority over others was only enhanced by his Auschwitz experiences and remained with him for the rest of his life.

Both Levi and Wiesel demonstrate a fear of limiting their freedom as human beings with dignity by becoming parts of a cruel, collective machine, be it a factory or a youth group or Auschwitz's hierarchy. This sentiment comes from a deep understanding of what true freedom is—not the power to order others around but the ability to follow one's own interior code of ethics, to become a "solid," not an "empty," person (see Chapter 3: "Thou shalt not steal").

Thomas Merton remarks, "the prohibition of idolatry is in fact one of the deepest roots of this Biblical doctrine of liberty, idolatry being in fact inseparable from servitude to human systems that exploit man's natural needs and appetites for their own ends, or seek to dominate him by brute force. Idolatry is, of course, a basic form of spiritual violence" (48). There was definitely idolatry occurring in the near worship of Adolf Hitler by some Germans between 1933 and 1945, and maybe thereafter. However, perhaps even more frightening than the unquestioning loyalty shown to one strong, charismatic leader is the ongoing, innate confusion that occurs when a bureaucracy with no one visibly in control prevails over its victims. Franz Kafka's *The Trial*, although presciently written at the beginning of the twentieth century, describes just such a bureaucratic nightmare that seems very real to many twenty-first century readers. Levi remarks, "Kafka comprende il mondo (il suo, e anche meglio il nostro d'oggi) con una chiaroveggenza che stupisce, e che ferisce come una luce troppo intensa" ["Kafka understands the world (his, and even better ours of today) with a clairvoyance that amazes, and that wounds like a too intense light"] ("Tradurre Kafka" III.921].

When in 1982 invited by Giulio Einaudi (Angier 630), Levi chose to translate into Italian this complicated text from the German (Kafka, a Jew, wrote in the language of the educated elite predominant in Prague under the Austro-Hungarian Empire), and Wiesel has taught this book at Boston University. He clearly loves to teach: "In Boston too, my students bring me joy. To witness the awakening of knowledge, that unique light of understanding, of recognition—is there a more beautiful moment for a teacher?" (*And the Sea Is Never Full* 106). In discussing the many themes and books he shares with his students, never teaching at Boston University the same course twice, he remarks, "And then there is my passion for Kafka: Kafka and Aesop, Kafka and theology, Kafka and psychology, Kafka and politics, Kafka the literary figure, Kafka the philosopher, Kafka and women, Kafka and the Jews" (*And the Sea Is Never Full* 107).

Kafka's *The Trial*, an unfinished novel, can be interpreted on many levels: Freudian, theological, sociological, and others. It portrays a seemingly innocent man, Josef K., succumbing to bureaucratic summons and threats in an enclosed society that replaces the rigid geographical boundaries of a prison. Unlike Levi and Wiesel, Josef K. is an "uomo vuoto" similar to those portrayed in Amelie Nothomb's novel discussed in Chapter 3 above. Kafka's anti-hero lacks what, it is worth repeating again here, psychiatrist Murray Bowen defines as a "solid self": "The solid self says, 'This is who I am, what I believe, what I stand for, what I will do or will not do,' in a given situation. The solid self is made up of clearly defined beliefs, opinions, convictions, and life principles" (365). Josef K. lacks the core value system that could make up his "solid self." Levi describes him poignantly: "la sua essenza (come quella di quasi tutti) consiste nell'essere incoerente, non uguale a se stesso nel corso del tempo, instabile, erratico, o anche diviso nello stesso istante, spaccato in due o piú individualità che non combaciano" ["his essence (like that of almost everyone) consists of the incoherent being, not equal to him himself in the course of time, unstable, erratic, and also divided in the same moment, broken into two or more individualities that do not fit closely together"] ("Tradurre Kafka" III.922). When Levi spoke about his Shoah experiences to school children, he wanted them to "understand that the Lager could be anywhere, even amongst themselves: since its essence was death, not by starvation, or the gas chambers, but by contempt: by the destruction of another's human dignity, after which his physical destruction is easy" (Angier 513).

Exemplifying this gradual "destruction of . . . human dignity," Kafka's "anti-hero" takes seriously the "arrest" he experiences upon waking up on the morning of his thirtieth birthday (4), even though he does not understand who or what is the power behind those arresting him and why he is being arrested. When he is not locked up anywhere but encouraged to go on to his job of Chief Clerk at his bank, he continues to believe that he is still under arrest, although the possibility has occurred to him that all of this may be a joke (4). He eventually realizes that "[w]hile he stayed quietly at home and went about his ordinary vocations he remained superior to all these people and could kick any of them out of his path" (58–59). One wonders why he does not retain his power and do just that—go about his ordinary business and remain quietly at home. The answer is that he has nothing within himself upon which to anchor himself calmly; his life revolves solely around externalities—his banking responsibilities, his evening visits to his favorite pub, his occasional meetings with Else the prostitute, and his rented room in Frau Grubach's home. Levi criticizes him sharply: Josef K. has wasted "la vita in meschine gelosie di ufficio, in falsi amori, in timidezze malate, in adempimenti statici e ossessivi" ["life in petty office rivalries, in fake loves, in sick shynesses, in static and obsessive fulfillments"] ("Tradurre Kafka" III.922). Hence he allows himself to get sucked into the nebulous bureaucracy that claims to have a reason to "arrest" him, although he continues to function freely outside of the confines of any prison.

Thus, even though he is not summoned a second time, he chooses to return to the sleazy slum and the filthy attic that claims to be waiting rooms, court, and offices the following Sunday simply out of "curiosity": "he had come only out of curiosity or, what was still more impossible as an explanation of his presence, out of a desire to assure himself that the inside of this legal system was just as loathsome as its external aspect" (66–67). The result is that he becomes so weakened and dizzy from stress and lack of air that he must be almost carried bodily down from the attic rooms out to the street by a male and female functionary who treat him not rudely, as might be expected of such a loathsome bureaucratic apparatus, but rather nicely (72–73). The "niceness" of these and other lower level officials pertaining to this strange organization is deceptive and invites him to cooperate with them even against his better judgment. However, here again at this point in the novel, he appears to decide to avoid this bureaucracy in the future: "he had made up his mind—and there he could advise himself—to spend all his Sunday mornings in future to better purpose" (73). The only problem with such a choice is that he really has no "better purpose" in life. He declares to the court painter Titorelli, "'I am completely innocent'" (149), but he never discovers what are the court's charges against him which could make him guilty, and he does not ask the painter to find this out for him.

Unlike Levi and Wiesel, Josef K. hopes for justice (this is apparent in some of his posturing speeches before participants in this strange tyrannical bureaucracy), but he does not act reasonably and compassionately to make justice happen for himself and others. He seeks allies such as, at the beginning of his "trial," Frau Gruber and Fräulein Bürstner, but they are not true compatriots because of his own power over them—Frau Gruber owes him a financial debt (28), and he sexually assaults Fräulein Bürstner (29–30) after telling her late at night the unnerving story of the Court of Inquiry's Inspector's visit to her room in her absence that morning. Unlike the egalitarian brotherhood Levi felt with Alberto when fighting the demonic powers of Auschwitz, or the loving, respectful relationship that Wiesel maintained with his father throughout their incarceration, Josef K. has no real friends. He is far from being a "Mensch" doing what is just and good and helping to alleviate the sufferings of others around him.

At the home of his lawyer, Dr. Huld, Josef K. meets Block who has been harried by his case proceedings for more than five years. Hoping to gain pertinent information about the court from him, Josef K. condescendingly chats with him, "feeling at ease now, at ease as one is when speaking to an inferior in some foreign country, keeping one's own affairs to oneself and discussing with equanimity the other man's interests, which gain consequence for the attention one bestows on them yet can be dismissed at will" (168). The power over others which he seeks, accentuated by his feeling of powerlessness before the court, renders impossible authentic, compassionate friendship.

The culminating expression of his emptiness as a human being is his passive preparation for and accompanying of his mechanical silent attendants to the barren location outside of the town on the night before his thirty-first birthday. Thus, unlike Block who keeps working on his case for years even when reduced to total abjection before his own lawyer and the court personnel, Josef K. has endured one year of anxiety and seems to welcome death, although he refuses to himself plunge the butcher knife into his own heart. He is much like the worn down old man seated on his stool outside the door in the often excerpted "parable of the doorkeeper" told to Josef K. by the "prison chaplain" (210) in the Cathedral. This poor creature waits daily for the doorkeeper to admit him through the door intended only for him (215) until he dies. Both the expectant man on his stool and Josef K. do not exert their free will to walk away from the doorkeeper and his door, and the court and its functionaries; they both are obsessed with and consumed by the systems that keep them psychologically and emotionally, but not physically, enchained.

It is exactly this kind of a modern bureaucratic system that Primo Levi, Kafka's Italian translator, and Elie Wiesel, teacher of Kafka's texts, want to alert their readers and students to—a system that captures one's free will with no one visible at the head of the realm, a bureaucratic "religion" without a charismatic godlike human figure or a "golden calf" to be worshiped. Modern idolatry occurs, instead, when people mindlessly submit to low level functionaries, incompetent, conniving lawyers, and superstitious gossipers, allowing whoever is most powerful to remain anonymously behind the scenes.

The priest Josef K. encounters in the dark Cathedral explains, '"it is not necessary to accept everything as true, one must only accept it as necessary.' 'A melancholy conclusion,' said K. 'It turns lying into a universal principle'" (220). With no access to the highest level of Judges and lawyers, if they really exist, and no certainty of truth, one is caught in an unreal world, searching here and there, as does this anti-hero, for fragments of what may be truth. Those employed by the court and benefiting from it somehow just fulfill their minimal duties, never seeing how what they do fits in with the whole "strategic plan" of the entire organization (119). Hence they need only follow orders, not their own personal ethics, if they still have any, to be exempted from responsibility, the plea of many criminals charged with war crimes after the Shoah. However, the person on the outside, like Josef K., accused and harassed without being told why, gradually wears down, losing more and more of his dignity and humanity: "a man . . . feels this thing secretly encroaching upon him and literally touching him to the quick,'" Josef K. explains to his lawyer (186) after only six months of anxiety. Even after being acquitted once, in this nightmarish system one may be "arrested" again, and so '"[o]ne must again apply all one's energies to the case and never give in'" (159).

Sadly Block explains, '"in these proceedings things are always coming up for discussion that are simply beyond reason, people are too tired and distracted to think and so they take refuge in superstition'" (174). Superstition, Block informs Josef K., acknowledges that '"you're supposed to tell from a man's face, especially the line of his lips, how his case is going to turn out. Well, people declared that judging from the expression of your lips you would be found guilty, and in the near future too'" (174). In 1915, long before Hitler's racial laws of the 1930s and the search for "semitic" faces and features, Kafka foresaw guilt assigned by physiognomy rather than moral and legal turpitude.

Dr. Huld tells Josef K., '"it's often better to be in chains than to be free'" (189), maybe because being "in chains" provides more certitude than nebulous freedom. K. nevertheless starts making some decisions freely, beginning with breaking with this lawyer and all of his household (189–90); he is humiliated in observing Block be humiliated by Dr. Huld: "The client ceased to be a client and became the Lawyer's dog" (193). In his later meeting with the "prison chaplain" of this evil court, Josef K. even wonders if there may be "a mode of living completely outside the jurisdiction of the Court. This possibility must exist, K. had of late given much thought to it" (212). Finally, he is, unlike the man on the stool by the doorkeeper in the parable (218), thinking of exerting his will to seek freedom far from the forces of the court.

However, he fails in the end because the court is inside of him as much as it seems to be outside of him. He passively cooperates with his two "nice" and polite executioners, and his final words in the novel show that he has fallen even below Block who wearily and humbly still keeps advocating for his case: Josef K. dies '"[l]ike a dog!' he said; it was as if the shame of it must outlive him" (229). Indeed, the shame of his slow death throughout the novel, culminating in this knife to his heart, does outlive him as Kafka's fragmented, incomplete text lives on almost one hundred years after its initial drafts. Levi in his short essay about translating Kafka affirms, "È finalmente un tribunal umano, non divino: è fatto di uomini e dagli uomini, e Josef, col coltello già piantato nel cuore, prova vergogna di essere un uomo" ["Finally it is a human, not divine, court: it is made of men and from men, and Josef, with the knife already embedded in his heart, feels shame at being a man"] (III.922).

Thus Western culture has evolved to the point where persons in power no longer create "any graven image" that can be identified; instead, an amorphous bureaucracy preoccupies its victims, wearing them down to the extent that they forget to even look for that "graven image" which, if found, might at least provide a focal point of attention and hence some relief for them. Overloaded with summons to obscure places, forms to be filled out, "nice" but unknowing functionaries who shift him from one office to another, literally "passing the buck," Josef K.'s fear increases in tandem with his frustration. Slowly the "court" occupies his mind continually, even when he is not physically present in it, thus wearing him down physically, emotionally, and intellectually so that he can no longer function well in his bank. He has already succumbed to it, even while still alive, when he stops fighting it and exorcising it from his inner being; rather, he gradually becomes like the broken elderly man whom Josef K. meets in the attic waiting room, who arrives at the court even when not summoned and provides documents not even requested, all in a humble attempt to please the anonymous, hidden, bureaucratic "powers that be": '"A month ago I handed in several affidavits concerning my case and I am waiting for the result,"' says the old man wearily (64). It is interesting to note that Josef K., at the beginning of his "trial," assaults this weary, broken man, as if to punish in him what he fears may occur in himself: "provoked without knowing it by the man's humility. . . . As a parting gesture he gripped the man with real force, flung him back on the bench, and went on his way" (65). This old man, Block, in the parable the doorkeeper's ever expectant man on the stool, and finally Josef K. succumb to the idol of a phantom bureaucracy with very real powers to enervate and kill. This phantom is the idol against which Levi and Wiesel most want to warn.

# Works Cited

Angier, Carole. *The Double Bond: Primo Levi a Biography.* New York: Farrar, Straus and Giroux, 2002. Print.
Bowen, Murray. *Family Therapy in Clinical Practice.* Northvale, New Jersey: Aronson, 1998. Print.
Cavaglion, Alberto, and Elisabetta Ruffini. *Primo Levi: I giorni e le opere.* Torino: Museo Diffuso della Resistenza della Deportazione, della Guerra dei Diritti e della Libertà, 2007. Print.
Kafka, Franz. *Il processo (Der Prozess).* Trans. Primo Levi. Torino: Einaudi (coll. "Scrittori tradotti da scrittori"), 1983. Print.
Kafka, Franz. *The Trial.* Trans. Willa and Edwin Muir. New York: Schocken Books, 1974. Print.
Levi, Primo. *If This Is a Man.* Trans. Stuart Woolf. New York: First Collier Books Trade Edition, 1993. Print.
Levi, Primo. *The Periodic Table.* Trans. Raymond Rosenthal. New York: Alfred A. Knopf, 1996. Print.
Levi, Primo. "Quaestio de Centauris." *Opere III: Racconti e saggi.* Torino: Einaudi, 1990. 119–30. Print.
Levi, Primo. *Il sistema periodica. Opere I.* Torino: Einaudi, 1987. 428–649. Print.
Levi, Primo. "Tradurre Kafka." *Operi III: Racconti e saggi.* Torino: Einaudi, 1990. 920–22. Print.
Merton, Thomas. *Opening the Bible.* Collegeville, Minnesota: Liturgical Press, 1986. Print.
Nothomb, Amélie. *Acide sulfurique: Roman.* Paris: Albin Michel, 2005. Print.
Thomson, Ian. *Primo Levi: A Life.* New York: Metropolitan Books Henry Holt and Company, 2002. Print.
Thomson, Ian. "Writing *If This Is a Man.*" *Primo Levi: The Austere Humanist.* Ed. Joseph Farrell. Bern: Peter Lang, 2004. 141–60. Print.
Wiesel, Elie. *And the Sea Is Never Full: Memoirs, 1969—.* Trans. Marion Wiesel. New York: Alfred A. Knopf, 1999. Print.
Wiesel, Elie. *A Beggar in Jerusalem.* Trans. Lily Edelman and the Author. New York: Schocken Books, 1970. Print.
Wiesel, Elie. *Et où vas-tu?* Paris: Éditions du Seuil, 2004. Print.
Wiesel, Elie. *Memoirs: All Rivers Run to the Sea.* New York: Alfred A. Knopf, 1995. Print.
Wiesel, Elie. Personal interview. 25 October 2004.
Wiesel, Elie. *Tous les fleuves vont à la mer: Mémoires I.* Paris: Éditions du Seuil, 1994. Print.
Wiesel, Elie. *Wise Men and Their Tales—Portraits of Biblical, Talmudic, and Hasidic Masters.* New York: Schocken Books, 2003. Print.

# Chapter 8: "Thou shalt not take the name of the LORD thy God in vain"

Moses' address to the Israelites in Deuteronomy 10: 12–13 includes God's expectations for them: "And now, Israel, what does the LORD your God ask of you but to fear the LORD your God, to walk in all His ways, to love Him, and to worship the LORD your God with all your heart and with all your being, to keep the LORD's commands and His statutes that I charge you today for your own good?" (Alter, *The Five Books of Moses* 932–33). In his commentary on these verses, Robert Alter notes their similarity to the words of the prophet Micah (Micah 6:8): "'He has told you, man, what is good and what the LORD requires of you—only to do justice and the love of kindness and walking humbly with your God'" (932). Primo Levi cannot love and worship God, although he definitely follows most of His Ten Words. Elie Wiesel fulfills the prophetic expectations, praying to God daily, observing the Decalogue and the laws relevant to Orthodox Judaism, but often reluctantly, for he can never accept God's seeming absence and silence during the Shoah. Since Levi refuses belief in God, he cannot really "take the name of the LORD [his] God in vain"; logically for him it is impossible because "[w]hen the name is spoken and drawn upon, one is claiming some knowledge of God or some claim on him" (Miller 80). As a reluctant believer in God, Wiesel has this possibility. Before exploring in detail how closely Wiesel may approach "tak[ing] the name of the LORD thy God in vain," we shall investigate Levi's rejection of God.

Carole Angier elucidates one of Levi's important childhood experiences:

> One interviewer asked him: did he enter the community of believers without believing? Primo answered: for months, that was a worry. And he *did* seek contact with God, for several months after the ceremony [*bar mitzvah*] he even believed; this happens to many, perhaps even most, Jewish boys ('I dare say,' he says, 'out of fear'). But when he'd sought that contact, he'd found nothing. His teacher ('who was probably not a very good one') presented him with a tyrannical, punishing God, a *Dio Padrone* who did not

appeal to him. She described an unknown, an unknowable, to whom nonetheless he was asked to pay homage, and in whom he must believe. '*Mi sembrava una violenza*,' he says: it seemed to him an act of violence. Slowly his other interests—his interest in the natural world, his reading of Darwin—helped him to break away. After the brief time of 'uncertainty' he withdrew from God completely, and put Him away among childish things. (77)

In addition, David Mendel relates:

> In reply to a question about [Levi's] being a fully paid-up member of the Turin Jewish community he said 'To tell the truth, for some months I was worried about it, but I put that behind me. I had even sought to bring myself into contact with God, without any success. I had been presented with a God the Master, a Punitive God, to whom I felt indifferent.' He goes on: 'After a short period of perplexity, I detached myself totally from him, keeping him at a distance as something from childhood which no longer concerned me. Not having ever interiorized God, I had no need to detach him from my mind nor to withdraw myself from his ambit.' (70)

However, Levi felt the need to educate his children about their Jewish roots, Joseph Sungolowsky notes, '"on the elementary level' with the view 'that they might be drawn back to an interest in Judaism' as happened to him" (84). Levi's concern for those persons needing love and justice is actually more in keeping with a sound theological understanding of God than is the concept of the almost cruel, "Punitive God" which had been presented to him as a child. This *"Dio Padrone"* or boss over his people whom He had redeemed from another overlord, Egypt's pharaoh, was not worthy of Levi's worship. His own loving and just actions as well as his obeying most of the Ten Commandments, as demonstrated in our chapters here, show him to be more in tune with the authentic, holy, loving, and just God of the Covenant than he might have realized during his lifetime. Always respectful of believers, he had to remain distant from his childhood "God the Master" in order to maintain the ethical stance intrinsic to his own moral character. The fearful, tyrannic *"Dio Padrone"* was less loving than he; he could not in good conscience worship such a God, even at the risk of being punished by Him if He really should exist. This ethical choice echoes his decision described in Chapter 6 not to pray during the terrifying *Selektion* in October 1943 at Auschwitz. Having rejected as a *"violenza"* worshipping the negative God presented to him by his teacher, he could not opportunistically call on that God for protection in this time of acute danger and vulnerability.

Nevertheless, Levi still declared himself to be a part of the Jewish community. He fits Wiesel's definition of a Jew: "A Jew is someone who links his or her destiny to the destiny of the Jewish people. And it is that linkage, that fusion of memory, the individual one and the collective one, that gives the identity to the individual and then to the people" (*A Journey of Faith* 44–45).

Alter in his *The Five Books of Moses* translates this commandment from the Hebrew as follows: "'You shall not take the name of the LORD your God in vain, for the LORD will not acquit whosoever takes His name in vain'" (430–31). The *New Revised Standard Version of the Bible* elaborates a bit more: "You shall not make wrongful use of the name of the LORD your God, for the LORD will not acquit anyone who misuses his name" (Ex. 20: 7). Perhaps those who misrepresented God to Levi as a child can be accused, indeed, of "tak[ing] the name of the LORD your God in vain," or "mak[ing] wrongful use of the name of the LORD" because Levi never understood God to be anyone other than what his teacher represented Him as; his dreadful experience at Auschwitz must have reinforced this negative image. In his translation and commentary on this passage in Exodus, Alter notes that "'[i]n vain' has the sense of 'falsely'" (*The Five Books* 430). Although the gist of this commandment is that one should neither make a promise using God's name that one does not intend to keep nor use "the potent divine name in adjuration and perhaps also in magical conjuration" (430), ramifications of dealing falsely with others also result from this commandment such as "'You shall not bear a false rumor'" (Exodus 23:1) which Alter glosses: "instead of pertaining to solemn oaths, it addresses the capacity of ordinary speech to do harm" (*The Five Books of Moses* 448). Levi's childhood teacher surely must not have intended for him to reject Judaism because of her negative conception of God, but, nevertheless, Levi's false understanding of God, impressed so strongly upon him in childhood, was foundational to his rejection of God throughout his lifetime. However, at least he remained an agnostic, one who cannot understand God, rather than a confirmed atheist, one who totally denies the existence of God.

A further reiteration of this commandment, "'You shall not swear falsely in My name, profaning the name of your God'" (Leviticus 19:12), links the false usage of words to "compromis[ing] God's own reputation of holiness through the malfeasance of the people purported to be God's special treasure" (Alter, *The Five Books of Moses* 626). Curiously, Levi's life of goodness, not "malfeasance," exemplifies much of what the commandments delineate as "holy" and pleasing to God, even though his actions are motivated by humanitarian or humanistic reasons rather than a submission to God. He embodies the question that some of Albert Camus's heroes in *La Peste* (*The Plague*) raise: can one be a saint without God? Judaism, of course, does not recognize saints, but it does honor the "*tzaddik*," whom Elie Wiesel defines as "[o]ne of the Righteous, who seeks social, moral, and religious perfection" (*Memoirs* 421). Was Levi such a man in spite of his agnosticism? He observably matured in his moral and social perfection, but not religiously. Given his false understanding of God, his ethical actions speak well for his integrity which might have been distorted if he had bowed to the "*Dio Padrone.*"

In his analysis of the Ten Commandments, Patrick D. Miller emphasizes the importance of God's name consisting of truth and power, in contrast to the empty or "vain" names of the idols of other people groups surrounding the Hebrews (71) on their journey out of Egypt through the desert and into the Promised Land. The places, altars, and statues or other iconic representations of these unreal, ineffectual gods (72) must be totally destroyed so that the Chosen People are not tempted into the false worship warned against in the two Commandments preceding this one: "I am the LORD thy God. . . . Thou shalt have no other gods before me" and "Thou shalt not make unto thee any graven image." YHWH, the LORD, is the name given by God in his self-revelation, and His merciful and just actions reveal His character as well as His desire to be in communion with His people.

Just before receiving the Ten Commandments Moses met God: "And the Lord came down in the cloud and stationed Himself with him [Moses] there [Mount Sinai], and He invoked the name of the LORD. And the LORD passed before him and He called out: 'The LORD, the LORD! A compassionate and gracious God, slow to anger, and abounding in kindness and good faith, keeping kindness for the thousandth generation'" (Ex. 34: 6–7a, Alter 508). The power, love, and justice of this LORD make clear why using His name falsely in any way is dangerous. His name, Miller continues, is what makes Him present whenever it is said; therefore, his presence cannot be confined to any specific location or object, unlike the "empty" gods. Hence the Book of Psalms and other Scriptures repeatedly mention believers calling upon "the name of the LORD" because "we trust in his holy name" (Ps. 33:21b, NRSV). "Through the use of the Lord's name, the human act of speaking becomes a speech event in which, to use [Emmanuel] Levinas's terminology, there is now a 'third party,' the Lord" (Miller 95). Alter concurs that particularly in Deuteronomy "God is not said to dwell in the sanctuary He will chose, . . . but rather an intermediary agency, God's name, dwells there" (*The Five Books of Moses* 941). It now is more apparent why Primo Levi cannot be considered in terms of this commandment since he believed in neither God nor His name.

Elie Wiesel, however, was raised in his *shtetl* in Sighet, Hungary, with a more balanced understanding of God than Levi had, and as a child he longed to be close to Him, fasting, praying, saying incantations, and studying Kabbalistic writings long before adulthood, against his father's wishes. When he found no answer to his prayers at Auschwitz, as noted in Chapter 4, he came close to rejecting this silent God completely. However, not having known any culture except his Hasidic one, he requested his prayer books after being liberated from Auschwitz and pursued his studies of Torah, "Hasidic works and treatises on mysticism" (*Memoirs* 118) which had been interrupted by the Nazis in May 1944. Although furious at God, he chose to remain within the Orthodox community as a believer in Him, always arguing with him similarly to Moses, Job, and Jeremiah. His choice to believe in God allows him to "take the name of the LORD [his] God in vain," if he so desires, a choice not open to the agnostic Levi.

Two verses from Psalms, Alter notes, use "the same idiom as in the Decalogue" to denounce those who engage in "swearing falsely" (Alter, *The Book of Psalms* 483): "O men of blood, turn away from me! — / Who say Your name to scheme, / Your enemies falsely swear." (Psalms 139:19b–20) Taking God's name in vain, however, means more than just using it falsely to confirm an oath. Is putting God on trial in a Purim play taking His name in vain? In his *The Trial of God* (*Le procès de Shamgorod*, 1979) Wiesel's characters do just that.

This play is set in 1649 in Shamgorod, "a lost village. . . after a pogrom" ("The Scene," no page number) with only two Jewish survivors remaining: Beresh, an innkeeper, and his young daughter Hanna who was gang raped by the persecutors during the pogrom on her wedding day and now remains gentle and sweet but confused and demented. A feisty, pretty Christian waitress, Maria, has witnessed the entire blood bath and remains faithful to her employer, Beresh, and exceedingly kind to Hanna whose mother, two brothers, and fiancé were all slaughtered before their eyes. Beresh is understandably furious at God for allowing all of this disaster (and others as well) to occur. When three traveling Purim minstrels, Mendel, Yankel, and Avrémel, appear, he suggests that they "play" the trial of God:

> BERISH
>
> You want to perform in honor of Purim? Good, let's stage a trial! Against whom? Imbeciles, haven't you understood yet? Against the Master of the universe! Against the Supreme Judge! That is the spectacle you shall stage tonight. It is that or nothing. Choose!
>
> MENDEL
>
> You mean a real . . . fake trial?
>
> BERISH
>
> Absolutely!
>
> MENDEL
>
> With God—blessed be His name—as . . . defendant?
>
> BERISH
>
> A trial like any other, except that this time, yes. Yes! With Him as defendant.
>
> YANKEL
>
> And what if the verdict is—
>
> AVRÉMEL
>
> —guilty?
>
> BERISH
>
> So what! It's Purim—on Purim, everything goes! (*Triumphantly*) Well? You agree? (55)

The players and Maria reluctantly agree, and parts are distributed to each participant, Berish serving as outspoken prosecutor, except that there is no one willing to defend God until an unobserved latecomer emerges from the shadows of the tavern and volunteers without hesitation. This is "SAM, the STRANGER. Intelligent, cynical, extremely courteous. Diabolical. His age? Still young. Neat, almost elegant. Self-controlled" ("Characters," no page number).

Sam's defense of God includes arguments that are common in discussions about "theodicy," "any attempt to justify, explain, or find acceptable meaning to the relationship that subsists between God (or some other form of ultimate reality), evil, and suffering" (Braiterman 4). For example, Sam does not deny that a major tragedy has occurred at Shamgorod, but he reasonably asks, "Who is to blame for all that? After all, the situation seems to me simple indeed: men and women and children were massacred by other men. Why involve, why implicate their Father in Heaven?" (128). Sam also suggests that the Jewish martyrs should thank God "for dying without prolonged suffering or shame. There are a thousand ways in which men die, you know" (131). Further, he piously affirms that he must choose God over suffering, dying Jews because "I'm his servant. He created the world and me without asking for my opinion. He may do with both whatever He wishes. Our task is to glorify him, to praise Him, to love Him—in spite of ourselves" (157).

All of these declarations in support of worshiping God no matter what befalls His creatures are turned upside down at the end of this drama when the Purim players put on their masks as does Sam—but his is "le masque du diable" ["the mask of the devil"] (137). More disaster follows, according to the final stage directions: "*Satan is laughing. He lifts his arm as if to give a signal. At that precise moment the last candle goes out, and the door opens, accompanied by deafening and murderous roars*" (161). The persecutors, about whom the village priest throughout the play has repeatedly warned, return, and the conclusion suggests that the two Jewish survivors of the earlier pogrom plus their three Purim guest actors will now also be slaughtered. The verdict on God will have to be postponed, as Mendel declares: "In truth, if I had to pronounce a verdict right now, it would be, I think, influenced by Berish the innkeeper... [sic] But we are not going to have enough time for our deliberations. The verdict will be announced by someone else, at a later stage. For the trial will continue—without us" (158).

The question arises again: are Wiesel's characters taking God's name in vain by putting on a strange Purim play (usually a repetition of Queen Esther's heroic efforts to save the Jewish community in exile under King Ahasuerus) that stages a court with an accuser and a defender of God, judges, and a public (played by Maria, the Christian servant)? Since Sam is the only one to volunteer to defend God, and he does so with the extremely faith filled statements indicated above, what does it mean when it turns out that it is the devil who affirms, "It's simple. Faith in God must be as boundless as God Himself. If it exists at the expense of man, too bad. God is eternal, man is not" (157)?

At the least, it means that Wiesel himself does not accept such simplistic, mindless statements. In fact, the devil's witness for God brings God very close to Levi's "*Dio Padrone.*" Neither Levi nor Wiesel can accept a God Who allows His people to be tormented repeatedly and then requires that He be worshiped mindlessly by pure faith. Wiesel's God is bigger than this concept, but He is also beyond words. Although admitting that God is present in all of his works, Wiesel refuses to "do theology" as such:

> God comes in here and there in my books. I oppose Him. I fight Him. I quarrel with Him. Some of my characters pray to Him. But when I say I don't speak *about* God, it means theologically, the whole theological art, which is a way of reaching the attributes of God: What is He doing? Who is He? . . . I am very concerned, even obsessed, with God. . . . I rarely speak about God. To God, yes. I protest against Him. I shout at Him. But to open a discourse about the qualities of God, about the problems that God imposes, theodicy, no. And yet He is there, in silence, in filigree. (*Conversations* 87)

Nevertheless, despite refusing to "theologize," Wiesel offers an interpretation of his puzzling, perhaps even blasphemous play. He says, "In my play *The Trial of God*, . . . I have Job return so that we may hear his protest. Does faith in God always, invariably, do honor to God? In other words, is religious fanaticism also a path that leads to God, and is that what He desires?" (*And the Sea Is Never Full* 358). After Beresh's numerous accusations against God for "hostility, cruelty, and indifference" (359), and Sam's steady defense of Him, Wiesel clarifies, "The fact that he defends God and even faith in God does not make him a man of faith, a man of compassion; in fact, he is the enemy of God and man. His fanaticism reveals who he is: the devil" (361). Thus, Wiesel places compassion for others ahead of faithful "fanaticism" which, he adds, he has been "fighting against . . . for years, wherever it appears. Be it religious or political, fanaticism is the real danger threatening the twenty-first century. Those who sow it today are provoking tomorrow's catastrophes" (361).

Wiesel's character "Sam" may be related to one of the lesser known archangels predominant in medieval Jewish folklore: Samael (Trachtenberg 251). It is significant that Wiesel shortens the name to just "Sam," thus removing "el," the "root term and a theophorous suffix" (Trachtenberg 260) indicating God, from his name. In this way the playwright avoids "tak[ing] the name of the LORD [his] God in vain," at least literally.

However, the leitmotif of this play is one phrase repeated by the angry Beresh and by Mendel, the more serious of the three Purim players: "Et Dieu dans tout cela?" ["And God in all of this?"] (*Le Procès de Shamgorod* 27). Beresh exclaims, "I want to understand why He is giving strength to the killers and nothing but tears and the shame of helplessness to the victims" (*The Trial of God* 43). In Act Two he reiterates, "What is the purpose of this trial? We know perfectly well that the outcome won't change anything: the dead will not rise from their graves. We judge because we wish to know. To understand" (*The Trial of God* 86). When one of the players suggests that he pity God, Beresh responds much more vehemently in the original French than in the English translation: "Moi je lui refuse ma pitié! Comme il m'a refusé la sienne! Je n'ai qu'un seul but: l'accuser, le juger et, si possible, le condamner! Sans pitié!" ["I, I refuse him my pity! Like he refused me his! I have only one goal: to accuse him, to judge him, and, if possible, to condemn him! Without pity!"] (77). Shortly thereafter, he affirms again his desire to understand "why human beings turn into beasts. . . . I want to know how good family men can slaughter children and crush old people" (*The Trial of God* 90).

In contrast to Beresh's heated words, Sam replies reasonably and coolly: "I dislike emotions. I prefer facts and cool logic. As far as I am concerned, we could open the proceedings right now. My client and I are ready" (122). In the opening stage directions, Wiesel indicates that "[t]he play should be performed as a tragic farce: a *Purimschpiel* within a *Purimschpiel*" ("The Scene," no page number). This tucking of the play within the enclosures of traditional farce and the drunken exuberance of celebrating Purim is a further protection against its author being charged with blaspheming the name of God on the stage.

However, an even stronger protection appears in Wiesel's explanation of the genesis of his play: "inside the kingdom of night, I witnessed a strange trial. Three rabbis—all erudite and pious men—decided one winter evening to indict God for allowing his children to be massacred. I remember: I was there, and I felt like crying. But there nobody cried" ("The Scene," no page number). Wiesel, like Beresh, his tavern owner, really wants to know why God acts as He does or, rather, refrains from acting when He is most needed. Satan's responses to Beresh and his companions are inadequate untruths. Wiesel and the original three rabbis seek truth, dare to call God to court for seemingly having broken His covenant with them and all of His people, and then return to their prayers to Him. Indeed, only God knows if they have "take[n] [His] name ... in vain."

In *A Journey of Faith*, his televised dialogue with John Cardinal O'Connor, Wiesel explains, "Where was God? But I'm asking the question from within faith, not from outside faith [unlike Levi]. If I didn't believe, where would be the problem? But if you do believe, then you have painful questions. And these questions remain open to this day [1990]" (2). Like Beresh, Wiesel wonders again, "Where is God in all that?" (7). Unlike Beresh, however, he adds, "We Jews don't blame God. We question God. I can blame human beings. And I do, and we should blame human beings when they do something wrong to other human beings. But to blame God, that's quite an act of arrogance. And we don't do that. But we question God" (12). Wiesel himself seems to specify the line between blasphemy—"blaming God"—and legitimately questioning Him. His Beresh, safely fictionalized and performing as prosecutor of God on Purim, can cross that line while the author remains on the questioning side of it.

Still, the ultimate blasphemer of God may be not Beresh but Sam himself who dares to present a *"Dio Padrone,"* to use Levi's term, who requires mindless faith in him, no matter what happens. God revealed Himself abundantly on Sinai via the Ten Commandments; His self-revelation says a lot about His own ethics which He wants to make foundational to His covenant. Following the second tablet of His ethics, He, like Beresh, must abhor what the pogromists did and will do (after the close of the play) to the Jews: "Thou shalt not kill." (Beresh has lost his entire family except for his now demented young daughter.) "Thou shalt not commit adultery." (The pogromists have torn Hanna away from her fiancé on her wedding day and destroyed her virginity, physical and emotional.) "Thou shalt not steal." (The pogromists have destroyed the Jews who owned Shamgorod's homes and businesses, and, much like those who took over Jewish homes, businesses, and household goods during the Shoah, they have allowed to fall into their own hands Jewish property and belongings.) "Thou shalt not bear false witness against thy neighbour." (Sam is bearing false witness against the God of the covenant by requiring mindless faith in Him.) "Thou shalt not covet thy neighbour's house." (As just noted, Beresh's tavern, which is also his home, will soon fall to the persecutors.)

Basically, "tak[ing] the name of the LORD thy God in vain" also means taking the God who ordained Ten ethical Commandments out of their (and His) Scriptural context and giving Him a new shape that must then be mindlessly worshiped, exactly what Sam does. Wiesel, in the end, is not blaspheming God but rather warning believers not to get sucked into honoring a god who does not fit the revealed description of the true God of Israel. Levi was right to reject the *"Dio Padrone"* wrongly taught to him before his *bar mitzvah*. Beresh's companions, on the contrary, unfortunately fall completely prey to, not only the pogromists outside their door, but also Sam whom they ultimately take to be a *"tzaddik,* a Just, a Rabbi, a Master" (*The Trial of God* 160); Mendel continues, "you [Sam] are endowed with mystical powers; you are a holy man. Do something to revoke the decree! If you cannot, who could? You are God's only defender, you have rights and privileges: use them! For heaven's sake, use them! O holy man, we beg you to save God's children from further shame and suffering!" (160).

Neither Sam nor Wiesel's God in this play save its righteous Jews at the end. Since God could also not be counted on to save His people at Auschwitz, despite His ethical character revealed in Scripture which would support the just causes of His people, then salvation must be dependent on men's and women's compassionate and just acts. Wiesel has repeatedly said that the opposite of love is not hate but indifference (*A Journey of Faith* 28). The fight for the salvation of the oppressed, including those even outside of Judaism, is humankind's task on earth, with God (as Wiesel acknowledges) and without God (as Levi affirms). This humanistic fight unites both authors.

# Works Cited

Alter, Robert. *The Book of Psalms: A Translation with Commentary.* New York: W. W. Norton & Company, 2007. Print.
Alter, Robert. *The Five Books of Moses: A Translation with Commentary.* New York: W. W. Norton & Company, 2004. Print.
Angier, Carole. *The Double Bond: Primo Levi a Biography.* New York: Farrar, Straus and Giroux, 2002. Print.
Braiterman, Zachary. *(God) after Auschwitz: Tradition and Change in Post-Holocaust Jewish Thought.* Princeton: Princeton UP, 1998. Print.
Camus, Albert. *La Peste.* Paris: Gallimard, 1947. Print.
Camus, Albert. *The Plague.* Trans. Stuart Gilbert. New York: Alfred A. Knopf, Inc., 1948. Print.
Mendel, David. "Primo Levi and the Jews." *The Legacy of Primo Levi.* Ed. Stanislao G. Pugliese. New York: Palgrave Macmillan, 2005. 61–73. Print.
Miller, Patrick D. *The Ten Commandments.* Louisville, Kentucky: Westminster John Knox Press, 2009. Print.
*The New Oxford Annotated Bible: New Revised Standard Version.* Bruce M. Metzger and Roland E. Murphy, ed. New York: Oxford UP, 1991. Print.
Sungolowsky, Joseph. "The Jewishness of Primo Levi." *The Legacy of Primo Levi.* Ed. Stanislao G. Pugliese. New York: Palgrave Macmillan, 2005. 75–85. Print.
Trachtenberg, Joshua. *Jewish Magic and Superstition: A Study in Folk Religion.* New York: Atheneum, 1970. Print.
Wiesel, Elie. *And the Sea Is Never Full: Memoirs, 1969—.* Trans. Marion Wiesel. New York: Alfred A. Knopf, 1999. Print.
Wiesel, Elie. *Conversations.* Ed. Robert Franciosi. Jackson: U of Mississippi P, 2002. Print.
Wiesel, Elie. *A Journey of Faith: A Dialogue between Elie Wiesel and His Eminence John Cardinal O'Connor, Based on and expanded from the WNBC-TV Broadcast.* New York: Primus, 1990. Print.
Wiesel, Elie. *Memoirs: All Rivers Run to the Sea.* New York: Alfred A. Knopf, 1995. Print.
Wiesel, Elie. *Le procès de Shamgorod tel qu'il se déroula le 25 février 1649.* Paris: Éditions du Seuil, 1979. Print.
Wiesel, Elie. *The Trial of God (as it was held on February 25, 1649, in Shamgorod).* Trans. Marion Wiesel. New York: Schocken Books, 1986. Print.

# Chapter 9: "Remember the Sabbath day, to keep it holy"

Elie Wiesel demonstrated his strict observance of the Sabbath when, shortly after having received the wonderful news that he had been awarded the Nobel Peace Prize in 1986, he twice refused the commissioner of baseball, Peter Ueberroth, the honor of throwing the first baseball of the World Series just beginning in New York, thus severely disappointing his adolescent son: "Elisha is devastated. He makes it clear that he'll never forgive me. I explain to him that though I have the right to violate all the laws of the Sabbath in order to save one life, any life, I do not have the right to violate the law for the—for me, dubious—pleasure of throwing a ball in front of a crowd of baseball fans" (*And the Sea Is Never Full* 260). Happily the conflict was resolved when the commissioner invited Wiesel a third time; Ueberroth explained, '"I've checked with an Orthodox rabbi. After nightfall you have the right to travel, so you can come to the stadium. With a police escort you'll get there in time'" (*And the Sea Is Never Full* 260). Wiesel concludes: "Elisha is jubilant" (*And the Sea Is Never Full* 260).

The commandment of Exodus 20:8–11 to observe the Sabbath derives from the creation story of Genesis 2:2–3 when God rested after six days of creating: "And God completed on the seventh day the task He had done, and He ceased on the seventh day from all the task [sic] He had done. And God blessed the seventh day and hallowed it, for on it He had ceased from all His task that He had created to do" (Alter 20). Even before the official Sabbath commandment is given in Exodus 20, Exodus 16 relates that the Hebrews in the desert were provided with a double portion of the miraculous bread from heaven so that they might rest on the seventh day: '"See, for the LORD has given you the Sabbath. Therefore does he give you on the sixth day bread for two days. Sit each of you where he is, let no one go out from his place on the seventh day'" (Ex. 16: 29, Alter 409). In his recent translation of *The Five Books of Moses*, Robert Alter explains in his commentary on Exodus 16 that "[t]he Sabbath—the word means 'cessation time'—... is assumed by the story (with the Creation story behind it) to be part of the very structure of nature" (409). Exodus 23:12, "'Six days shall you do your deeds and on the seventh day you shall cease, so that your ox and your donkey may rest, and your bondman and the sojourner catch their breath,'" Alter explains, provides a humanitarian purpose for the Sabbath: rest for "the laborer panting from his work and longing to draw a long breath of relief after labor" (450–51).

Jon D. Levenson remarks that "[t]he reality that the Sabbath represents—God's unchallenged and uncompromised mastery, blessing, and hallowing—is consistently and irreversibly available only in the world-to-come. Until then, it is known only in the tantalizing experience of the Sabbath" (123). Christian author Wayne Muller adds, "The Sabbath is a patch of ground secured by a tiny fence, when we withdraw from the endless choices afforded us and listen, uncover what is ultimately important, remember what is quietly sacred" (143).

The Sabbath is a part of essential Jewish spirituality because it embodies eternity; it is, indeed, a piece of eternity available in this life. Abraham Joshua Heschel explains, "That the Sabbath and eternity are one—or of the same essence—is an ancient idea. A legend relates that 'at the time when God was giving the Torah to Israel, He said to them: My children! If you accept the Torah and observe my mitzvoth, I will give you for all eternity a thing most precious that I have in my possession. –And what, asked Israel, is that precious thing which Thou wilt give us if we obey Thy Torah? –The world to come. –Show us in this world an example of the world to come. –The Sabbath is an example of the world to come'" (73). The prohibitions of the Jewish Sabbath are intended to cultivate the sacred while diminishing the influences of the mundane so that one can learn to enjoy eternity before being immersed in it "in the world to come" (74). The other six days of the week are a pilgrimage to this moment of eternity, and the sustained joy of (and from) the Sabbath should be the leitmotif experienced throughout these working days (90).

Heschel continues, "There is much that philosophy could learn from the Bible. To the philosopher the idea of the good is the most exalted idea. But to the Bible the idea of the good is penultimate; it cannot exist without the holy. The good is the base, the holy is the summit. Things created in six days He considered *good*, the seventh day He made *holy*" (75). This distinction illuminates Primo Levi's and Elie Wiesel's differing attitudes and observances of the Jewish Sabbath. Levi, strongly educated in Greco-Roman rationalistic philosophy and literature, experiences delight in God's good creation, the chemical elements and their interesting combinations, including human beings, but cannot believe in their Creator. Hence, it would be hypocritical for him to seek connection with that Creator by following Sabbath worship rituals and traditions. Wiesel, on the other hand, educated to obey God, recalls fondly the joy of his childhood Sabbaths up to May 1944, the time of his and his family's deportation to Auschwitz. He cannot ignore or surrender these Sabbaths and often shared them with Heschel and his family (*Tous les fleuves* 514). He would agree with him that "[t]he Sabbath is an ascent to the summit. It gives us the opportunity to sanctify time, to raise the good to the level of the holy, to behold the holy by abstaining from profanity" (Heschel 75).

Sadly, the honoring of the weekly Sabbath became a part of the early medieval Church's *adversus Iudaeos* critique. As Church fathers, well trained in Greco-Roman rhetorical skills, built a doctrine upon the Pauline scriptural polarity of "flesh" and "spirit," celebration of this sacred day fell into the category of "fleshly" observance, along with circumcision, dietary laws, Passover rituals, and other practices described in the "Law" of the Five Books of Moses. As professor of Scripture Paula Fredriksen remarks, Justin Martyr, writing in the second century, had hoped that after the fall of the Temple in 70

> [s]urely the Jews would (finally!) realize now that Moses' law was never meant to be fulfilled in a 'carnal,' literal way (*Trypho* 18). Yet incredibly, stubbornly, the Jews persisted, circumcising fleshly foreskins rather than their hearts, observing the Sabbath carnally as a day of feasting and of physical repose. Having missed the Christological meanings of the 'old law,' they now failed to understand that, through Christ and his church, a 'new law' had been given (*Trypho* 11–12). No wonder the Jewish nation was broken, scattered, and powerless. (Fredriksen 85–86)

Sadly the roots of anti-Semitism are already evident within the first century and a half after Jesus's death: "By the mid-second century, Justin Martyr taught that all Jews everywhere, in every generation since the crucifixion, were guilty of the crime of killing the Son of God" (Fredriksen 83). The *adversus Judaeos* rhetoric would only increase and eventually become legalized under Constantine and his followers (Fredriksen xv) who could never have imagined that its outcome would be Auschwitz.

Significantly, "no correspondingly robust tradition *contra Christianos* appears in extant Jewish literature of the same period, from the second to the early fifth century" (Fredriksen xv). Jewish scholars were occupied with the Mishnah, the Talmud, and *midrashim*, seeking God's presence and holiness rather than engaging in rhetorical attacks on Christians. They did, however, support some separation of Jews from "heathen" during "religious festivals," as Saul Lieberman, one of Wiesel's beloved teachers of Torah, describes: "the Rabbis enacted a series of laws for their co-religionists restricting their association and negotiations with the heathen during the latter's religious festivals. They prohibited all action by the Jews which may result in conferring any benefit on idols (or a heathen temple) or in deriving any profit from them" (128). He does not specify if worshipers of Christ would have fallen under the category of "heathen."

Defense of Jewish obedience to the Law, Fredriksen argues, came from Augustine who diverted from the *adversus Iudaeos* attacks when he affirmed "that traditional Jewish practice truly conformed to divine intention" (244). Jews had been criticized for "Sabbath behavior deeply antisocial" (244), when "they had done just what God had commanded them to do ([Augustine] *Against Faustus* 12.9, and frequently)" (244). In fact, Jesus had not only honored the Sabbath during his life on earth, but "[s]o vigilant was Christ in keeping the Law's commands *as the Jews traditionally had understood and enacted them* that he remained in the tomb, his body 'resting from all its works' during the Sabbath. For this reason he rose again only 'on the eighth day,' once the Sabbath had passed ([Augustine, *Against Faustus*] 16.29)" (Fredriksen 255).

Unfortunately, Augustine's later *Sermons on John* revert back to typical *adversus Iudaeos* rhetoric, "when he criticizes the Jews' 'fleshly,' unspiritual day of rest. (... *Sermons on John* 3.19. . . )" (Fredriksen 306), and other of his sermons contain the usual invective against Jews (Fredriksen 311). Brutal acting upon these hateful affirmations followed for centuries leading to the explosion of the First Crusade advocated by Pope Urban II in 1095. In his recent book on *Rashi* Elie Wiesel comments on the violence that occurred during his subject's lifetime: "For the Jews of Western Europe the century ended in a deluge of blood, fire, and death, all in the name of a man who was born Jewish of Jewish parents, whose beautiful dream was to bring love into the hearts and souls of believers" (81).

Wiesel's ongoing respect for Jesus reveals itself here again in stark contrast to Augustine's momentary honoring of the Jews, their Law, especially their Sabbath, followed by his reappropriation of the *adversus Iudaeos* tropes. Wiesel affirms that "Israel is wedded to the *Shekhinah*" whose presence accompanies His people (*Rashi* 65). "Contrary to what the first Christians and some of their relatives [like Augustine] claimed, the God of Israel did not change people and He never will: the people of Israel remain the *true* Israel for all time" (*Rashi* 65). Lest Wiesel's comment in defense of his people sound like the beginning of a *contra Christianos* doctrine, to use Fredriksen's term from above, this tiny book about Rashi, which will probably have a predominantly Jewish audience due to their love of this medieval Jewish sage and many Christians' ignorance of him, includes a reminder to love that echoes authentic Christian ethics: "Rabbi Akiba says, '"And thou shall love thy neighbor as thyself' is a great precept of the Torah."' Rashi: this law applies to all men, not just to Jews" (*Rashi* 70).

Persuading worshipers of God, both Jewish and Christian, that God's chosen people are no longer Jews but now Christians has had disastrous results. Massimo Giuliani sees this replacement doctrine to be revealing a deep sense of insecurity among Christians: "De-legitimizing Israel: this is the content and form of Christian anti-Judaism that witnessed the contradiction between two chosen people and posed the problem of the authenticity of the election in exclusive terms, that is, terms of absolute and unique truth. But the roots of that de-legitimacy of the other were (and still are, in every theology of substitution) in the emptiness of its own legitimacy, in the lacking of a clear and unequivocal self-legitimacy of the Church" (163). One of the tragedies resulting from the disdaining of God's covenant with His Jewish people was the shameful murder of a rabbi who refused to work at Auschwitz on the Sabbath: Sarah Kofman's father Berek was brutally murdered because he would not renounce celebrating "le shabbat... enterré vivant à coups de pioche" ["the Sabbath... buried alive from blows of a pickax"] (Kofman 41–42).

Giuliani sees the "de-legitimization" issue evolving into Hitler's insane Aryan ideology:

> Hitler ... said: 'Two chosen people cannot exist. We are the people of God. These words define everything.' The entire complex language of the supremacy of the Aryan ideology and all of the hate for the non-Aryan (or better, the fear that the Aryans could be delegitimized and lose the natural and Divine right to supremacy, in one word, the fear of losing the election) justified the elimination of the Jew. For Nazism, as for Christian theology, (but for Nazism, at extreme levels unknown in Christianity), the elimination of the Jews was the only possible guarantee never again to be delegitimized, the certainty that Germans were the only chosen people entitled to exercise their mission of civilization on the rest of the world. (164)

This Nazi ideology, under the guise of a Christian theology, ignored an important aspect of both Jewish and Christian teachings: God loves and protects the poor and the weak. Both Levi and Wiesel have written stories about the Jewish folk hero, the Golem, whom God may allow to arise in order to help save these very poor and weak from excruciating oppression. Giuliani describes how words breathe life into clay: "Artificial life is also born from a combination of letters, as seen in the legend of Golem who had the word *emet*—truth—written on his forehead. The word creates, therefore, constitutes, and gives existence" (77). This is one way of activating a golem; there are others.

Alter signals Exodus 23:20–21 as the first mention of the divine name being "a potent agency in its own right" (452): "Look, I am about to send a messenger before you to guard you on the way and to bring you to the place that I made ready. Watch yourself with him and heed his voice, do not defy him, for he will not pardon your trespass, for My name is within him." Wiesel's and Levi's Golems are activated by the divine name, so important, as we have seen in the previous chapter, to the third commandment, "Thou shalt not take the name of the LORD thy God in vain." Both authors' Golems do indeed protect the poor and the oppressed, but they end their existences in radically different ways, Wiesel's in a gentle sleep and Levi's following an exhausting temper tantrum on the Sabbath.

Golem legends appear to have existed since the Middle Ages, resurfacing in the nineteenth and twentieth centuries with Frankenstein being perhaps a version of that legend. These stories capture the desire of clever humans to create a nearly human being as God did Adam. Alden Oreck explains that "golem" in Hebrew means "shapeless mass" and that the Sefer Yezirah ("Book of Creation"), "often referred to as a guide to magical usage by some Western European Jews in the Middle Ages, contains instructions on how to make a golem." After that clay mass resembling a person is shaped and baked, then "God's name," whose significance is explored in the previous chapter, is used "to bring him to life, since God is the ultimate creator of life."

One way to energize the clay mass is to put the precious name on a parchment and then insert it into the creature's mouth. Levi's Golem in "Il servo," first appearing in *Vizio di forma* in 1971 (Angier 693), is controlled by the wise, righteous Rabbi Judah Loew ben Bezalel, the Maharal of Prague (1513–1609), inserting a box with such a parchment into his creature's mouth and withdrawing it when he wants the figure to sleep inactively.

Wiesel's Golem in *The Golem: The Story of a Legend* (1983) is activated and deactivated in yet another way which Oreck describes: "one would shape it out of soil, and then walk or dance around it saying combination of letters from the alphabet and the secret name of God. To 'kill' the golem, its creators would walk in the opposite direction saying and making the order of the words backwards." Wiesel's tale, dedicated to his son Elisha and to Michael, the son of this text's illustrator, Mark Podwal, is a gentle narration about the good deeds of the Prague Rabbi's silent servant as he helps the Jews of this city's ghetto survive through his strength, daring, invisibility, sense of justice, and power to fly.

For example, when the Jewish community is accused of killing a Christian child in order to use its blood for its upcoming Passover ritual, the Rabbi hopes to avert a terrifying pogrom by instructing Yossel, his beloved Golem, to vindicate the innocent Jews:

> "We have a week. We must solve the mystery before the first Seder. . . . "
> Scour the neighboring cemeteries and search for an empty grave, since the enemy had undoubtedly removed from its grave a child who had just died. By identifying the child, the Golem would unmask those who had defiled the grave. . . . He finally found the empty grave. How? Not limited by his senses, he could see souls and not just their bodies. And, as everyone knows, the soul likes to hover about the body it has just abandoned. The Golem noticed the soul of a child that seemed in deeper mourning than the others. When told, the Maharal called for the police. They opened the grave. Someone remembered having seen two peasants wandering nearby, during the night. Someone else added that the two peasants had sworn revenge on the Jewish merchant, to whom they owed five hundred crowns. They were questioned; they broke down. That year the Jews of Prague celebrated Passover with more joy than ever. (29–31)

Wiesel's Golem is charitable, sensitive, and intelligent; in fact, "he was not less human than we, but more human" (34). He lives for ten years (92), and his remains reside in the attic of the Maharal's synagogue in Prague, a place to which the Rabbi forbade entry: "the Maharal had forbidden access to the attic because, in truth, the Golem had remained alive. And he is waiting to be called" (96).

Wiesel's charming story makes no mention of the Golem working on the Sabbath or dying then, unlike Levi's short version of the tale. This author praises the Rabbi for his intellectual and physical powers, announcing that some of his descendants may include Karl Marx, Franz Kafka, Sigmund Freud, and Albert Einstein ("Il servo" III.338). Fearful that he might be breaking the commandment forbidding the creation of graven images, the Rabbi makes his Golem a courageous worker, faithful and strong but without too much intelligence (339). He would hopefully live after the Rabbi's death to continue to defend the Jews of Prague (339).

The ineffable name of God is inscribed on a parchment and placed in a silver case, which is then inserted into the clay figure's mouth. Vivified, the Golem's first words are "Perché prospera l'empio?" ["Why does the impious man prosper?"] (342). Unlike Wiesel's mute figure, this creature speaks with a subdued anger burning within him and has the power to spit out the box when he does not wish to do menial chores such as cutting wood in a forest or fetching water home from a fountain. He much prefers enterprises that call on his courage and valor; for many years he is indeed the powerful defender of the Jewish community in Prague (342–43).

However, "nel suo petto d'argilla indurita dal fuoco ardeva una collera tesa, quieta e perenne, la stessa che aveva lampeggiato nella domanda che era stata il suo primo atto vitale" ["in his clay chest hardened by fire burned a tense, quiet, and ongoing anger, the same that had flared up in the question that was his first living action"] (342). This deep latent anger explodes on the Sabbath.

The Rabbi is unsure if his Golem falls under the commandment to honor the Sabbath, but, just in case the creature should, he does not have him work then. However, one fateful Friday the Golem, angered by the master's command to chop wood in the attic of his home, furiously chops the tree trunks apart with his bare clay hand and then will not halt when sunset, hence the beginning of the Sabbath, arrives (344). Worse, he shoves the Rabbi away when he tries to remove the silver box from his mouth and then proceeds to chop apart everything in his home as the Rabbi watches helplessly from under a staircase. At dawn of the Sabbath morning, the exhausted Golem allows the box with the parchment to be removed from his mouth (345), hence deactivating the creature. When the Rabbi tries to resurrect him Saturday evening after the end of the Sabbath, in order to help clean up the shattered house, the Golem crumbles to dust (346). Unlike Wiesel's Golem who may arise to help Jews again, this Golem's fragments are gathered up by the Rabbi and placed in the attic of his humble home on Strada Larga in Prague (346).

Wiesel's tale for children ends gently and hopefully. As an assimilated, secular Jew, Levi shows that his Golem servant, as he gradually takes on more human characteristics while powerfully defending his community, is angered by the flourishing of the impious and by the imposition of subhuman tasks on him. As time passes, the creature becomes more human in his willfulness, exhibited in his preference for virtuous, courageous actions rather than hard slave labor: "Accettava invece, con un lampo lieto negli occhi, tutte le imprese che richiedono coraggio e valentia, e le conduceva a termine con un suo tenebroso ingegno. Per molti anni fu un valido difensore della comunità di Praga contro l'arbitrio e la violenza" ["Instead, he accepted, with a happy light in his eyes, every undertaking that required courage and valiance, and led them to ends through his dark mind. For many years he was a fit defender of the community of Prague against injustice and violence"] (343). However, his anger flares uncontrollably when he carries to the extreme his master's order to chop wood by demolishing furniture, curtains, windows, dividing walls, strong boxes, and shelves lined with sacred books (345). It is clear that the Golem wants to be treated as a human being with dignity, not as a robot in servitude. (Levi himself remarks, "the golem itself, his creature, was nothing more than a robot" ["Beyond Survival" 17]). His tantrum cannot be stopped by the onset of "il sabato," either the Sabbath or Saturday in Italian. Levi's humanism permeates this medieval tale; treating the Golem as a slave, even with a caring master, is worse than keeping the Sabbath day holy. Perhaps "Il servo" could also have been entitled "Se questo è un uomo" ["If this is a man"], like his first memoir.

Stanislao G. Pugliese has noted that Levi "spoke no Hebrew until late in life, did not observe the dietary laws, and only occasionally visited the Moorish-style synagogue in his native city on high holy days" (3). He died on Saturday, April 11, 1987, on a Sabbath which he obviously did not observe since he received the mail from his building's concierge, perhaps telephoned the Rabbi of Rome, and awaited his wife's return from getting groceries. Even so, he had been sensitive to those who did observe the Law, for example avoiding eating *prosciutto* (ham), which he thoroughly enjoyed, in their presence, and he was respectful of their beliefs, including Wiesel's Hasidism. It would be out of character for him to kill himself on the Sabbath as if he were making a horrific agnostic statement against God; his Golem could go out of control and thus communicate to his readers an infinite respect for the dignity of man, but the author himself needed no such dramatic event to exit from this life. In his private life at home, as an unbeliever, Levi could certainly choose to omit Sabbath worship and traditions, but it is highly unlikely that he would be insensitive to the additional shock a Sabbath suicide would create among observant Jews. Levi's respect for his community argues again against his fall being an act of suicide.

# Works Cited

Alter, Robert. *The Five Books of Moses: A Translation with Commentary.* New York: W. W. Norton & Company, 2004. Print.

Angier, Carole. *The Double Bond: Primo Levi a Biography.* New York: Farrar, Straus and Giroux, 2002. Print.

Fredriksen, Paula. *Augustine and the Jews: A Christian Defense of Jews and Judaism.* New York: Doubleday, 2008. Print.

Giuliani, Massimo. *Theological Implications of the Shoah: Caesura and Continuum as Hermeneutic Paradigms of a Jewish Theodicy.* New York: Peter Lang, 2002. Print.

Heschel, Abraham Joshua. *The Sabbath: Its Meaning for Modern Man.* New York: Farrar, Straus and Giroux, 1995. Print.

Kofman, Sarah. *Paroles suffoquées.* Paris: Éditions Galilée, 1987. Print.

Levenson, Jon D. *Creation and the Persistence of Evil: The Jewish Drama of Divine Omnipotence.* San Francisco: Harper & Row Publishers, 1988. Print.

Levi, Primo. "Beyond Survival." Trans. Gail Soffer. *Prooftexts* 4.1 (January 1984): 9–21. Print.

Levi, Primo. *Se questo è un uomo. Opere I.* Torino: Einaudi, 1987. 1–212. Print.

Levi, Primo. "Il servo." *Opere III.* Torino: Einaudi, 1990. 338–46. Print.

Lieberman, Saul. *Hellenism in Jewish Palestine: Studies in the Literary Transmission Beliefs and Manners of Palestine in the I Century B.C.E. – IV Century C.E.* New York: The Jewish Theological Seminary of America. 5722–1962. Print.

Muller, Wayne. *Sabbath: Finding Rest, Renewal, and Delight in Our Busy Lives.* New York: Bantam Books, 2000. Print.

Oreck, Alden. "The Golem." *Jewish Virtual Library.* A Division of The American-Israeli Cooperative Enterprise, 2010. Web. 24 Mar. 2010. <http://www.jewishvirtuallibrary.org/jsource/Judaism/Golem.html>.

Pugliese, Stanislao G. "Trauma/Transgression/Testimony." *The Legacy of Primo Levi.* Ed. Stanislao G. Pugliese. New York: Palgrave Macmillan, 2005. 3–14. Print.

Wiesel, Elie. *And the Sea Is Never Full: Memoirs, 1969–.* Trans. Marion Wiesel. New York: Alfred A. Knopf, 1999. Print.

Wiesel, Elie. *The Golem: The Story of a Legend as told by Elie Wiesel and illustrated by Mark Podwal.* Trans. Anne Borchardt. New York: Summit Books, 1983. Print.

Wiesel, Elie. *Rashi: A Portrait.* Trans. Catherine Temerson. New York: Schocken, 2009. Print.

Wiesel, Elie. *Tous les fleuves vont à la mer: Mémoires I.* Paris: Éditions du Seuil, 1994. Print.

# Chapter 10: "Honour thy father and thy mother"

It is time to review all of the Ten Commandments from Exodus 20 in their correct order. Robert Alter in his *The Five Books of Moses* provides in his commentary the shortened version that Moshe Weinfeld posits which could have fit on stone tablets. Alter notes, "The use of stone tablets . . . is most probably dictated by the fact that these Ten Words amount to the text of a pact between God and Israel, and such covenantal texts were typically recorded on tablets of metal or stone" (429). Weinfeld's hypothetical shortened "original" version follows:

1. I am the LORD your God; you shall have no other gods beside Me.
2. You shall make you no carved likeness.
3. You shall not take the name of the LORD your God in vain.
4. Remember the Sabbath day to hallow it.
5. Honor your father and your mother.
6. You shall not murder.
7. You shall not commit adultery.
8. You shall not steal.
9. You shall not bear false witness against your fellow man.
10. You shall not covet. (Alter 428)

Alter continues, the fifth commandment, "Honor your father and your mother," "effects a transition, as Nahmanides nicely observes, from obligations vis-à-vis God to obligations vis-à-vis human beings, beginning with the human pair through whom each of us comes into the world" (421). How one treats one's parents often shapes how one will conduct his or her life in broader society.

Both Primo Levi and Elie Wiesel have honored their fathers according to Jewish traditional rites as best they could. On March 23, 1942, Levi's father died from stomach and liver cancer (Thomson 104) at 75 Corso Re Umberto, only sixty-three years old. Although Levi tried to arrive from his work by the mine at San Vittore as quickly as possible, his father was already dead when he entered his home. Cesare Levi had suffered more than necessary because "[t]he doctor tending him, Giuseppe Diena, had been jailed on anti-Fascist charges at the beginning of January, and since then Cesare had insufficient medical attention. He had been denied morphine and the family watched helpless as he was consumed by pain" (Thomson 109). Significantly, despite his agnosticism, "Primo, as the family's first-born son, had to recite at the graveside the Jewish prayer for the dead" (Thomson 109). Although Cesare's pain was intense, he at least died at home watched over by his wife and daughter, unlike Elie Wiesel's father who was murdered cruelly at Buchenwald in January 1945.

While Levi prayed the *Kaddish* for his father, only he knowing how much he believed in the God to whom it was addressed, Wiesel, the Hasid and also only son of Shlomo, was unable to follow this rite at Buchenwald, and yearly thereafter he struggled with it, a conflict he poignantly describes in his essay "The Death of My Father" found in *Legends of Our Time*. He says that his father was "robbed of his death" (2) since it "had nothing to do with the person he had been" (2):

> Stretched out on a plank of wood amid a multitude of blood-covered corpses, fear frozen in his eyes, a mask of suffering on the bearded, stricken mask that was his face, my father gave back his soul at Buchenwald. . . . he gave it up, not to the God of his fathers, but rather to the imposter, cruel and insatiable, to the enemy God. They had killed his God, they had exchanged him for another. How, then, could I enter the sanctuary of the synagogue tomorrow and lose myself in the sacred repetition of the [*Kaddish*] ritual without lying to myself, without lying to him? (2)

Wiesel reveals his internal dialogue about this ethical issue, including his ongoing arguments with God: "Perhaps, after all, I should go to the synagogue to praise the God of dead children, if only to provoke him by my own submission" (2). The act of proclaiming God's holiness and greatness before the Jewish community seems incongruent with the horrors and loss of God's presence at Auschwitz and with the cruel way his father had died. Yes, he concludes, "All things considered, I think that tomorrow I shall go to the synagogue after all. I will light the candles, I will say *Kaddish*, and it will be for me a further proof of my impotence" (7).

## Chapter 10

Gershom Scholem, whom Wiesel knew in Israel and whose expertise on Jewish mysticism he greatly admires (*Tous les fleuves* 579), provides hope that Wiesel's father might have received comfort from those who had already died: "For we know that when the hour comes for a man to leave this world, he finds himself surrounded by his father and his relatives, and he looks at them and recognizes them, and sees all who were his companions in this world, and they escort his soul to the new abode it is to have" (Scholem 53–54). Whether or not Wiesel believes that such an escort was provided for his father dying in the most wretched conditions imaginable, he does draw strength from his father daily: "mon père.... sa présence reste un repère, un soutien, un soleil noir devenant refuge mais non collation. Chaque fois que, à la croisée des chemins, je dois prendre une décision, c'est son visage que je contemple.... comment faire pour qu'il n'ait pas honte de son fils?" ["my father.... his presence remains a benchmark, a sustenance, a black sun becoming a refuge but not a refreshment. Each time that, at a crossroads, I must make a decision, it is his face that I contemplate.... how to act so that he will not be ashamed of his son?"] (*Et où vas-tu?* 239)

Wiesel even claims to have seen his father standing behind his son just as he was about to begin his Nobel Prize acceptance speech in 1986:

> Commençant son discours, il s'adressa d'abord au roi et à la reine avant de saluer la présence de Danielle Mitterand, de sa dernière soeur survivante, Hilda, puis de sa femme 'my wife and ...' A ce moment précis, il fut comme paralysé ne pouvant plus prononcer le mot suivant et demeura peut-être trente secondes ou davantage bouleversé et muet. Enfin, il arriva à arracher du plus profound de sa mémoire ce mot: 'my son...' —mon fils. Parce qu'il le relie à son père, et qu'en cette occasion plus qu'en nulle autre, les morts étaient présents devant lui, étaient *visibles*.
>
> Il expliqua par la suite que durant ce silence à peine soutenable, il revit devant lui son père et sa mère, sa petite soeur, Dodye Feig, son grand-père et sa grand-mère, ses maîtres Shoushani et Lieberman compris, et d'autres visages disparus, tout Sighet. 'Avec ce racourci que le president Aarvik a fait entre mon père et mon fils, c'était toute l'histoire de ma vie et j'ai vu mon père et j'ai vu mon fils, et j'étais tellement bouleversé que je n'ai pas pu prononcer une parole...' [Beginning his discourse, he first addressed the king and the queen before honoring Danielle Mitterand, his last surviving sister Hilda, then his wife, 'My wife and ...' At this exact moment, he was paralyzed, unable to speak the next word, and he remained for perhaps thirty seconds or more overcome and mute. Finally, he drew out of the depths of his memory this word: 'My son...' Because he [President Aarvik]

linked him to his father, and on this occasion more than any other, the dead were present before him, they were *visible*.

He later explained that during this almost insufferable silence, he saw again before him his father and his mother, his little sister, Dodye Feig, his grandfather and his grandmother, his teachers including Shoushani and Lieberman, and other faces long disappeared, all of Sighet. 'With this connection that President Aarvik made between my father and my son, it was the whole history of my life, and I saw my father and I saw my son, and I was so overcome that I could not pronounce a word. . . ']. (de Saint Cheron 220)

Wiesel mentions briefly this stunning mystical experience in his televised conversation with John Cardinal O'Connor, but unfortunately Gabe Pressman, the dialogue's moderator, does not follow up on his revelation by asking him to explain more clearly what actually happened during this unusual occurrence (Wiesel, *A Journey of Faith* 56). It obviously was a very real and moving moment for Wiesel.

He was also deeply honored shortly after the Nobel Peace Prize ceremony when "Rabbi Menashe Klein, [his] friend since Buna, Buchenwald, and Ambloy [in France] announce[d] the creation of a Beit Hamidrash, a house of study and prayer [in Jerusalem], that will bear [Wiesel's] father's name. . . . This house of study and prayer means more to me," he says, "than any laurels I could receive, for my parents' dream had been for me to become a *rosh yeshiva* (head of a yeshiva)" (*And the Sea Is Never Full* 273). Wiesel obviously continues to honor his father and his mother.

Levi and Wiesel grieved the loss of their mothers. Wiesel surmises that his grandmother, mother, and little sister Tsipouka were asphyxiated by Zyklon-B gas at Auschwitz II-Birkenau the night of the family's arrival from Hungary in May 1944. Unlike his frequent references to his father, he rarely speaks of these loved ones except in his memoirs. He recalls his last hours with them on the terrible train trip from Sighet, Hungary, to Poland—the sound of his grandmother's murmured prayers, his mother's tender gestures, and his little sister's heroism as she "refused to show her fear" (*Memoirs* 76). He notes, "My mother was my sole ally and support. She alone understood me" (*Memoirs* 13).

On April 19, 1993, the day of the official opening of the United States Holocaust Memorial Museum in Washington, D.C., cold rain having ruined his prepared speech, Wiesel was obliged to tell a story extemporaneously:

> I evoke the genesis of the project under President Carter, the deep reasons that impelled me to give it form with the words: 'For the dead *and* the living—we must bear witness.' I tell the story of a woman in her kitchen, preparing for Passover in 1943, discussing the news from Warsaw [the Warsaw Ghetto uprising on April 19, 1943]. She wonders: 'Why did the young Jews there think it necessary to rebel? Couldn't they have waited quietly for the end of the war?' My speech ends with this small sentence: 'That woman was my mother. . . .' (*And the Sea Is Never Full* 249)

Wiesel's impromptu anecdote reveals the gentle spirit of his mother, the Hungarian Jews' ignorance of the horrible events really occurring in the Warsaw ghetto in 1943 and before, and their inability to imagine their own deportations soon to happen in May 1944. Primo Levi has written an essay entitled "Defiance in the Ghetto" which describes the heroism of its inmates. He notes, "On April 18, 1943, it was learned that the Germans were preparing a mass deportation. The following day, about a thousand SS men who had entered the Ghetto were received by rifle fire and incendiary bottles flung at them, and they pulled back in disarray" (*The Mirror Maker* 170). Later the rebels were exterminated and the ghetto was leveled.

Levi watched his mother slowly decline into dementia and immobility; he did not live to witness her death in 1991, four years after his (Thomson 477). Germaine Greer met *Signora* Levi when she visited the author for an interview. "Everything about the woman, recalled Greer, bespoke the 'most loving care and attention'" (Thomson 446). When Greer asked Primo Levi if he feared dying, "Levi replied that he could bear his own pain, but not that of others" (446). He compared his mother to a "*Muselmann*" at Auschwitz (446), a person dead within but still physically surviving, the gleam of the eye having already disappeared.

Philip Roth who visited Levi in his home in September 1986 also witnessed Levi's pain because of his mother's deteriorating condition: "His sense of entrapment and subservience to his mother disturbed Roth greatly. 'I've known some Jewish sons, [Roth said] but Levi's filial duty and devotion was stronger than anything I'd ever seen'" (Thomson 479). Some of Levi's friends and biographers have criticized him for overly caring for his mother (Angier 730); however, this was not their choice, but his. His care for her as she became more demented, more like the "*Muselmänner*" of Auschwitz, beginning in the late 1970s, was preceded by his respectful yet humorous descriptions of his extended family and ancestors in "Argon," the first chapter of *The Periodic Table* (*Il sistema periodica*, 1975), his unusual autobiography, unique because of its organization around elements found on the Periodic Table of chemical elements.

Although much of "Argon" is devoted to analyzing briefly words that have emerged as combinations of Hebrew and the dialect of Piedmontese, a few anecdotes about worthy ancestors emerge. For example, Levi narrates the tale of his great-grandfather Leonin:

> *Barakhà* is the benediction a pious Jew is expected to pronounce more than a hundred times a day, and he does so with profound joy, since by doing so he carries on a thousand-year-old dialogue with the Eternal, who in every *barakhà* is praised and thanked for His gifts. Grandfather Leonin . . . lived at Casale Monferrato and had flat feet; the alley in front of his house was paved with cobblestones, and he suffered when he walked on it. One morning he came out of his house and found the alley paved with flagstones, and he exclaimed from the depths of his heart, ' *'N abrakha a coi goyim c'a l'an fait i losi!*' ('A blessing on those unbelievers who made these paving stones!'). (15)

This little episode demonstrates not only the linguistic mélange that emerged among Jewish settlers in the Piedmont area of Italy but also the tensions between Jews and Christians there, as elsewhere, alleviated momentarily by the paving of an alley. Levi's style honors his ancestor while retaining good humor and understanding of his daily frustrations.

At the close of "Argon," he finally describes his eccentric paternal grandmother whom as a child he visited regularly on Sunday mornings with his father. He states that "Grandmother Malia. . . . survives in the figure of an overdressed, tiny vamp in some studio poses executed around 1870, and as a wrinkled, short-tempered, slovenly, and fabulously deaf old lady in my most distant childhood memories" (21). Reputed to have been unfaithful to her husband, who committed suicide, as an older woman she married "an old Christian doctor, a majestic, taciturn, bearded man, and from then on inclined to stinginess and oddity, although in youth she had been regally prodigal, as beautiful, much loved women usually are" (21).

Part of her "oddity" was to save everything and to attend both the synagogue and the parish Catholic church, "[p]erhaps out of a fear of making a mistake in her definitive choice" (21). The voice of a scared child creeps into the adult narrator's concluding remarks about his grandmother:

> When we arrived at the tenebrous landing of the apartment on Via Po, my father rang the bell, and when my grandmother came to open the door he would shout in her ear: 'He's at the head of his class!' My grandmother would let us in with visible reluctance and guide us through a string of dusty, uninhabited rooms, one of which, studded with sinister instruments, was the doctor's semi-abandoned office. One hardly ever saw the doctor, nor did I certainly want to see him, ever since the day on which I had surprised my father telling my mother that, when they brought him stammering children to be treated, he would cut the fillet of skin under the tongue with his scissors. When we got to the good living room, my grandmother would dig out of some recess the box of chocolates, always the same box, and offer me one. The chocolate was worm-eaten, and with great embarrassment I would quickly hide it away in my pocket. (23)

Levi's confession about this strange grandmother lacks the humor found in many of his earlier descriptions of his eccentric ancestors. He closes this chapter with this image of an embarrassed little boy hiding the weekly gift of "worm-eaten" chocolate with no further comment. Nevertheless, his tone is respectful; he still honors his grandmother as he did his father who had his own "oddities."

On the way to visit Grandmother Malia, his father "stopped to caress all the cats, sniff at all the truffles, and leaf through all the secondhand books" (22), his own pockets already bulging with books. Levi's father enjoyed prosciutto, using his engineer's logarithmic ruler to check "the multiplication for the prosciutto purchase" (22). Levi kindly notes, "superstitious rather than religious, he felt ill at ease at breaking the *kasherut* rules, but he liked prosciutto so much that, faced by the temptation of a shop window, he yielded every time, sighing, cursing under his breath, and watching me out of the corner of his eye, as if he feared my judgment or hoped for my complicity" (23). Levi shows respect for his father's weaknesses, while revealing them in detail. He honors his father by balancing truth and love as he describes their weekly Sunday walks to his eccentric grandmother's apartment.

He also honors his father by omitting mention of his adultery. Never does Levi reveal in his writings the dark truth about his father which his biographers uncovered: that his father was unfaithful to his mother for many years (Angier 62–64; Thomson 36) with a secretary: "According to Anna Yona [Levi's cousin in Boston], Cesare's ill-treatment of Ester explains why Primo grew to be so overattached to his mother. 'In a way, Primo felt he had to provide Ester with the love she didn't have as a wife'" (Thomson 36). Ian Thomson disregards this comment as lacking plausibility, but Levi's compassion for the wounded and oppressed makes it quite possible that he felt unusually protective of his mother.

Extremely vulnerable are the demented, especially those who descend into dementia after living active, productive lives. Both Levi and Wiesel feared this outcome for the elderly, including themselves (Amsallem 195, Thomson 489), Levi witnessing it happening before his eyes with his mother in his home and Wiesel dreading it because it destroys the survivor's memory, his ability to accurately witness to the past, while he or she lives on. Wiesel explains, "Is there a disease worse than Alzheimer's? It is a cancer of identity, of memory. In the novel [*The Forgotten*] I compare it to a book whose pages are torn out one by one, until all that remains is the cover" (*And the Sea Is Never Full* 362).

Wiesel acknowledges that his most depressing novel is *L'oublié* (*The Forgotten*, 1989) which he wrote in response to his deep concern about Alzheimer's disease and then kept in a drawer until he could find some kind of hopeful, not devastating, ending for it. It describes the gradual descent of Elhanan Rosenbaum, born in 1926 (98), an accomplished therapist, professor, and Shoah survivor, into a fragmented consciousness which results in his depending more and more on his son Malkiel, a journalist for the *New York Times*, forty years old in 1988 (11). Although beset with his own problems, Malkiel shows committed devotion to his declining widowed father as his only child, fulfilling what Ecclesiasticus, or the Wisdom of Jesus Son of Sirach, recommends: "My child, help your father in his old age, / and do not grieve him as long as he lives; / even if his mind fails, be patient with him; / because you have all your faculties do not despise him" (*New Revised Standard Version*, Sirach 3.12–13). Indeed, Wiesel begins this dark novel with a poignant quote from the Talmud: "Respect the old man who has forgotten what he learned. For broken Tablets have a place in the Ark beside the Tablets of the Law."

Like Wiesel, perhaps Levi had a similar idea of trying to cope with his mother's progressive dementia by eventually writing about it in some form. Carole Angier notes:

> [After his return home from prostate surgery in March 1987] [h]e hardly went out. He did nothing: just waited for sleep, as he had told David Mendel. He sat for hours in front of his computer, doing nothing. And he sat for hours by his mother's bedside, as he had done for months, even years. But there, perhaps, he did something. . . . To Edith [Bruck] he said that he

was writing down the things his mother said: 'annotating', Edith wrote in her own book, 'his mother's sensations'. 'Do you understand?' he asked her hurriedly. 'I don't know if they'll make a book.' (713)

Writing is an author's way of gaining control of a situation, especially a challenging, difficult circumstance. Daniela Amsallem records that in one of his last interviews Levi states, '"Jour après jour, au contraire, je vis une vie différente, hélas bien moins méthodique et systématique. Ecrire est un moyen de mettre de l'ordre. Et c'est le meilleur que je connaisse, même si je n'en connais pas beaucoup'" ['"Day after day, on the contrary, I live a different life, unfortunately much less methodical and systematic. Writing is a way of putting things in order. And it is the best way that I know, even if I do not know a lot of them'"] (202).

A turning point occurs in Wiesel's *The Forgotten* when Malkiel and his girlfriend Tamar persuade Elhanan to tell them the pieces of his life's story that he can remember: '"Do you see?' Malkiel asked him. 'When you talk, your brain works better. Why not try to tell us more about your life?'" (150).

Malkiel, in caring for his increasingly demented father, puts in question all of his own actions up until this huge responsibility falls upon him, for now he has become his father's parent (24), always a difficult transition in a family. "Have I been a good son? Malkiel stood before the house of his father [in Romania]. Most of the time surely yes, but not always" (130). Naturally he feels guilt for the moments when in the past he did not honor his father, particularly in the transgressive love relationships he kept from him, knowing that Elhanan would have disapproved: there was Leila the Muslim Tunisian who protests for students' and Palestinians' rights in the 1960s (Malkiel wonders "if his father's illness was not a punishment for the love he himself had born for an Arab woman," 141–42); there was Inge the German (90–91) whom he dares not ask what her parents were doing during the War; there was his cousin Rita (138), and finally there is the temptation to form a liaison with Lidia, his interpretor, when, because of his father's insistence (92), he visits his father's hometown Feherfalu in Romania (26), trying to fill in the pieces of a tragedy that Elhanan can no longer fully remember, sadly rarely having spoken of his past before his disease struck him (132).

Elhanan can recall enough of that event, however, to make him feel guilty also. Lucid scholar that he is (or was), he still wonders if his disease is a punishment for having forgotten an important concept of Jewish law:

> In his moments of lucidity, which would later become increasingly rare and painful, he suggested an explanation of what was happening to him: 'I am a guilty man. That is why I am being punished. . . . I saw a sin committed . . . [sic] a crime. . . . [sic] I could have, I should have, done something, called out, shouted, struck a blow. I forgot our precepts, our laws, that require an individual to struggle against evil wherever it appears. I forgot that we can never simply remain spectators, we have no right to stand aside, to keep silent, to let the victim fight the aggressor alone. I forgot so many things that day. . . . [sic] That is why I am forgetting other things now.' (51)

That dementia is a punishment to be attributed either to father or son is a fallacious concept. It is a progressive, neurological disorder that can strike anyone, its etiology, despite years of research, still being unknown. Regardless of its cause, its outcome is certain, as Elhanan understands it, after receiving his doctor's diagnosis: "slowly, and then not so slowly, but at an unforeseeable pace, I was going to forget my whole existence, forget all that I had been" (144). Malkiel will find the missing pieces for his father and, in a profound sense, become his memory, keeping his father's narrative intact so that it can be passed on to his and Tamar's children—Tamar being the one woman Elhanan approves of Malkiel marrying because she resembles Talia, his wife who died in giving birth to Malkiel. This dark novel, which demonstrates Wiesel's uncanny understanding of Alzheimer's disease without his having lived it or served as a caregiver of one of its victims, ends hopefully, although with an unfinished sentence that Malkiel (and perhaps also the reader) will have to complete:

> They say that before dying a man sees his whole past. Not I. All I see is bursts and fragments. But perhaps that is because I am not yet going to die, not physically, at any rate. Is that why I still cannot recall the essential thing that I want so much to pass on to you, Malkiel?
> That doesn't matter, my son.
> Even as I speak to you I tell myself that you will discover in your own way what my lips cannot say.
> God cannot be so cruel as to erase everything forever. If He were, He would not be our father, and nothing would make sense.
> And I who speak to you cannot say more, for (316)

Wiesel's faith in an eternal, loving God allows him to conclude his novel in this way and to publish it since he refuses to publish anything that is totally despairing. He affirms that Malkiel, Tamar, and Elhanan "will proceed with a memory transfusion just as patients are treated with blood transfusions. In the end Malkiel will remember even an episode his father had repressed" (*And the Sea Is Never Full* 364).

Levi's lack of faith in such a God gave him no relief from his depression after his prostate surgery as he sat by his mother's bed taking notes on her utterances. His novel or essay about her and her dementia remained unwritten since he died a few weeks later. It showed magnificent courage that he even considered writing it; probably it would have honored her.

# Works Cited

Alter, Robert. *The Five Books of Moses: A Translation with Commentary*. New York: W. W. Norton & Company, 2004. Print.

Amsallem, Daniela. *Primo Levi au miroir de son oeuvre: Le témoin, L'écrivain, Le chimiste*. Lyon: Editions du Cosmogone, 2001. Print.

Angier, Carole. *The Double Bond: Primo Levi a Biography*. New York: Farrar, Straus and Giroux, 2002. Print.

Levi, Primo. *The Mirror Maker: Stories and Essays*. Trans. Raymond Rosenthal. New York: Schocken Books, 1989. Print.

Levi, Primo. *The Periodic Table*. Trans. Raymond Rosenthal. New York: Alfred A. Knopf, 1996. Print.

Levi, Primo. *Il sistema periodico. Opere I*. Torino: Einaudi, 1987. 428–649. Print.

*The New Oxford Annotated Bible: New Revised Standard Version*. Bruce M. Metzger and Roland E. Murphy, ed. New York: Oxford UP, 1991. Print.

Saint Cheron, Philippe M. de. *Elie Wiesel: Pèlerin de la mémoire*. Paris: Plon, 1994. Print.

Scholem, Gershom. *Zohar, The Book of Splendor*. New York: Schocken Books, 1949. Print.

Thomson, Ian. *Primo Levi: A Life*. New York: Metropolitan Books Henry Holt and Company, 2002. Print.

Wiesel, Elie. *And the Sea Is Never Full: Memoirs, 1969 —*. Trans. Marion Wiesel. New York: Alfred A. Knopf, 1999. Print.

Wiesel, Elie. "The Death of My Father." *Legends of Our Time*. New York: Holt, Rinehart and Winston, 1968. 1–7. Print.

Wiesel, Elie. *Et où vas-tu?* Paris: Éditions du Seuil, 2004. Print.

Wiesel, Elie. *The Forgotten*. Trans. Stephen Becker. New York: Schocken Books, 1992. Print.

Wiesel, Elie. *A Journey of Faith: A Dialogue between Elie Wiesel and His Eminence John Cardinal O'Connor, Based on and expanded from the WNBC-TV Broadcast*. New York: Primus, 1990. Print.

Wiesel, Elie. *Memoirs: All Rivers Run to the Sea*. New York: Alfred A. Knopf, 1995. Print.

Wiesel, Elie. *L'oublié*. Paris: Éditions du Seuil, 1989. Print.

Wiesel, Elie. *Tous les fleuves vont à la mer: Mémoires 1*. Paris: Éditions du Seuil, 1994. Print.

# Conclusion

In the Introduction we defined "ethics" as "a system of moral principles" and noted that, according to ethicist John K. Roth, "[e]thical imperatives direct attention and guide action" (*Ethics* 66). In response to the question of whether or not there can be ethics after Auschwitz, Primo Levi and Elie Wiesel emphatically affirm verbally and demonstrate consistently throughout their lives that the ethics of the Decalogue are still worthy standards of conduct. This book has examined their actions and writings in terms of each of the Ten Commandments; despite living in a postmodern and post-Holocaust era, Levi and Wiesel still adhere to the ancient proclamations from Sinai.

Roth affirms:

> In our pluralistic world, where cultural, religious, and philosophical perspectives vary considerably, a widely held belief is that values are so relative to one's time and place that the 'truth' of moral claims is much more a result of subjective preference and political power than a function of objective reality and universal reason. The relativistic outlook meets resistance in the Holocaust, for there is a widely shared conviction that the Holocaust was wrong. An assault not only against Jewish life but also against goodness itself, the Holocaust should not have happened, and nothing akin to it should ever happen again. (*Ethics* 26)

Adherence to the Ten Words can help to prevent anything like the Shoah recurring. In a postmodern era, ethics remain. Tragedies happen when they are absent. The shocking reality of the Shoah demonstrates this powerful truth.

Primo Levi also reveals in his last book completed before his death, *The Drowned and the Saved* (*I Sommersi e i salvati*, 1986), a sensitivity to postmodern relativism similar to Roth's: "A skeptical generation stands at the threshold of adulthood, bereft not of ideals but of certainties, indeed distrustful of the grand revealed truth: disposed instead to accept the small truths, changeable from month to month on the convulsed wave of cultural fashions, whether guided or wild" (199). Such young skeptics may indeed find difficulty accepting the ancient Ten Commandments though they have stood the test of time in Judeo-Christian culture.

The Decalogue, however, is only one system of ethics. In a recent book entitled *Hitler's Ethic: The Nazi Pursuit of Evolutionary Progress* historian Richard Weikart argues that Adolf Hitler also followed a clearly defined ethic throughout his life, an evolutionary ethic obviously quite different from the Judeo-Christian commandments, as he sought "to foster upward evolution" (5). Weikart affirms that the Nazi dictator's "overriding goal, shaped by evolutionary ethics, was to improve the human race biologically. In order to achieve this goal, he clung to the following positions throughout his career" (8):

1. An expanding population is biologically beneficial, so the state should promote pro-natalist policies.
2. The biological quality of the German people should be improved through eugenic policies.
3. Germany needs more living space to accommodate the expanding population, and this can only be obtained through military action.
4. Inferior races must give way to superior ones in the struggle for existence, so policies should favor the superior Aryan or Nordic race.
5. Jews are an inferior race, especially in their moral characteristics, so they need to be eliminated—one way or another—from German society.
6. Racial mixture with inferior races must cease, because it leads to biological decline. (8–9)

Weikart concludes, "Hitler never deviated from these six basic principles during his career" (9). What ethics one chooses to live by is indeed decisive in determining one's words, actions, and influence on others. Although other historians and critics may disagree with Weikart's claims or find them to be an oversimplification of Hitler's life and Germany's policies, they nevertheless stand as an example of an ethical system dangerously opposed to the compassion, justice, and goodness of the Ten Words.

Particularly disturbing is the fifth affirmation above: "Jews are an inferior race, especially in their moral characteristics, so they need to be eliminated—one way or another—from German society" (9). Who determined that Jews were "an inferior race" when sacred Judeo-Christian Scriptures declare them to be God's chosen people? Who dares to denigrate their moral characteristics when, according to those sacred Scriptures, God has given them the Decalogue, in fact twice

(Exodus 20 and Deuteronomy 5), and much of Western civilization has been built upon these foundational standards, even when examples of their violation abound? Finally, since there really is no truth in the Jews' moral inferiority, who can logically connect a fallacious statement with mass genocide, couched under the abstract terms "eliminated... from German society"?

Of course, Hitler never overtly announced his ethical system; if he had, the bluntness indicated above would have shocked at least some serious German thinkers and moved them to strong actions opposing the dictator following such an ethic. Weikart draws this list from much research into Hitler's readings, words, and actions over his lifetime, including his public speeches which often revealed half-truths and his private meetings with advisors and military officers where he was blunter about his intentions. Weikart's book serves to demonstrate the power of *idées fixes*, wrapped up in a frightening "ethic," to change, indeed annihilate, lives on an international scale.

It may be valuable to compare and contrast Hitler's ethic to the one followed by Levi and Wiesel. The foundation of both ethical systems is a concept of God. As Levi matured, he sought understanding of God, as did Wiesel, Levi, however, as an agnostic, one who could not seem to find God, and Wiesel as a Hasidic Jew, one who, within Judaism, persistently challenged the mysterious God beyond words. Their concepts of God derive from Jewish Scriptures and commentaries as well as their own harsh, and also at times blessed, life experiences.

Hitler's concept of God derived, according to Weikart, from the writings of Darwin, not the Austrian Roman Catholicism in which he was raised. However, the dictator dared to define "Nature," the overpowering force behind all life, in his own terms; for example, he stated in a May 1937 address to construction workers:

> ... nature has granted the stronger and healthier the right to life. And rightly so. Nature knows no weakling or coward, it knows no beggar, etc., but rather nature knows only those who stand firm on their soil, who sacrifice their life, and indeed sacrifice it dearly, and not those who give it away. That is an eternal law of nature. You see it if you gaze into the forest, you see it in every meadow, you see it in the struggle of individual organisms in the world, and you see it throughout the millennia of human history.... (quoted in Weikert 3–4)

Hitler's rhetoric smoothly elides the "nature" seen in one's physical surroundings with the "nature" at work in history, an illogical jump in thinking hidden in his repetitive rhetoric. His belief system denies compassion for the weak, a central focus of Judeo-Christian beliefs. As Ulf Schmidt concludes, "'Nazism reveals a fundamental break with Judaeo-Christian ethics, an attack on a traditional belief system based on altruism and compassion'" (quoted in Weikert 201). The starting points of these two contrasting belief systems will influence all that follows.

"I am the LORD thy God. . . . Thou shalt have no other gods before me" and "Thou shalt not make unto thee any graven image" are irrelevant to Hitler as he exalts "nature" which propels the survival of the fittest in all forms of life; God, indeed, has been replaced by "nature" whose chief interpreter is Hitler, for he determined that the so-called Aryan Germans were the fittest and should be provided the conditions in life that would assure their propagation and ongoing strengthening and perfecting. Whatever commandments that prevent Hitler's "nature's" goal must be eschewed so that the evolution of Aryans may move forward.

"Thou shalt not take the name of the LORD thy God in vain." Since "nature" replaces God, it is its name which will be repeatedly evoked by Hitler to justify countless acts of aggression, murder, theft, and manipulation of populations. For example, he believed and stated in *Mein Kampf* that there must not be a mixing of non-white races and certain European populations with the Aryans because such a racial mélange "leads to lowering the level of the higher race, both physically and intellectually. Racial mixing, then is 'nothing else but to sin against the will of the eternal creator' and 'to rebel against the iron logic of Nature'" (quoted in Weikart 139). Apparently "Nature" has now become '"the eternal creator'".

**"Remember the Sabbath day, to keep it holy"** was unnecessary for Hitler since "Nature" was at work every day. **"Honour thy father and thy mother,"** however, took on immense importance since Aryan parents were the propagators of Hitler's sacred race. Weikart notes, "On Mother's Day in 1939 about three million [German] women received their medallions [the German Mother's Cross]: bronze for four children, silver for six children, and gold for eight or more children. Hitler Youth were instructed to snap to attention and salute women wearing their medals" (130).

"**Thou shalt not kill.**" Hitler's murder of millions of Jews, gypsies, homosexuals, political prisoners, religious persons (rabbis, Catholic priests and nuns, Jehovah's Witnesses, Protestant pastors, and others), prisoners of war, children, elderly, mentally and physically disabled persons, and others has been well documented. All of these, in his mind, were obstacles to the evolutionary growth of Aryans. The historian Hans-Walter Schmuhl states chillingly, '"By giving up the conception of humans in the image of God through the Darwinian theory, human life was construed as a piece of property, that—contrary to the idea of a natural right to life—could be weighed against other pieces of property'" (quoted in Weikart 180).

"**Thou shalt not commit adultery**" was more nebulous in Hitler's interpretations of it. Maintaining a family where the Aryan spouses did not "commit adultery" could be helpful to promoting the evolution of purer Aryans. However, the suitability of the marriage partners had at first to be assured. Hitler's Marriage Health Law permitted only those with health certificates documenting that they were not carriers of genetic diseases already signaled in the Law for the Prevention of Hereditarily Diseased Offspring to marry (Weikart (156). As World War II progressed and more exemplary Aryan men were lost in combat, he favored propagation of his mythical race outside of marriage in order to replenish the racial stock.

"**Thou shalt not steal.**" Hitler's regime's theft of property from the Jews and others whom he murdered or forced to exit from Germany and its extended Reich has also been well documented by historians. It was often a legal, bureaucratized plundering built into Nazi law and governing bodies. Primo Levi describes its effect on a local level:

> We cannot know whether this procedure was based on a regulation or whether the functionaries in charge had a free hand. Constant was the hypocritical advice (or order) to bring along as much as possible [on the deportation journey]: especially gold, jewels, valuable currency, furs, in certain cases (certain transports of Jewish farmers from Hungary and Slovakia) even small livestock. 'It's all stuff that will come in handy,' the escort personnel said out of the side of their mouths and with an air of complicity. In fact, this was self-plunder, a simple and ingenious ruse to bring valuables into the Reich, without publicity, bureaucratic complications, special transports, or fear of thefts in route—and sure enough, upon arrival, everything was seized. (*Drowned* 109)

The Nazis' unjust stealing is still being contested, even some sixty-five years after the War, by family members of those who were victimized in reparation trials with international repercussions.

"**Thou shalt not bear false witness against thy neighbour.**" All of the devastating policies described above were facilitated by "false witnessing" about the importance to the Aryan race of eugenics, pronatalism, and geographical expansion in order that this particular race could grow. Hitler's "ethic," which—to those inculturated with a Western European tradition that honors justice and the dignity of all human beings—now looks like a cruel "anti-ethic," was reinforced by his appointment of scholarly theorists and medical doctors to important positions in his government, in research institutes, and in universities; their propagation of what Hitler believed was then supplemented by their articles in scholarly journals and the creation of seemingly well researched documentaries about their apparent findings relevant to the superiority of Aryans over all others (Weikart 201). This pseudo-research plus German pride, among many other complex variables, contributed to Hitler gaining a committed following and hence obedience when his frightful policies were implemented in the Third Reich. All of those involved in this propagation of lies did indeed bear "false witness" against reality. For example, Weikart reports that "Emil Abderhalden's journal *Ethics* reached an audience of scientists and especially physicians with social Darwinist and eugenics views paralleling Hitler's own ethical views. Other scientific journals devoted to eugenics, racism, and biology purveyed Nazi ideals to the educated elites" (201).

Hitler, of course, was elated that his power could impose his views on both the well educated and the lesser instructed. His enthusiasm was high in 1937 as Weikart reports:

> Pro-natalism, prohibitions against miscegenation, and eugenics were part of a coordinated program to improve the German people biologically. At the Nuremberg Party Congress in September 1937, Hitler bragged about the racial and eugenics policies his regime had pursued. He stressed the sweeping significance of these policies, stating that 'the greatest revolution Germany has undergone was that of the purification of the *Volk* and of race hygiene, which was launched systematically in this country for the first time ever.' He continued, 'The consequences of this German racial policy will be more significant for the future of our *Volk* than the effects of all the other laws together. For they are what is creating the new man.' (Quoted in Weikart 157)

Hitler was convinced of his understanding of "Nature" and the pseudo-research that supported that comprehension as the "new man" evolved. As Primo Levi remarks:

> the entire history of the brief 'millennial Reich' can be reread as a war against memory, an Orwellian falsification of memory, falsification of reality, negation of reality. All of Hitler's biographies, while disagreeing on the interpretation to be given to the life of this man so difficult to classify, agree on the flight from reality which marked his last years, especially beginning with the first Russian winter. He had forbidden and denied his subjects any access to truth, contaminating their morality and their memory; but, to a degree which gradually increased and attained complete paranoia in the Bunker, he barred the path of truth to himself as well. Like all gamblers, he erected around himself a state set woven of superstitious lies and in which he ended by believing with the same fanatical faith that he demanded from every German. His collapse was not only a salvation for mankind but also a demonstration of the price to be paid when one dismembers the truth. (*Drowned* 31–32)

**"Thou shalt not covet thy neighbour's house."** The "new man" "naturally" is entitled to his neighbor's land and home (Hitler's *Lebensraum* theory), simply because he is superior and stronger, and it is Nature's law that the strong prevail over the weak. In *Mein Kampf*, published in 1926, he could already state:

> Nature as such has not reserved this [European] soil for the future possession of any particular nation or race; on the contrary, this soil exists for the people which possesses the force to take it and the industry to cultivate it. Nature knows no political boundaries. First, she puts living creatures on the globe and watches the free play of forces. She then confers the master's right on her favorite child, the strongest in courage and industry. (Quoted in Weikart 163)

Hitler's "Nature" is a frightening G/god which honors the mightiest. Primo Levi shows the personal outcome of this abstract policy: even if Jews might manage to escape a concentration camp's electrified barbed wire, sentries with machine guns on towers, and dogs well trained to hunt men, "[t]hey no longer had a country (they had been deprived of their original citizenship) or a home, confiscated for the benefit of citizens in good standing. But for a few exceptions, they no longer had a family, or if some relative of theirs was still alive they did not know where to find him or where to write to him without putting the police on his tracks" (*Drowned* 154). Since harboring Jews was punishable by death, Jews could expect little help from those who lived in the area surrounding the camp. Hence, those who are so deprived that they must yield to the mightiest who "covet" their lands and homes are reduced to landlessness, homelessness, poverty, and eventually dust and ashes.

This brief review of Hitler's ethic filtered through the Decalogue demonstrates frightfully the annihilating effects of Hitler's "antiethic" which somehow gained the support of many Germans and others during his lifetime. His loss of World War II and his suicide in his Berlin bunker close the case on his belief system, or so it seems. Remnants, most unfortunately, of his belief system still survive, and Primo Levi and Elie Wiesel have fought against these throughout their lives.

They demonstrate that the Decalogue can be followed by both agnostics and believers in God. Levi's texts show that, despite his assimilated Jewish upbringing, he somehow had absorbed the profound meaning of each of the Ten Laws in childhood, long before his Auschwitz experience when he was plunged into ethical chaos, indeed the tragic outcomes of the six points of Hitler's ethics listed above. Elie Wiesel also continued to follow the Commandments even after being profoundly shocked by his dehumanizing and frightening experiences occurring during his first night at Auschwitz and continuing thereafter. Regardless of their readers' religious stance, the preceding chapters demonstrate that there is much to be learned from both authors about how to live life in cruel chaos and afterward.

Both writers have embraced the concept of being a "Mensch" and honoring every other human being as such. A "Mensch" may be defined as one who has profound compassion for others; Jack Kolbert's definition bears repeating: "someone endowed with honesty, fairness, justice, integrity, respect for the sanctity of human life, and with compassion for the underdog" (147). Such a person contrasts with the feared and rejected *Muselmann*, whom Levi defines as "the worn out man, whose intellect is dying or dead" (Levi, *Drowned* 142) and "the weak, the inept, those doomed to selection" (*Survival in Auschwitz* 88). At Auschwitz the *Muselmann* was particularly abhorred because the inmates, committed to "organizing" to save their own lives, were terrified of them themselves turning into what appeared to be a passive subhuman human. Hence they scorned and avoided the *Muselmänner*. Levi must have recognized the ethical fallacy in this behavior when his mother, through no fault of her own but due to her strokes, began to turn into such a human being. His compassion forbade him to avoid her; hence his ongoing refusal of friends' suggestions that he place her in a convalescent home (Angier 709; Thomson 483). His final text, *I Sommersi e i salvati* (*The Drowned and the Saved*), acknowledges that the *Muselmänner* were indeed the "true witnesses" of Auschwitz: "we, the survivors, are not the true witnesses. . . . we are those who by their prevarications or abilities or good luck did not touch bottom. Those who did so, those who saw the Gorgon, have not returned to tell about it or have returned mute, but they are the 'Muslims [*Muselmänner*],' the submerged, the complete witnesses, the ones whose deposition would have a general significance. They are the rule, we are the exception" (83–84).

Wiesel also learned later in life that physical illness, like his Elhanan Rosenbaum's Alzheimer's disease in *L'oublié* (*The Forgotten*), can create *Muselmänner*, as much as the victim and his or her family members try to fight its onset and progression. Hence, both authors' ethics had to expand to include love and profound compassion for the seemingly less than human, *Muselmann* like person. The Hitlerian doctrine of "evolutionary ethics" would have, of course, eliminated such persons at the onset of their mental and physical incapacitation in order to make room for the fittest.

Wiesel believes that God resides in all human beings regardless of their race, ethnicity, gender, and physical and mental capacities (*And the Sea Is Never Full* 94); they are all made in His image and worthy of respect. Repeatedly he finds renewed spiritual strength from studying the Torah and following the traditions and additional laws of Orthodox Hasidism—observing all of the Sabbath rituals, eating kosher, praying daily—while Primo Levi had only himself to rely upon for internal strength to follow the Law. Wiesel argues with God from within belief, while Levi searched for God from outside of it. Indeed, to both of them, the ways of God are often incomprehensible.

Elie Wiesel, as a literary artist, can no longer believe "in art for art's sake":

> For me literature must have an ethical dimension. The aim of the literature I call testimony is to disturb. I disturb the believer because I dare to put questions to God, the source of all faith. I disturb the miscreant because, despite my doubts and questions, I refuse to break with the religious and mystical universe that has shaped my own. Most of all, I disturb those who are comfortably settled within a system—be it political, psychological, or theological. If I have learned anything in my life, it is to distrust intellectual comfort. (*Memoirs* 336–37).

Primo Levi's ethics pervade all of his writings, but he avoided making such a sharp statement like Wiesel's above. Levi hoped to expand his writing repertoire to include topics beyond his incarceration at Auschwitz, hence his attempts to write science fiction stories and other creative tales which do not always reveal that he is a Shoah survivor.

Roth chronicles Primo Levi's struggle for (or maybe against) faith shortly before his death: "less than a year before his own death, Primo Levi checked the typescript of a series of interviews he had granted to Ferdinando Camon. At the end of one of the interviews, Levi had said, 'No, I have never been [a believer]. I'd like to be, but I don't succeed. . . . I must say that for me the experience of Auschwitz has been such as to sweep away any remnant of religious education I may have had'" (Roth, "Deliver" 251). However, Roth notes that "Levi had penciled a margin note beside his not-quite-final comment: 'I don't find a solution to this dilemma,' Levi had added; 'I keep looking, but I don't find it'" (Roth, "Deliver" 252).

Thomas Merton affirms:

> Agnosticism leads inevitably to moral indifference. It denies us all power to esteem or to understand moral values, because it severs our spiritual contact with God Who alone is the source of all morality and Who alone can punish the violation of moral laws with a sanction worth our attention. That is why there was something peculiarly strange and funny about the feeble efforts of the bourgeois generations of the late nineteenth and early twentieth centuries to bring up their progeny with a respect for moral and social obligations but with no belief in God. . . . 'Why should I worship the fictions you have imposed on me in the name of Nothing?' (112).

Levi was raised to be a highly assimilated Italian Jew by parents much like Merton describes, but he obeyed the Law given by Moses; for him, the agnosticism he claimed did not lead to "moral indifference." If Merton is correct that "God . . . is the source of all morality," then Levi may have been more connected to the true God, not the empty figure taught to him by his synagogue instructor before his *bar mitzvah*, than he himself realized, the true God Who is the Mystery that Wiesel disputes with daily. Indeed, Wiesel's wise father Elhanan in *The Forgotten* (*L'oublié*) tells his son Malkiel, "Never forget what the ancients taught us: God exists in contradictions, too. He is the limit of all things, and He is what extends the limit" (281).

Like Wiesel, Levi advocated for justice and could not find in God an advocate of equal intensity. Carole Angier remarks, "The rejection of injustice is one of Primo Levi's greatest themes, in both life and work. He had a passion for equality; it was the one point on which he allowed himself to feel—and speak, and write—almost violently. Equality of respect, the equal right to dignity of all creatures . . . was his highest personal principle, and the single greatest motor of all his writing" (154–55). It was easier to doubt God's existence than to acknowledge Him to be less just than His creature, man.

In contrast to "religion," which involves participating in the practices and rituals emanating from a specific belief system, "spirituality" may be defined as a transcendental personal notion of meaning and purpose; it includes living with the highest values possible and moving toward an authentic self. Despite his misgivings about God, Levi's ethics, based on the Decalogue of Exodus 20, provided him with standards upon which he could act and thus move into his authentic Jewish identity. Regardless of his minimal participation in Jewish rites, he exhibited throughout his life a *spirituality* which embraced the concept of honoring each person's dignity and right to be treated with respect, free from abuse.

Elie Wiesel's *spirituality* and ethics, as we have shown in this book, are very similar to Levi's. Wiesel, however, also is "religious" since he does indeed daily pray and practice the rituals foundational to Judaism. This very practice makes him the provocative figure he described himself as above: he is annoying to some believers, even fellow Hasidim, because he is not observant enough and because he persists, like Job and Jeremiah, in challenging God relevant to His love and justice; he is also annoying to agnostics and atheists because he has not given up on God and refuses to depart from his Hasidic practices. Although obviously thus located in a painful place, Wiesel is true to himself and his values by remaining there.

Wiesel has noted that many of the "kapos" were "liberal intellectuals" and that "many of the intellectuals were sadists" ("Solitude" 5). This was in contrast to those with "religious convictions"—resistance priests and rabbis, for example ("Solitude" 5). Indeed, Levi concurs with Wiesel's judgment: "the nonagnostic, the believers in any belief whatsoever, better resisted the seduction of power, provided, of course, they were not believers in the National Socialist doctrine" (*Drowned* 145). He continues:

> the believers lived better. . . . Catholic or Reformed priests, rabbis of the various orthodoxies, militant Zionists, naïve or sophisticated Marxists, and Jehovah's Witnesses—all held in common the saving force of their faith.

> Their universe was vaster than ours, more extended in space and time, above all more comprehensible: they had a key and a point of leverage, a millennial tomorrow so that there might be a sense to sacrificing themselves, a place in heaven or on earth where justice and compassion had won, or would win in a perhaps remote but certain future: Moscow, or the celestial or terrestrial Jerusalem. (*Drowned* 146)

Some have called Levi a "liberal intellectual," even with leftist leanings (unlike Wiesel), but his conduct at Auschwitz and his careful analysis of its inmates in *The Drowned and the Saved* (*I Sommersi e i salvati*), "son testament spiritual" ["his spiritual testament"] (Amsallem 276), show him to fit behaviorally into the realm of those with "religious convictions." Indeed, Levi admits that he is uncomfortable with the term "liberal intellectual" being used to describe him both at Auschwitz and afterward: "I may be an 'intellectual' today, even though the word fills me with vague discomfort; I certainly was not one then [at Auschwitz], because of moral immaturity, ignorance, and alienation; and if I became one later on, paradoxically I owe that precisely to the Lager experience" (*Drowned* 132).

Levi never fell prey to "the power of evil and its contagiousness," which Wiesel sorrowfully chronicles:

> Here was brutality in its purest state. Why did human beings act like savage wolves? Why were even inmates so sadistic? I 'understand' the savagery of the Germans, for savagery was their 'vocation,' their politics, their ideology, their education—I was about to say their religion. But what about the others? The Ukrainians who beat us, the Russians who struck us, the Poles who humiliated us, the Gypsies who slapped us, the Jewish kapos who clubbed us? Why? To show the killers they could be just like them? (*Memoirs* 85)

Although Levi acknowledges that "the greatest responsibility lies with the [Hitlerian] system" (*Drowned* 44), he also provides some possible answers to Wiesel's "Why?": "the [concentration camp inmate] functionary-prisoner. . . . wants to tame you, extinguish any spark of dignity that he has lost and you perhaps still preserve. . . . Privilege, by definition, defends and protects privilege" (*Drowned* 41). He adds that these privileged, now already incriminated by having compromised themselves as lower level workers in the concentration camp system, "thus establish[ed] a bond of complicity so that they [could] no longer turn back" (*Drowned* 43). He notes that power "attracted the human type who is greedy for power," provided "many material advantages," and, of course, "offered them [the Jews] the only possible escape from the 'final solution'" (*Drowned* 47). There were also, of course, those who did indeed identify with their oppressors (*Drowned* 48).

Levi himself insisted that believers of any kind—Jews, Jehovah's Witnesses, committed communists—supported better, more than others, the camp's challenges and survived at a higher number than nonbelievers (Amsallem 109). In addition to Levi acting more like a religious person in the camps than the sadistic "liberal intellectuals," Levi's view of the Shoah is shared by many Orthodox Jewish thinkers, more so than that of Wiesel, the Hasid. Specifically, Wiesel is more "modern" than Levi in his view that the Shoah represents a complete break with the covenant, something horribly new and unexplainable in God's relationship with His people, an affirmation that many Orthodox scholars and rabbis try to deny. "The *novum* too is part of the process of the covenant," remarked Irving Greenberg (quoted in Giuliani 237); to preserve the covenant, the *novum tremendum* must somehow be incorporated into it and Jewish history. Curiously, Primo Levi, the agnostic Jew, tries to make some sense of this tragedy, not believing it to be somehow mystically outside of his people's chronology. Hence his efforts align with those of the orthodox rabbis while those of Wiesel, the Orthodox Jew, oppose them.

The issue is crucial, as Massimo Giuliani explains: "From an Orthodox perspective, refusing to consider the Shoah as a caesura in and of the tradition often comes from the fear that the continuity of this very religious tradition could be questioned by the threat of the 'modern exposition of history'" (249). He continues, "And the root of the Shoah, its historical and, at the same time, theological explanation, must be searched for in the 'sin of modernity,' that is, in assimilation and rejection of the tradition" (249). Wiesel refuses to believe that the sins of the Jewish people in any way were responsible for the Holocaust. Levi would agree with him here (Amsallem 111–112, 263).

Both authors also agree on the abomination that the Nazis presented as they lorded themselves over the Jews: "it was the SS, not God, who governed our world and whose shadow fell upon us. The SS wanted their victims to see them not as superior men but as gods, and they acted like sovereign, omnipotent gods. They had every right; we had none. They knew everything; we knew nothing. They fed us or killed us with the merest gesture, but we had no right even to look at them. He who looks God in the face must die" (*Memoirs* 83). In their own ways, as we have seen in the preceding chapters, Levi and Wiesel refused this abomination.

Giuliani affirms:

> All of the theologies that do not accept justifying God for evil—or that do not accept evil as necessary in God's plan but that 'celebrate God' hoping that He will show His justice in the world—are theologies that look at man as the last hope in order to permit God to win His battle against the forces of chaos. In doing so, they not only give man the task of redeeming the world (*tikkun ha'olam*) but also of redeeming that part of God which evil dispersed in the world (a kind of *tikkun haShem*). And finally, they celebrate the human partnership in the fight against injustice. (55–56)

Levi was not aware of redeeming the world or God, unlike Wiesel, who, as noted in the Introduction, practices a mystical *tikkun* through his good works, but his actions demonstrate his participating in "the human partnership in the fight against injustice." Both Levi and Wiesel have fought this "fight against injustice" by following the Decalogue.

Levi's fall in April 1987 silenced his physical voice, but his writings continue to challenge his readers to think and act ethically in this ongoing "fight against injustice." Wiesel continues to speak and write, advocating for peace built upon authentic compassion and justice. Public intellectual and political commentator Alan Wolfe said in 2007, when discussing the need for "conscience driven prophetic voices, probably coming from religious people," that "Elie Wiesel is a prophetic voice who walks through mine fields unscathed" ("Who's Afraid of American Religion?"). Wiesel speaks out wherever he sees injustice—Soviet and Ethiopian Jews, victims of *apartheid* in South Africa, Argentina's *desaparecidos*, Nicaragua's Miskito Indians, Kurds, and others. His advocating did not stop after he received the Nobel Peace Prize in 1986.

He has also tried to increase understanding between Jews and Christians, always remaining true to the verities he sees. For example, he remarks, "During a conference of Catholic intellectuals a speaker declares that the Holocaust presents as serious a problem for Jews as it does for Christians. I feel the need to correct him. And I remember the shock I provoked when I said: 'Just a moment, my friends. The situation is not the same: The victims may be my problem; the killers are yours'" (*And the Sea Is Never Full* 146). On the other hand, he pleads for understanding: "Speaking in Stockholm's cathedral, I say: 'You must understand that the Jew that I am cannot look upon the cross as you do. For you, it represents mercy and love. For us, it evokes terror and persecution'" (*And the Sea Is Never Full* 146). His personal history attests to this poignant reality of which many Christians are unaware.

Finally, he affirms, "The truth is that all mystical traditions have similar origins. It is only on the surface, on their most superficial levels, that religions seem opposed to one another or even incompatible" (*Memoirs* 223). He dared to declare to a predominantly Polish Catholic readership in 1996, "Nous avons en commun le même Père qui s'adresse à nous dans notre langue à nous, et qui nous offre des clés différentes pour ouvrir la même porte" ["We have in common the same Father who addresses us in our own language, and who offers us different keys to open the same door"] (. . . *Et la mer* 255). However, as he explained to his friend the Roman Catholic Archbishop of Paris, Jean-Marie Cardinal Lustiger, whose Jewish mother died at Auschwitz (*And the Sea Is Never Full* 170), "One cannot belong to two religions [Roman Catholicism and Judaism]. True, it is the same God who governs our lives, but the paths that lead to Him are different" (*And the Sea Is Never Full* 171).

Sadly, both Levi (Thomson 374) and Wiesel have received hatemail, Wiesel's from "anti-Semites, pro-Palestinians, and [Holocaust] deniers" (*And the Sea Is Never Full* 162), and Wiesel's even includes death threats (*Memoirs* 337). He is now accompanied by a body guard after having been assaulted in a San Francisco hotel corridor by a Holocaust denying youth in 2007. None of these threats have silenced him. Like Levi, he states, "I believe in remembrance more than anything else. I have more trust in education than in the work of politics or in the organized religions" (*Conversations* 158). Hence, well into his eighties, he continues to teach two courses annually at Boston University. I shall close my book with his impassioned plea which no doubt Levi would affirm:

> Will we ever understand the meaning of the phenomenon called Auschwitz or Sachsenhausen? Friends who read these words, know this: *never* will you understand what your brothers and sisters endured there.
> The forced labor, the long 'Roll Calls,' the public floggings, the hangings, the shouts of the Kapos, the last gasps of the dying, the fixed gaze of the 'Muselmaenner' [sic], the Selektion nights: never will you see what some of us have seen and witnessed. But you must learn about it. Our survival and yours is at stake. It would be a betrayal to forget: if we have survived to betray the dead, it would have been better not to have survived at all.

> That is why we have never stopped shouting, reminding, whispering: 'we must not forget, above all, do not forget. . .' It is easy to say. Even though it is linked to the events that occurred, it all ends up becoming blurred and indistinct. How can I be sure that I shall always remember all the emaciated faces which throng through my mind? How can I guarantee that I shall always recall the gestures, the phrases, the unfinished lives and destinies which haunted me for years and entered my harmless, easy pleasures? Once I swore: 'I shall never forget!' I will continue to make that vow, I shall swear that oath. But in the depth of my being, I am afraid. I am afraid of forgetting. That is why I appeal to you: 'Brothers, help me. Help me not to forget.' (Wiesel and Friedlander, *The Six Days of Destruction* 58–59)

**We shall not forget.**

# Works Cited

Amsallem, Daniela. *Primo Levi au miroir de son oeuvre: Le témoin, L'écrivain, Le chimiste.* Lyon: Editions du Cosmogone, 2001. Print.
Angier, Carole. *The Double Bond: Primo Levi a Biography.* New York: Farrar, Straus and Giroux, 2002. Print.
"Ethics." *The Random House College Dictionary.* Revised Edition. 1983. Print.
Giuliani, Massimo. *Theological Implications of the Shoah: Caesura and Continuum as Hermeneutic Paradigms of a Jewish Theodicy.* New York: Peter Lang, 2002. Print.
Hitler, Adolf. *Mein Kampf.* München: Zentralverlag der NGDSB, 1940. Print.
Hitler, Adolf. *Mein Kampf.* Trans. Ralph Mannheim. Boston: Houghton Mifflin, 1943. Print.
Kolbert, Jack. *The Worlds of Elie Wiesel: An Overview of His Career and His Major Themes.* Selinsgrove: Susquehanna UP, 2001. Print.
Levi, Primo. *The Drowned and the Saved.* Trans. Raymond Rosenthal. New York: Vintage International, 1989. Print.
Levi, Primo. *I Sommersi e i salvati. Opere I.* Torino: Einaudi, 1987. 651–822.
Levi, Primo. *Survival in Auschwitz: The Nazi Assault on Humanity.* Trans. Stuart Woolf. New York: A Touchstone Book Simon & Schuster, 1996. Print.
Merton, Thomas. *The Ascent to Truth.* New York: A Harvest Book, Harcourt, Inc., 1981. Print.
Roth, John K. "Deliver Us from Evil? Kuhn's Prayer and the Masters of Death." *Fire in the Ashes: God, Evil, and the Holocaust.* Ed. David Patterson and John K. Roth. Seattle: U of Washington P, 2005. 243–58. Print.
Roth, John K. *Ethics During and After the Holocaust: In the Shadow of Birkenau.* New York: Palgrave Macmillan, 2007. Print.
Thomson, Ian. *Primo Levi: A Life.* New York: Metropolitan Books Henry Holt and Company, 2002. Print.
Weikart, Richard. *Hitler's Ethic: The Nazi Pursuit of Evolutionary Progress.* New York: Palgrave Macmillan, 2009. Print.
Wiesel, Elie. *And the Sea Is Never Full: Memoirs, 1969 —.* Trans. Marion Wiesel. New York: Alfred A. Knopf, 1999. Print.
Wiesel, Elie. *Conversations.* Ed. Robert Franciosi. Jackson: U of Mississippi P, 2002. Print.
Wiesel, Elie. *. . . Et la mer n'est pas remplie: Mémoires 2.* Paris: Éditions du Seuil, 1996. Print.
Wiesel, Elie. *The Forgotten.* Trans. Stephen Becker. New York: Schocken Books, 1992. Print.
Wiesel, Elie. *Memoirs: All Rivers Run to the Sea.* New York: Alfred A. Knopf, 1995. Print.
Wiesel, Elie. *L'oublié.* Paris: Éditions du Seuil, 1989. Print.
Wiesel, Elie. "The Solitude of God." *Elie Wiesel: Between Memory and Hope.* Ed. Carol Rittner. New York: New York UP, 1990. 1–7. Print.
Wiesel, Elie, and Albert H. Friedlander. *The Six Days of Destruction: Meditations toward Hope.* New York: Paulist Press, 1988. Print.
Wolfe, Alan. "Who's Afraid of American Religion?" Azusa Pacific University, Azusa, CA. 30 Oct. 2007. Responses to Questions.

# Index

## A

Abderhalden, Emil, 160
*Accident, The* (Wiesel)
    home in, 86
    sainthood in, 43, 49
    sexuality in, 43–44, 45
*Acide sulfurique* (Nothomb), 54–57
adultery
    of father of Levi, 155
    of grandmother of Levi, 148, 149
    in literature of Levi and Wiesel, 42–45
    Nazism and, 159
    relationship to theft and murder, 45–46
*adversus Judaeos* rhetoric, 133–34, 135
agnosticism
    atheistic humanism and, 5
    ethics and, 164
    of Levi, 95, 99–100
    Ten Commandments and, 162
Alberto (friend of Levi), 7, 50, 51
Alter, Robert
    on metaphor in Bible, 45
    on name of God, 119, 121, 123
    on Sabbath observance, 131–32
    on swearing falsely, 123
    on use of stone tablets for Ten Commandments, 143
*Alto Solo* (Volodine), 54
altruism and survival, 7–8
Angier, Carole, on Levi
    bearing witness, 9–10
    centaur image and, 107
    coping with dementia of mother, 8, 150–51
    death, 31, 32, 33
    justice and, 11, 164–65
    rejection of God, 119–20
    suicide, 70–71
    wife's background, 39
Anissimov, Myriam, on Levi, 5, 6
anti-Semitism
    as bearing false witness, 73
    Crusades, 134–35
    delegitimization of Judaism and, 133, 135–36
    early Christian, 133–34
    as rational, 26
"Argon" (Levi), 147–48
asceticism and mysticism, 83
atheistic humanism, 5, 114, 139
Augustine, 134
Auschwitz II-Birkenau
    bombing by Allies, 63
    dehumanization process, 66–67
    destruction of dignity as essence, 113
    hangings, 68–69
    inability to leave psychologically, 81, 83, 86
    infirmary, 69–70
    layout, 67
    *Muselmann* in, 162
    overview of life at, 15
    prayer in, 11–12
    revolt, 69
    roll calls, 67
    *Selektions*, 9, 69
    survival at, 7–8, 15, 49–50, 103
    theft, 49–50, 68
    women in, 41

## B

Bauman, Zygmunt, 27, 28, 37
bearing witness
    as burden of survivors, 9–11, 84

importance of, 169–70
*Muselmann* as truly, 163
primacy of, 14
as purpose of literature, 163
reasons for, 9–11
bearing witness falsely
   anti-Semitism as, 73
   Holocaust distortions as, 52–59, 73–74
   by thieves of time, 52–59
   as tool of Nazis, 160–61
beauty, as co-opted by Nazism, 26–27
*Beggar in Jerusalem, A* (Wiesel), 24, 29, 109
Berger, Peter L., on Levi, 99–100
"Beyond Survival" (Levi), 71
Bible
   affirmation of human life, 23, 71
   concept of being human, 25
   influence on Levi, 5, 94
   influence on Wiesel, 5
   metaphors for sin in, 45
   purpose of, 109–10
   Sabbath observance in, 131–32
   translations, 6, 121
   translations of use of name of God, 121–22
   *See also* Ten Commandments
Blumenthal, David R., 11
Book of Creation, 136–37
Bowen, Murray, 56, 112
Braiterman, Zachary, 11
Bruck, Edith, 41
Buchenwald, 70, 144
business ethics, 52

## C

Camus, Albert, 4, 122
Cavaglion, Alberto, on Levi, 5
centaur image, 107–8
"Cerio" (Levi), 50
chance and survival, 97, 103
chosen people concept, 133, 135–36
Christianity
   anti-Semitism as root of Holocaust, 93
   Christians as Judas, 24
   Crusades anti-Semitism, 134–35
   dialogue with Judaism, 168–69
   early anti-Semitism, 133–34
   grandmother of Levi, 148
   Holocaust as problem of, 23–24
   Jews as killer of Jesus, 133
   Nazism and, 23–24, 135–36
   replacement doctrine, 133, 135–36
Cicioni, Mirna, 4, 97
compassion and rationalism, 15
*Conquest of Happiness, The* (Russell), 4
credibility
   of truth, 63
   use of objective narration in Holocaust literature and, 65, 68
Crusades, 134–35

## D

Dantec, Maurice G., 54
Darwinism
   dignity of individual and, 101
   Nazism and, 157
   role of humans in, 93
   Ten Commandments through lens of, 158–62
*Dawn* (Wiesel), 28
*Day, The* (Wiesel). *See Accident, The* (Wiesel)
the dead
   comfort from those that preceded, 145
   prayer for, 144
   prayers for, before death, 71, 72
   relationship with, 145–46
"Death of My Father, The" (Wiesel), 144
Decalogue. *See* Ten Commandments
"Defiance in the Ghetto" (Levi), 147
dehumanization
   Darwinism and, 93
   delegitimization and, 135–36
   destruction of dignity as, 113
   extermination and, 23, 26
   hunger and, 67, 68
   process at Auschwitz, 66–67

delegitimization of Judaism, 133, 135–36
dementia, 150–53
Dick, Philip K., 53–54
dignity
    Darwinism and, 101
    destruction of, as essence of Auschwitz, 113
    Golem and, 139
    Mensch concept and, 3–4, 51
    survivor's guilt and, 51–52
*Dio Padrone* concept, 119–20, 122, 126, 128–29
*Drowned and the Saved, The* (Levi)
    acceptance of truth, 155
    *Muselmann* as true witnesses, 163
    as spiritual testament of Levi, 166
    survivor's guilt, 51
Druker, Jonathan, 31
*Due stanze vuote* (Bruck), 41

## E

education, importance of, 169–70
the elderly and dementia, 150–53
equality. *See* justice
eternity and Sabbath, 132
ethical imperatives, role of, 155, 156
ethics
    agnosticism and, 164
    defined, 4, 155
    of former slaves, 3
    God as source of all, 164
    of Hitler, 156–58, 163
    memory and, 10
    post-Holocaust structure of, 3
    as system of moral principles, 4
    *See also* goodness ethic
*Ethics* (Abderhalden), 160
eugenics. *See* Social Darwinism
evil
    as contagious, 166
    God and, 125, 168
    hatred as visible face of, 6–7
    as inverted by Nazism, 27, 28, 49
    silence as indifference to, 9
    *See also* goodness ethic
evolutionary ethics, 156–62, 163

exaggeration and Holocaust literature, 65

## F

*Faith and Fratricide* (Ruether), 73
false witness. *See* bearing witness falsely
family
    commitment to, 8–9
    as foundation of society, 40–41
    Nazism and, 159
fanaticism, 126–27, 128–29
Farrell, Joseph, 94
fascism. *See* Nazism
*Fifth Son, The* (Wiesel), 29
First Crusades, 134
*Five Books of Moses, The* (Alter), 121, 131–32, 143
forgiveness, as Christian value, 12–13
*Forgotten, The* (Wiesel), 150, 151–53, 164
Frankenstein, 136
Frankfurter, Felix, 63
Fredriksen, Paula, 133, 134
freedom
    definition of complete, 63
    essence of true, 111
    of former slaves, 3
    idolatry and, 111
    truth as precursor, 64
    uncertainty of, 116
friendship
    being human and, 101
    betrayal of, 108
    home and, 88
    between Levi and Wiesel, 2, 13–14
    between Levi and women, 40, 41
    of parents, 7–8
    role of, in survival at Auschwitz, 7–8
*fumo di Birkenau, Il* (Millu), 41

## G

Gambetta, Diego, 31, 32, 33–34
*Gates of the Forest, The* (Wiesel), 87–88
Germans, hatred of, 6–7

Giuliani, Massimo
  on anti-Semitism and delegitimization of Judaism, 135–36
  on fascism, 93
  on Golem, 136
  on Levi, 1, 51, 97
  on replacement doctrine, 135–36
  on responsibility for Holocaust, 167, 168
God
  belief in
    anger at and, 72–73, 144
    as choice, 123
    comfort of, 100, 152–53
    desire for, 96, 103
  chance/luck vs., 103
  chosen people of, 133, 135–36
  concepts of, 119–21, 157
  concretized in Ten Commandments, 5
  different paths to, 169
  in each human being, 29–30, 79–80, 163
  ethics and
    goodness ethic as embodiment of, 103–4
    goodness ethic as expectation of, 119, 122
    justice, 73, 96, 129
    as source of all, 164
  evil and, 125, 168
  expectations of, 119, 122
  fanaticism as enemy of, 126–27, 128–29
  as giver of life, 26
  Hitler as, 26, 111
  humanity's partnership with, 11, 129, 168
  love and, 96, 109, 110, 119–21
  murder and death of, 29–30
  Nature as, 158, 161
  nature of, 71–72, 164
  Nazism and death of, 144
  prayer and, 120–21, 148
  responsibility for Holocaust and, 167–68
  silence during Holocaust, 3, 91, 94, 99, 110, 128
  on trial, 123–29
  *See also* Levi, Primo; name of God; Wiesel, Elie
Golem, 136–39
*Golem: The Story of a Legend, The* (Wiesel), 137–38, 139
goodness ethic
  as basis of Judeo-Christian ethics, 158
  as embodiment of God and Ten Commandments, 103–4
  as essence of being human, 100–2
  as expectation of God, 119, 122
  as inverted by Nazism, 25–27, 28, 49, 158
  justice as foundation, 11
  Mensch concept and, 27
  need for holy, 132–33
  origins, 82
  respect for the other, 6, 7
  shared by Levi and Wiesel, 1–2
  *See also* evil
Gordon, Robert S. C. on Levi, 3, 78
gray zone theory, 51
Greeks, ancient, 25
Greenberg, Irving, 167
Greer, Germaine, 147

# H

Haas, Peter J., 4, 25, 28
Hasidism, 2, 37, 101
hatred, 6–7
Heschel, Abraham Joshua, 25, 26, 132
*History, Religion, and Antisemitism* (Langmuir), 73
Hitler, Adolf
  as creator of new man of Nazism, 160–61
  ethics of, 156–58, 163
  as God, 26, 111
  Nature as defined by, 157–58, 161
  Ten Commandments and, 158–62

*Hitler's Ethic: The Nazi Pursuit of Evolutionary Progress* (Weikart), 156
holiness and goodness, 132–33
Holocaust
    approaches to studying, 1
    behavior of believers vs. nonbelievers, 165–66, 167
    Christian anti-Semitism as root, 93
    as Christian problem, 23–24
    distortions of, 52–59, 73–74
    following orders and, 115
    as inversion of good and evil, 28
    Jewish partisans, 82
    responsibility for, 166, 167–68
    silence of God during, 3, 91, 94, 99, 110, 128
    situation of Jews during, 161–62
Holocaust literature
    approach of Levi, 64, 65, 66–67
    approach of Wiesel, 64–65
    bearing witness as burden of survivors, 9–11, 84
    distortions as theft, 53–58
    use of objective narration and credibility, 65, 68
home
    exile and, 78
    finding, 16
    friendship and, 88
    as within human heart, 79–80, 82–83, 85
    as human need, 77, 83
    in literature of Wiesel, 85–88
    postwar journeys to, 79–81
    "simple" life as, 83
homeless people, 78–79
homogeneity and purity, 101–2
Horowitz, Sara R., 3, 9
human, being
    Biblical concept, 25
    desire for the ordinary and, 82
    elements of, 16, 100–2
    Greek concept, 25
    *Muselmann* as less than, 162–63
    *See also* dehumanization; "Mensch" concept

humanism, 5, 109, 114, 139
humanity
    fragility of, 10–11
    God in, 29–30, 163
    home within heart each person, 79–80, 82–83, 85
    idolatry of, 16
    individual as property, 159
    love of, and goodness, 82
    love of God and love of, 109, 110
    need for home, 77, 83
    partnership with God, 11, 129, 168
    structure of post-Holocaust ethics and, 3
    *See also* dehumanization
human life
    Biblical affirmation, 23
    God as giver of, 26
    primacy in Judaism, 23, 71
    as property, 159
humility, 109, 110
hunger and dehumanization, 67, 68
Hurbinek, 9

# I

idolatry
    of bureaucracy, 16
    freedom and, 111
    Golem and, 138
    of Hitler, 26, 111
    of humanity, 16
    modern, 111, 115, 117
    name of God and, 122–23
    of Nature, 158, 161
    of self, 109, 110
    as spiritual violence, 111
*If Not Now, When?* (Levi), 30, 44–45, 83, 99
*If This Is a Man* (Levi), 49, 65, 71, 94
    *See also Survival in Auschwitz* (Levi)
indifference and evil, 9
inductive reasoning, use of, 4
injustice
    Bible and, 109–10
    hatred and, 7
    as inverted by Nazism, 49

literature and, 7
Wiesel protesting current, 168
See also justice
*Iron Dream, The* (Spinrad), 54
Israel, 2, 81–82
Ivaldi, Franca Mussa, 41

## J

Jesus, 24, 133, 134
Jews
    anti-Semitism and, 26, 73, 133–36
    as chosen people, 133, 135–36
    denial of humanity and extermination, 23, 26
    dialogue with Christians, 168–69
    in ethics of Hitler, 156
    exile and loss of home, 78
    exile and love for stranger, 101
    Jesus and, 24, 133
    Levi relationship with, 120, 121
    situation of, during Holocaust, 161–62
    statelessness, 79
    Wiesel definition of, 121
*Jew Today, A* (Wiesel), 23
Job, commentaries on, 5
Jogmin, Otto, 27
*Journey of Faith, A* (television program), 128
Judah Loew ben Bezalel, 137, 138–39
Judaism
    Bible as central core of, 5
    ceremonial laws, 4–5
    delegitimization of, 133, 135–36
    dialogue with Christianity, 168–69
    early Christian Church and, 133–34
    emphasis on life, 23, 71
    forgiveness and, 12–13
    rejection of suffering, 71
justice
    Bible and, 109–10
    as foundation of goodness, 11
    God and, 73, 96, 119, 122, 129
    as inverted by Nazism, 49
    of nonbelievers, 96
    as passion of Levi, 164–65
    as task of humanity, 129
    *tikkun* as foundation, 11
    See also injustice
Justin Martyr, 133

## K

kabbalism, 11, 103
*Kaddish*, 71, 72, 144
Kafka, Josef, 16, 94, 111–17
kapo syndrome, 110–11, 166, 167
Karski, Jan, 63–64
King James Version of Bible, 6
Klein, Menashe, 146
Kolbert, Jack, 50–51, 162
Krankenbau, 69–70

## L

Langmuir, Gavin I., 57–58, 73
Lanzmann, Claude, 63–64
*Legends of Our Time* (Wiesel), 144
Leonin (great-grandfather of Levi), 148
Levenson, Jon D., 132
Levi, Cesare (father), 17, 143–44, 155
Levi, Ester (mother)
    death, 147
    depression of Levi and, 8, 12, 17, 32, 42
    love and devotion of Levi, 8, 147, 149–51
    as *Muselmann*, 8, 17, 147
Levi, Lucia (wife)
    background and characteristics of, 39–40
    death of Levi as suicide, 31
    Levi's love for, 42
    as mother, 41–42
Levi, Malia (grandmother), 148–49
Levi, Primo, 2
    as anti-Wiesel, 1
    approach to studying Holocaust, 1
    as atheistic humanist, 5, 114, 139
    Auschwitz and, 7–8, 15, 50, 66–67, 70
    on bearing witness, 10

in business, 52
as character in *Sulphuric Acid*, 54–57
death of, 8, 30–31, 33, 140
definition of *Muselmann*, 162
definitions of theft, 49
depression and mother's health, 8, 12, 17, 32, 42
depression when translating *The Trial*, 94
family background of, 4
as follower of Ten Commandments, 119
on forgiveness, 12–13
friendship at Auschwitz, 7–8
friendship with Wiesel, 2, 13–14
friendship with women, 40, 41
God and
    agnostic or believer, 5, 95, 99–100, 119–21, 123
    concept of, 157
    desire to believe, 96, 164
    envy of believers, 100
    survival, 96
hate mail received, 169
hatred of Germans and, 6
on Hitler and truth, 161
importance of home, 77–78
influential books, 4, 5, 6, 94
Israeli treatment of Palestinians, 2
justice as passion of, 164–65
as liberal intellectual, 166
love and admiration for wife, 40, 41–42
love for mother, 8, 147, 149–51
love for others and rejection of prayer, 11–12
love of children, 95
as member of Jewish community, 120, 121, 140
occult and, 108
as pacifist, 30
pain of others and, 147
postwar journey home, 80–81
prayer and, 95–96, 97–98, 144
in Resistance, 30
as saint, 49
search for scientific truth, 93

spirituality and, 108–9, 165
as supervisor, 110
survivor's guilt and, 51
on theft of property of Jews, 159
as "*tzaddik*", 122
use of inductive reasoning, 4
values shared with Wiesel, 1–2, 3–4
view of Holocaust, 167–68
Levi, Primo, writings of
    adultery and sexuality in, 44–45
    approach to Holocaust, 64, 65, 66–67
    Biblical influence in, 71–72, 94
    genres, 164
    Golem in, 137, 138–39
    Nobel Prize for Literature rumor, 3
    style, 2, 14
    translating *The Trial*, 94, 112
    use of centaur image, 107–8
    wariness of poetry, 98
Levi, Renzo (son), 31, 32
Levinas, Emmanuel, 27–28, 123
"liberal intellectuals," 165–66
Lieberman, Saul, 134
literature
    cathartic effect of writing, 9
    Holocaust distortions in, 53–58
    Nazi ideology in, 54
    purpose of, 7
    as testimony, 163
    *See also* Holocaust literature; Levi, Primo, writings of; Wiesel, Elie, writings of
Lollini, Massimo, on Levi, 98
Lorenzo (friend of Levi), 7
love
    description of "successful," 37
    as essence of Hasidism, 101
    of fellow human beings, 28, 82, 101, 109, 110
    God and, 96, 109, 110, 119–21
    indifference as opposite of, 129
    for *Muselmann*, 162–63
    necessity of, 28
    *See also under* Levi, Primo; Wiesel, Elie
luck and survival, 97, 103
Lucretius, 4

Lustiger, Jean-Marie Cardinal, 24

## M

magic, 108
Maharal of Prague, 137, 138–39
*maître du Haut Château, Le* (Dick), 53–54
man, conception of. *See* human, being
Mandas, Roberto, 30–31
*Man in the High Castle, The* (Dick), 53–54
Matt, Daniel Chanan, 103
Mauriac, François, 24
*Mein Kampf* (Hitler), 158, 161
*Memoirs* (Wiesel)
    occult, 108
    Sighet in, 83
    survival at Auschwitz, 49–50
memory and ethics, 10
Mendel, David, 31, 49, 97, 120
"Mensch" concept
    defined, 50–51, 162
    dignity and, 3–4, 51
    goodness ethic and, 27
Merton, Thomas, 111, 164
"mia casa, La" (Levi), 77–78
Micah, on goodness and justice, 119
Miller, Patrick D., 45–46, 122–23
Millu, Liliana, 41
Mingelgrün, Albert, 15, 53–58, 57
*Monkey's Wrench, The* (Levi), 83
Montalcini, Rita Levi, 31
moral principles, 4, 27
    *See also* ethics
Morpurgo, Lucia. *See* Levi, Lucia (wife)
Muller, Wayne, 132
murder
    adultery and, 45–46
    death of God and, 29–30
    Holocaust deniers as committing, 58–59
    of inferior to protect superior, 159
    justifiability, 28–29
    removal from humanity and, 23
    survivor's guilt and, 51
*Muselmann*
    defined by Levi, 162
    Ester Levi as, 8, 17, 147
    homeless people as, 78–79
    original use of word, 17
    as subhuman, 162–63
    Wiesel as, after death of father, 8, 70
mysticism
    asceticism and, 83
    origins, 169
    presence of dead, 145–46

## N

name of God
    blessing, 73
    to justify violence, 158
    Levi's unbelief and, 123
    potency of, 122–23, 136, 137, 138
    translations of use of, in Bible, 121–22
    in *The Trial of God*, 123–29
    as truth, 122–23
narrative ethics, described, 4
Nature
    as defined by Hitler, 157–58, 161
    as God, 158, 161
Nazism
    believers of religion and, 165–66, 167
    Christianity and, 23–24, 135–36
    death of God and, 144
    ethics of, 156–58, 163
    goodness ethic inverted by, 25–27, 28, 49
    homogeneity and purity and, 101–2
    ideology in literature, 54
    Nietzsche and, 94
    spirituality and, 93
    Ten Commandments and, 158–62
new man of Nazism
    bearing false witness to prove superiority, 160–61
    entitlements of, 161
    Hitler as creator, 160–61
    honoring parents of, 158
    Nature and, 157–58
    sanctioning murder to protect, 159
*New Revised Standard Version of the Bible*, 121
Nietzsche, Friedrich, 94

*Night* (Wiesel), 15
   anger at God, 72
   silence of God during Holocaust, 99
   writing style, 65–66
Nobel Prizes, 3, 145–46
Nothomb, Amélie, 54–57

## O

objective narration, 65, 68
occult, 108
*On Nature* (Lucretius), 4
the ordinary, 3, 82
Oreck, Alden, 136–37
"organizing," 49, 50
the other
   honoring differences/diversity and, 101–2
   love for, 28, 101
   respect for, 6, 7
*oublié, L'* (Wiesel), 150, 151–53, 164

## P

Palestinians, 2
parents
   caring for, 8, 69–70, 147, 149–51
   child as parent of, 151
   as friends, 7–8
   honoring in Nazi ethic, 158
   in literature of Wiesel, 150, 151–53
Parussa, Sergio, 100
*Periodic Table, The* (Levi)
   Auschwitz chapter, 50
   fall from height, 32
   family in, 147–48
   honoring the other, 101–2
   love for wife, 40
   purpose of Bible study, 109–10
*Peste, La* (Camus), 122
Piacenza, Aldo, 30
*Plague, The* (Camus), 122
Podwal, Mark, 137
*Portes de la forêt, Les* (Wiesel), 87–88
power, 110–11, 165–67

prayer
   for dead, 144
   for the dead before death, 71, 72
   God and, 120–21
   as joyful dialogue with God, 148
   secular rationalism and, 95–96, 97–98
   *Shemà*, 97–99
   spirituality without, 11–12
   Wiesel and, 12, 13, 98–99, 165
*Primo Levi's Ordinary Virtues: From Testimony to Ethics* (Gordon), 3
privilege, defense of, 166
*procès de Shamgorod, Le* (Wiesel), 123–29
Pugliese, Stanislao, 139

## Q

"Quaestio de Centauris" (Levi), 107–8

## R

*racines du mal, Les* (Dantec), 54
*Rashi* (Wiesel), 134–35
rationalism
   compassion and, 15
   as failure and betrayal, 26–27
   of Greek teachings, 25
   in literature of Levi, 65, 66–67
   morality and, 27
   of Nazism, 25–26, 27
   Sabbath observance and, 133
   secular, 1, 95–96, 97–98
   study of Holocaust, 1
*Reawakening, The* (Levi), 80
relativism and truth, 155
religion and spirituality, 165
*Rêve de fer* (Spinrad), 54
revenge, justifiability of, 28–29
*Roots of Evil* (Dantec), 54
Rosenbaum, Mordechai, 27–28
Roth, John K., 4, 64, 155, 164
Roth, Philip, 147
Rubenstein, Richard L., 1
Ruether, Rosemary Radford, 5, 73
Russell, Bertrand, 4

## S

Sabbath observance
  belief and, 132–33
  in Bible, 131–32
  death of Levi and, 139–40
  early Christian view of, 133, 134
  Golem and, 138–39
  Jesus and, 134
  Levi and, 6
  Nazism and, 158
  rationalism and, 133
  by Wiesel, 5–6, 131
saint, designation as, 43, 49, 122
salvation, 71–72, 129
Schmidt, Ulf, 158
Schmuhl, Hans-Walter, 159
Scholem, Gershom, 11, 145
Scroppo, Erica, 95
secular rationalism
  prayer and, 95–96, 97–98
  study of Holocaust, 1
  *See also* rationalism
*Sefer Yezirah* (Book of Creation), 136–37
*Selektions* (at Auschwitz), 9, 69
self-adoration, 109, 110
self-reliance, 110
*Se non ora, quando?* (Levi). *See If Not Now, When?* (Levi)
*Se questo è un uomo* (Levi), 71
  *See also If This Is a Man* (Levi); *Survival in Auschwitz* (Levi)
*Serment de Kolvillag, Le* (Wiesel), 23
*Sermons on John* (Augustine), 134
Servadio, Gaia, 42
"servo, Il" (Levi), 137, 138–39
sexuality, in literature of Levi and Wiesel, 42–45
*Shemà*, 97–99
"Shemà" (Levi), 97–98
Shoah. *See* Holocaust
*Shoah* (movie), 63–64
Shoushanie, 27–28
Sighet, Romania (currently), 83, 84–85, 88
silence as indifference to evil, 9
*sistema periodico, Il* (Levi). *See Periodic Table, The* (Levi)
*Smoke of Birkenau, The* (Millu), 41
Social Darwinism, 94, 157, 158–62
"solid self," 112
Solzhenitsyn, Alexander, 102
*Sommersi e i salvati, I* (Levi). *See Drowned and the Saved, The* (Levi)
Spinrad, Norman, 54
spirituality
  fascism and, 93
  humanism and, 109
  of Levi, 108–9, 165
  religion and, 165
  of Wiesel, 165
  without prayer, 11–12
statelessness, 79
suffering, rejection in Judaism of, 71
suicide
  death of Levi as, 8, 30–31, 140
  in literature of Wiesel, 86
  as murder, 23
*Sulphuric Acid: A Novel* (Nothomb), 54–57
Sungolowsky, Joseph, 120
"superstite, Il" (Levi), 51
*Survival in Auschwitz* (Levi), 11–12, 15, 65–66, 100
  *See also If This Is a Man* (Levi)
survival of the fittest philosophy, 93, 94, 101
survivors
  bearing witness as burden of, 9–11, 84
  guilt of, 51–52, 96
  inability to bear witness completely, 163
  role of luck/chance, 97, 103
"Survivor, The" (Levi), 51

## T

Ten Commandments
  acceptance by modern skeptics, 155–56
  agnostics and, 162

dementia as punishment for
forgetting, 152
as followed by Levi and Wiesel, 119
God concretized in, 5
goodness ethic as embodiment of,
103–4
Hitler and, 158–62
interconnectedness among, 45–46
as summary of Torah moral
standards, 4–5
translated (shortened version), 143
use of stone tablets for, 143
*teshuva* concept, 100
theft
adultery and, 45–46
in Auschwitz, 49–50, 68
Holocaust distortions/denials and,
52–59
legitimized in Nazism, 159–60
survival as, 51, 69, 96
thieves of time, 15, 52–59
"This Side of Good and Evil" (Levi), 94
Thomson, Ian, on Levi
in business world, 52
centaur image and, 107
credibility in writings, 65
death as accident, 33
exerting authority, 110
friendship with Wiesel, 13–14
love for mother, 149–50
magic and, 108
parody of Nietzsche, 94
in Resistance, 30
Solzhenitsyn and, 102
spirituality, 108
wife's characteristics, 39–40
*tikkun*, 11, 129, 168
Toaff, Elio, 12
Torah, 4–5, 103
*See also* Bible; Ten Commandments
*Toward a Definition of Antisemitism*
(Langmuir), 73
*Town Beyond the Wall, The* (Wiesel), 86–87
*Trial, The* (Kafka), 16, 94, 111–17
*Trial of God, The* (Wiesel), 123–29

truth
as co-opted by Nazism, 26–27
credibility of, 63
discovery methods, 97
Golem and, 136
Levi on Hitler and, 161
as liberator, 64
name of God as, 122–23
relativism and, 155
search for scientific, 93
*See also* bearing witness
Turkov, Mark, 84
*Two Empty Rooms* (Bruck), 41
"*tzaddik*", 122, 129

# U

Ueborroth, Peter, 131

# V

*Ville de la chance, La* (Wiesel), 86–87
violence, justifiability of, 28–29, 30
Volodine, Antoine, 54

# W

Warsaw ghetto uprising, 147
Weikart, Richard, 156, 157, 158, 160
Wiesel, Elie, 2
Auschwitz and, 50
on dehumanization process at,
66, 67
departure for other camps, 15
overview of life at, 15
prayer in, 12, 13
survival at, 7–8, 49–50
basis of activism, 11
on bearing witness, 10–11, 169–70
Christians and, 23–24, 168–69
current injustices and, 168
on Darwinism, 93
definition of Jew, 121
definition of "*tzaddik*", 122
on forgiveness, 13

God and
- anger at, 72–73
- on nature of 157, 164
- necessity of, 99
- relationship with, 119, 126
- silence during Holocaust of, 128

hate mail received, 169
hatred of Germans and, 7
on Holocaust distortions/denials, 52–53, 58–59
on idolatry, 109
influential authors/books for, 4, 5
Israeli treatment of Palestinians, 2
Levi, friendship with, 2, 13–14
Levi, values shared with, 1–2, 3–4
Levi as opposite, 1
Levi as suicide and, 32
love for and pride in work of wife, 37–38
as *Muselmann*, 8, 70
Nobel Prize for Peace, 3, 145–46
occult and, 108
postwar home, 79
religion and, 4
- as follower of Ten Commandments, 119
- as Hasid, 2
- prayer and, 12, 13, 98–99, 144, 165
- Sabbath observance by, 5–6, 131

Sighet, 83, 84–85, 88
spirituality and, 165
as supervisor, 110–11
survivor's guilt and, 51, 52
teaching *The Trial*, 112
view of Holocaust, 167–68
*See also* Wiesel, Shlomo (father)

Wiesel, Elie, writings of
- adultery and sexuality in literature of, 42–44, 45
- approach to Holocaust, 64–65
- Golem in, 137–38, 139
- honoring parents in, 150, 151–53
- on purpose of, 163
- style, 2–3, 14

Wiesel, Marion (wife), 37–39
Wiesel, Sarah (mother), 8–9, 146–47

Wiesel, Shlomo (father)
- death of, 8, 70, 144
- prayer and, 12, 144
- survival of Wiesel and, 7–8
- Wiesel relationship with after death, 145–46
- Wiesel's care of, 69–70

witness. *See* bearing witness
Wolfe, Alan, 168
women
- in Auschwitz, 41
- Hasidism and, 37
- Levi friendship with, 40, 41

## Z

Zionism
- challenges of, 83–84
- Marion Wiesel and, 37
- postwar journey to Israel, 81–82